THE PREMIER LEAGUE

THE PREMIER LEAGUE

25 YEARS

Lloyd Pettiford

URBANE
Publications

urbanepublications.com

First published in Great Britain in 2017 by Urbane Publications Ltd
Suite 3, Brown Europe House, 33/34 Gleaming Wood Drive, Chatham,
Kent ME5 8RZ

A CIP catalogue record for this book is available from the British Library.

ISBN 978-1-911583-09-7
MOBI 978-1-911583-11-0
EPUB 978-1-911583-10-3

Design and Typeset by The Invisible Man
Cover by The Invisible Man

Printed and bound by CPI Group (UK) Ltd, Croydon, CR0 4YY

urbanepublications.com

For Emma, William, Steve & Carol

(He was <u>never</u> offside)

CONTENTS

---

[1] This 'joke', repeated endlessly through the book is homage to the bloke that used to do the football results on the radio who never seemed sure where this word ought to end.

[2] He used to do it to Wycombe too.

FORE FOREWORD

Why Should I Buy This Book?[1]

This book is as much about fans as it is about teams. Although the fans are almost exclusively of teams who have played in the Premier League, for the most part you will recognize the same pain, superstition and irrational hatreds at all levels of football. Whilst commending it to you all therefore, here is a special note for Manchester United fans:

Because you are special (in so many ways) and there's lots of you and if you don't pick up this book just to have a quick glance then who will? You've won the Premier League more often than not (13 of 25 times), and if Millwall fans think no one likes *them* and they don't care, well you have even more reason to feel like that. As far as I know there are no equivalents of ABU for other teams. So this book's admiration of your team's achievement is, on occasion, grudging I'll admit...but I'm sure you'll take that as a compliment, even if not intended. If you just imagine it was Liverpool who won it so often, that'll give you an idea of how we all feel. None of the occasional invective applies to you personally dear Manchester United supporting reader, and certainly not the lovely people who contributed to this book; but there *are* plenty out there that find some Man U fans just a teensy bit 'entitled, spoilt and arrogant' (Baker, 2017) so please just regard anything less than fawning admiration as a corrective to Sky.[2] But don't let that put you off.

---

[1] If you want to get a flavour of why this book might be of interest, go to: **https://www.youtube.com/watch?v=81bv_gF4j5k** (accessed 30/10/16) or **https://www.youtube.com/watch?v=AgoEWtB3fA0** (same thing differently presented)

[2] For further excellent background reading, see Shindler, 1998.

So this is a book for everyone, and I hope you'll really like it. And even if you don't, you'll know someone who will really like it, and that's one less Christmas present you need to worry about isn't? Indeed after exhaustive analysis...nearly 50 teams and 100,000 words, the book's overall conclusion is that: *this is probably the perfect Christmas or birthday present for your grandchildren, nephews, nieces and, indeed, anyone at all younger than you. Or older.*

Here's just a little bit of what you'll be getting:

- Genre: Informed 'comedy non-fiction', originally entitled "Premier League: You're Having A Laugh"

- Basic premise: An irreverent 'celebration' of the EPL's first quarter century through fan produced content: narrative account, facts, jokes, stories and quizzes. Except quizzes. Covers all teams who ever made it, including the latest additions of Bournemouth, Brighton and Huddersfield.

- Benefit 1: Using extensive contacts, it's a genuinely fan-built book tapping into news and views not accessible via programmes and newspapers. Ordinary people like you have been involved: aristocrats, professors, poets, ex-professional players, pop-stars – oh and just plain old fans.

- Benefit 2: When you find 'the error' (all sports books contain them, and we're all gleeful and indignant in equal measure when we spot them) you can tweet me (@UrbanePL25Book) or wordpress me (premierleaguefanshistory.wordpress.com) and it will be corrected in subsequent versions with a full apology offered and credit (moral) given!

Some Chapters or Features are:

- The First 25 Years: An irreverent journey from the official 'start of football' to the present day including analyses of money and songs.

- The good, the bad and the ugly: winners, losers, cheaters. Best league in the world it may be, but the Premier League experience (the move from fans to audiences) is not unproblematic.[3]

- Teams – all 49 of them - making use of extensive fan contacts throughout the country. Even Pompey. This may include as examples:
  - Best/worst players or matches

---

[3] As Uncle Bob says 'I can't say that the football is any better in the premier league with all that money; mind you I watched West Ham win the F.A. Cup, European Cup Winners Cup and the World Cup, when they started out at 6 pounds a week and we had had only 4 Managers since the Club was formed.'

- PL Dream Team
- Quotes
- Most incredible PL match/season
- Funniest songs and incidents
- Awards (including best PL team ever - which objectively might get Matt Le Tiss on the bench, but probably no other SFC players I promise).

Please note that whichever team you support, if you are a genuine fan, you will be convinced that this book is part of a global conspiracy against your team. And you might just be right you know.

And why shouldn't I buy this book? Billy Ivory, previously owner of a faulty garden conveyancing system, makes the case in the Foreword he kindly supplied.

FOREWORD

I have been following Notts County for over forty five years. Which makes me uniquely qualified to write a foreword for a book about the Premier League - uniquely, because, of course, Notts have never bathed in the warm and luxuriant waters of the World's Greatest League (which is what Sky kept telling me it was when I first indicated I wanted to cancel my Sports subscription a few years ago). In fact, Notts, rather famously, got relegated from the old First Division at the end of the 1991-92 season, on the very eve of soccer's bright new dawn, and therefore missed out on the torrents of TV cash, parachute payments and good old fashioned bungs which I'm pretty certain would have seen them challenging for Champions' League glory by now. But we'll let that pass. The point is, *because* of that exclusion and the very nearness, the *almost across the line-ness* of the Magpies' fall from grace, down into the lower reaches of the EFL, I have always kept a very close eye indeed on the World's Most Watched League (see above).

Now, if you detect a slight sarcasm in some of what I've written so far, particularly, a slight reticence to swallow whole the massive TV hyperbole which inevitably follows the Premier League wherever it goes, then I must admit some culpability. The endless images of players diving into tackles in super slo mo whilst accompanied by great chunks of overlaid Coldplay, all delivered at the behest of a Murdoch apparatchik, desperately trying to convey THE PASSION OF THE WORLD'S MOST DRAMATIC LEAGUE, is something which *does* trouble me – and almost at once sends me straight back to Meadow Lane where I can watch professional footballers moving that slowly in real time - and I don't have to do so with Gwinnie's ex yelling in my ear.[1]

---

[1] Main author's note: I may be dim, OK I am dim, but I didn't get this reference at first. Then I showed it to someone intelligent and they didn't get it either. So we asked Billy. It is an obvious reference to Gwynneth Paltrow, ex-wife of Coldplay front man Chris Martin. He said I could put in this footnote. If you still don't get it, I can't help.

But it's not the football, you understand?

The imported players, the revamped stadiums, the more accommodating kick off times, the grass on top of the soil - it has *all*, genuinely, led to a version of high-end football in this country which is more skilful, more athletic, more watchable than ever before. And I've no doubt that for an eleven year old fan of Liverpool or Arsenal, following their team in the new format is just as engrossing, just as exciting, as it was for me following mine (briefly) in the old First Division. Nevertheless, for those of us who do remember earlier times, who can recall standing on the terraces prior to the advent of the Premier League, then the anniversary of the launching of this great megalith, twenty five years ago, comes with a joy not completely unalloyed.

Why?

Well, let me start by going back to Notts. I remember some long time past but very clearly, hearing a disgruntled fan crying out one Saturday afternoon: "Mek an effort you idle bastard. I pay your wages!" Now whatever you may think about this particular method of motivational encouragement, an important point was being made: the players were of our orbit. They earned more than us, probably, but without us there, that very afternoon, they wouldn't be in the amiable position they were. ..So get your bloody finger out.

And the players knew this to be true, too: the line which divided those on the pitch from those watching, was thin indeed. So much so, in fact, that the ex-England centre forward Tommy Lawton once told me, just before his death, that he recalled an occasion when, on international duty and *en route* to play for his country at Wembley, he had to stand on the train all the way to London since there were no seats left which might allow him to rest his pre-match legs. Despite his pleas to the stuffed carriage that quite soon, he'd be running around on their behalf, the gathered fans simply took the view that they were *all* men with tiring jobs and it was just a question of luck as to who got a decent rest on the way down.

Can you imagine that today? Of course not. Because the surge of money which flooded into the game post 1992, turned the Premier League's players into millionaires overnight and with that wealth came distance. No longer could a fan shout "I pay your wages", not unless he was earning two grand an hour, because the salary garnered by top flight footballers was now of a different scale, a different league. And that pay packet was no longer linked (at least not in the first instance) to those actually turning up at the ground – rather, it was linked to those taking out TV packages all around the world – and an ever widening gap between the doers and the watchers, started to develop.

For some, this is not a concern. They argue that football has always been a business and the Premier League has merely done well what the old first division did rather badly, which is to exploit the game for profit. They further posit that footballers have always been idols; they have always been worshipped and adored and the Premier League has merely ensured that box office potential has morphed into box office actuality – and the fact that footballers are now ensconced in the popular conscience as entertainers and celebrities, as much as they are athletes, is the simple result of their paymasters doing their jobs properly, rather than any sinister realignment of the role of the footballer in modern society. They point out, also, that the birth and rampant growth of the Premier League has occurred alongside the explosion of on-line communication and social media interaction - and *this* has done as much as anything to elevate the national game to its current ubiquitous level (don't get me started on those player Tweets on Match of the Day). They say, quite correctly, that the technology which keeps the Premier League so much in our lives, 24/7, would have been available *whatever* the shape of our football leagues today.

But the fact remains, for me, that as much as I love so much of what the Premier League has brought with it - the quantum leap in the quality of football on display, the chance to see, first hand, players I would normally only witness in European cups or in international games, even the improved standard of refereeing, despite all of that, the Premier League has taken something from me, too. And it is that sense of connection; with the players, even with the spirit of football itself – because I've never regarded soccer as the beautiful game. Football is about raw emotion, commitment, skill, tenacity and the ability to stick the ball in the net more times than your opponent. And that's enough. It's more than enough. Bollocks to those who insist that our national game was somehow inchoate in the past and only now is it starting to realise its true potential – as a quasi religious, life enhancing, soul nourishing, multimedia experience situated somewhere between a Frederick Ashton ballet and the poetry of Lorca. It's not that, it's a load of lads leathering a ball about and trying to stuff it over a line painted on the grass. Just as you and I did, or still do. And that's not to decry the potency of the game. In fact, from that simple, shared, understandable truth comes the primal connection with *our* national pastime, with a game which, however it's played, is as pure, as exciting, as inspiring as any which has ever been invented; a game, too, which *does*, naturally, throw up any number of heroes. As well as villains.

Yet, that's somehow not enough. That truth. Since, with the huge wages which came as a result of the huge influx of money which came as a result of the starting of the Premier League in 1992, there came the need to embellish the truth, to make it brighter, sharper; to give us 4K truth, rather than to tell it like it is. So, in the manner of the boxing promoter who needs to sell tickets to the most tawdry of bouts, we're informed that every game, every tackle, every goal, is critical, stunning, majestic – hyperbole *does* become the language of the day and that bloody super slo mo is utilised to an indecent level. Because it's all about the money. The players as stars, the games as spectacle - everything is designed to shift product. *Everything* is packaged in an attempt to persuade us that what we are seeing (wherever we may be in the world) is worth the cost of admission. And the cost of that admission is high, indeed.

Anyway, that's just what I think. And of course, this is written by a man whose team has never graced the Premier League, so you may consider it all sour grapes. And you may be right...[2]

William Ivory - writer of the 'Diary of a Football Nobody'

May, 2017

---

[2] With Billy's permission, I'm inserting here a link to a spoof Sky advert from 'That Mitchell and Webb Look' which encapsulates some of what he's saying: **https://www.youtube.com/watch?v=MusyO7J2inM** (accessed 5 January 2017). If you don't have the time, or energy to go and look, David Mitchell gets more and more climactic. For instance: 'Constant, dizzying, 24 hour, year-long, endless football, every kick of it massively mattering to someone...presumably'. I also love the idea of the 'battle for the North West' (Shrewsbury versus Macclesfield) and the giants of Charlton taking on the titans of Ipswich Town 'making them both seem normal size'. Watch it! Watch the football!

THE PREMIER LEAGUE YEARS[1]
INTRODUCTION

Let me emphasise then that this is a book for fans with lots of contributions *from* fans. My job has been to try and stitch it all together. There is of course some coherence in a season by season narrative, but inevitably there is some randomness too. I have embraced difference, rather than seek uniform coverage and contribution, to try and avoid what is known as the 'Rimmer Effect'. In the recently revived comic series *Red Dwarf* we find (series 4; Ep: Meltdown) the following dialogue between irritating hologramatic 'smeghead', Arnold Rimmer, and the only human left alive, Dave Lister:

Rimmer: *So there we were at 2.30 in the morning; I was beginning to wish I'd never come to cadet training school. To the south lay water; there was no way we could cross that. To the east and west two armies squeezed us in a pincer. The only way was north; I had to go for it and pray the gods were smiling on me. [pause] I picked up the dice and threw 2 sixes [pause] Caldicott couldn't believe it, my go again, another 2 sixes!*

Lister *(exasperated): What's wrong with you? Don't you realise that no one is even slightly interested in anything you're saying? You've got this major psychological defect that blinds you to the fact that you're boring people to death! How come you can't sense that?*

Rimmer *(grinning inanely and without hesitation): Anyway, I picked up the dice again. Unbelievable, another 2 sixes...*

Lister *(interrupting): Rimmer! No one wants to know some stupid story about how you beat your cadet school training officer at Risk.*

---

[1] The Premier League has had various sponsors and sometimes gone by the name 'Premiership'; this book refers to it by the name Premier League throughout, unless directly quoting a source who has used the term Premiership.

Rimmer *(without noticing): Then disaster! I threw a 2 and a 3. Caldicott picked up the dice and threw 'snake eyes' – I was still in it! Anyway to cut a long story short I threw a 5 and a 4 which beat his 3 and a 2...another double 6 followed by a double 4 and a double 5 after he'd thrown a 3 and a 2, I threw a 6 and a 3.*

It just occurred to me that without fan input, without trying to capture some of the fans' excitement (or desperate misery), a history of the Premier League could easily go the same way: 'After Manchester United beat Leeds 1-0 on Saturday March the 3rd, Arsenal needed to get something at Sheffield Wednesday, on Tuesday. They drew 1-1, but won their next 3 matches to put the pressure back on Fergie's boys who stuttered to a draw at Selhurst Park but then thrashed Sunderland, West Ham and Southampton in their next three games.' And so on. I'm going to try and avoid that, but since I'm relying on fans to provide the information, if this all leaves you in a state of what Lister terms profound 'un-gripp-ed-ness', then you've only your smegging selves to blame.

As I began to think about the possibility of this book, I was reading 'The Philosophy of Walking' by Frederic Gros. So inspired, and in an attempt to mimic the profound lunacy of Nietzsche, Rimbaud and others, I found myself limping and crying with blister pain in locations as exotic as the Isle of Wight, the Peak District, the Laugavegurinn Trail in Iceland and the banks of the River Trent, Nottingham. Ultimately this thinking time allowed me to conclude that embarking on this book was probably a very silly idea; thus reassured, I set to work immediately.[2]

A walk along the Trent in Nottingham does, in fact, offer plenty of inspiration to the sporting enthusiast. Trent Bridge Cricket ground, for instance, evokes some wonderful memories: Jimmy Anderson bowling balls with the trajectory of a particularly curved – EU approved - banana; Gary Pratt's moment in the sun, running out Ricky Ponting in 2005's Ashes test (how we laughed as the poisoned dwarf muttered off, and on... and on); and Stuart Broad cleaning up the Aussie's 11-man tail for a trifling 60 first innings runs ten years later. An innings short enough (111 balls) that it could be covered in one tweet. So @rameshsrivats did just that: "04W24W0W04100000W40000110W02 0000401000W0000000000101000011W0011200010040040000W1W300000000000 00400000000000001004W: Aus innings in one tweet."[3]

On the same side of the Trent as the cricket ground is the City Ground of Nottingham

---

[2] Every previous book on football I have attempted has been roundly criticised by someone that didn't like it being somewhat silly, even though I never claimed anything else and the word 'irreverent' was put in the blurb by a careful publisher. So here, clearly in the small print, please note: some of this is quite silly.

[3] An honourable mention to @SgtArthurWilson for a photo of Skippy the Bush Kangaroo whispering in the boy's ear, with the caption: "What do you mean Skip? Australia all out for 60...why that sounds like Pomicide."

Forest FC. Although looking smarter now, this was the place where Brian Clough took a team of journeymen to 2 European Cups at the end of the 1970s, a fact it is still difficult to believe. It's also impossible to avoid for more than 60 seconds in conversation with those of a red (apparently in tribute to Italian revolutionary Garibaldi) persuasion.[4] As the Premier League era dawned, Forest's triumphs were still recent enough history for them to be considered a big club. Arriving in the city in 1994, I found Forest 3rd in the top flight, and although the last 20 years have been tougher, the big club delusion will not be shifted.

On the other side of the river sits Meadow Lane where big club delusion is an illness no longer found even in the very old. Not for Notts County though the mimicry of Italians, but being mimicked by them, as Juventus' famous black and white stripes were merely copying. If you sit with the 5000 or so fans (not that snug in a 20,000 seat stadium) it is more much difficult to recall the glory day, unless you actually have history books with you – but it happened. However, you look up at the twinkling Christmas tree style floodlights and the sign on the Jimmy Sirrel Stand which for years said 'otts County' and it doesn't feel like a big club because, I'm afraid, it isn't. Fans of 'the 'Pies' almost revel in their fierce and perverse devotion to a club where things may never get better again.[5] Singing 'I had a wheelbarrow, the wheel fell off' recognises the über-fragility of a half-time lead or even their proud status as the oldest football league club in the world. Most of all it urges caution that something is likely to go wrong. Soon. But perhaps, as with fans of Queen's Park in Scotland, at least everyone knows that once upon a time 'we' set the standard and that continues to mean something.

Notts County's last relegation from the English top flight was the season before the Premier League was born (a fate coincidentally shared by Luton Town). It thus required me to crow-bar them into this introduction as epitomising the great mass of clubs that one assumes will never play at this level. Perhaps, as Billy Ivory suggests, that relegation has defined County's future. And yet over half of the teams in the football league *have* played in the Premier League. Bournemouth's incredible ascension for the 2015/16 season took us beyond 50% of the top 4 divisions who have had their moment(s) in the sun and Brighton became the 48th for 2017/18 having been cruelly denied a place in 2016/17. The once mighty Huddersfield Town (and on a modest budget) then became the 49th after a 45 year absence from the top flight. And the fact that Wimbledon *were* there, that Bournemouth *are* there surely gives hope to Fleetwood or Accrington or even Notts County.

---

4   The 2015 DVD *I Believe in Miracles* is well worth a watch.

5   Yet another winding up order at the time of writing and 90th in the football league.

That said, as money seems to filter up the pyramid, such dreaming might be considered ever more madness; there is even occasional talk of a more US-style approach where relegation is eliminated altogether. No dreaming just cash. And whilst this might still be exciting as a Man Utd, Liverpool, Chelsea or Arsenal fan in Thailand or Sweden or the USA, without this dream the Premier League is, perhaps, looking ever more predictable and alienating great swathes of grassroots football support in its own country. Even with promotion/relegation it's still generally the case that promoted teams struggle to stay up and relegated teams often bounce back with extensive parachute payments.

So is money now everything? At the start of the Premier League era, you might have predicted that wealthy northern industrialist Jack Walker would have just enough brass to make his dream come true of helping Blackburn Rovers to become English champions for the first time since they had had to play the mighty Glossop North End just 80 years previously, and before the phrase 'World War' was even common currency. You might not have predicted, however, that 25 years later their fierce local rivals Burnley – perpetual doldrum dwellers and last day escapologists to even remain a league club – would look the stronger outfit and more likely Premier League material. Indeed Rovers became the first Premier League champions to be relegated to the third tier.

In the 1992/93 first season of the Premier League, you would also have predicted correctly that the semi-domination of the East Midlands in the 1970s (in the form of championships for Derby County (2) and Nottingham Forest (1)) was unlikely ever to be replicated. But no-one saw the possibility, even a year before it happened, that in 2015/16 Leicester City would finally eclipse their sensational 1928/29 season, when they were runners up in the quaintly named First Division and had players with nicknames like 'Bunny' and 'Todger' leading the line. I'll be clear, I've never liked Leicester. Perhaps it was the unfriendly 'welcome' of Filbert Street, but I always saw them (all blue shirts and slobbering Neanderthals) as the Pompey of the north. Even so, their winning the Premier League with a well organised team, a whippet up front and that fabled 'team spirit' – it certainly had the whiff of it - was a shot in the arm for all the dreamers of any kind and even I was ambivalent about Saints 'letting' them have 3 points on the run in.

My determination to have a pop at Pompey is known, but I should say at the outset that this book is not going down that direction (at the insistence of the publisher). Few and far between will be my opportunities also for needling the Scots, not that I really understand these virulent hatreds in any case, which is why I make fun of them. Anyway, this fans' book will treat Portsmouth no differently. With the help of over 100 contributors, I will be aiming to capture the Premier League experience, not just of the high achievers (the Mans City and Utd, Chelsea and Arsenal) and the stable also-rans (Everton, Tottenham, Liverpool), but those who jump in from time to time and even those who dipped their toes in and found it too cold but nonetheless played in the best league in the world *once upon a time*.

As well as aimlessly tramping around in walking boots, I began research for this book by reading a serious football book. I thought that would be a sensible precaution. David Goldblatt's excellent *The Game of Our Lives* is a great place to go for full consideration of corruption, racism, misogyny, class discrimination and other blights on the game, ancient and modern. Those are touched on here, especially in the opening chapters, and are obviously important, but not with the same detail and precision. Nonetheless Goldblatt's effort highlights the dangers of even trying to be too serious, or sounding too authoritative. In his discussion of football in the midlands, he notes Clough's Derby County winning the league in 1973. Wrong! As a glory-hunting small boy at the time I followed Derby (I won't say I was a true fan) and can say with confidence that Clough's Derby won in 1971/72 and Dave Mackay's Derby did the same in 1974/75. This is not a mistake a fan is likely to make, and so I commend the approach of this book to you even if it lacks the scholarly weight of Goldblatt's detailed socio-economic analysis.[6] Goldblatt then goes on to point out the subsequent (post '1973') pathetic-ness of football in the midlands, including the Leicester City who would soon give us faith once more that anything was possible by triumphing in 2015/16. Indeed, rewind a season and a half and I saw Southampton beat Hull to go 2nd in the Premier League in November-ish. We sang 'now you gotta believe us, we're gonna win the league' and of course no one did, believe us that is. I speculated about how a couple of results going our way would see us top, and if we could just hold on to that until Christmas anything was possible...and I was accused of 'football wanking'. But after Leicester's triumph, I wish we simply had believed a bit more.

In a different vein, I also started my research at the other end of the spectrum. Colchester and Notts County et al, may currently wonder how they will ever join those who have played in the Premier League, but I wondered what football was like down where it's not even a dream. Where the kick-off really is delayed when you call to say you'll be late. Well, maybe not quite that bad, but I went to Oakham United ('Pride of Rutland'), just down the road from the then Premier League champions Leicester

6 There are, of course, dangers inherent in relying on fan memory. The Sutton United fan who put a clip on YouTube and an entry in Wikipedia clearly thought his team deserved extra-time in the 1981 FA Trophy final, so he just invented it and the minute of the winning goal (114). For the record, Terry Sullivan scored in the last minute of normal time (89) as Bishop's Stortford triumphed 1-0. The authoritative version of events can be found in Stephens, 2001. I thought crow-barring Notts County into this book would be difficult, but getting the mighty BSFC in here too...now there is an achievement.

5

City and surely with greater odds of getting to League 2 than even Leicester's much quoted 5000-1 Premier League triumph. This was a trip to see football for football's sake, like it was almost exclusively before the moneyed last quarter century. I have done plenty of ground-hopping over the years but had never before sunk this low before. No tell a lie, I did once go and see Vancouver Whitecaps (obviously before money raised MLS to the level of Conference National[7]). The trip to Oakham did nothing in terms of the book, but it's a nice club, deserves a mention, and oddly the football was enjoyable. A trip to that level does allow you to appreciate more fully the range of expletives used by players and managers; tone it down eh boys?

Finally, I had a chat with Steve Ogrizovic or 'Oggy'. As a player, his career spanned significant time before and after the start of the Premier League so he seemed a good person to ask about changes and developments. He's got two European Cup Winners medals (as Liverpool reserve keeper), but unlike Nottingham Forest fans he doesn't go on and on about it all the time. Steve played most of his career with Coventry City where he helped them win the exciting FA Cup final of 1987, something which – 30 years on – people still mention and thank him for on a daily basis. Despite a great career, he's clearly still very happy to have been awarded a Coventry and Warwickshire lifetime achievement award. In other words, a genuinely nice guy who was good enough to reflect on all things football for an hour. I, meanwhile, was good enough not to bring up any sensitive subjects, most notably Sutton United.[8]

The over-riding impression I got, apart from talking to someone who feels genuinely privileged to have made a living from football, and still has a passion for it, is that our conversation had very little to do with 1992/93. Oggy notes with a rueful smile that the Chairman didn't suddenly waltz into the dressing room with bags of cash and enhanced contracts, even as the game itself did get swamped with cash. Reflecting on high points of his career, Steve recalls more things from the 1980s than the 1990s. Things changed more slowly. More money, more foreign players; less violence, less racism; different player lifestyles, but nothing overnight. But after the dark days of the 1980s when it was not safe to go to the football, something was going to have to change anyway.

Both my visit to Oakham and chat with Oggy made me realise that the idea of having 'Premier League' records (that only go back 25 years) has no meaning and is a fact which angers particularly Liverpool fans. It's still the same game, and the passion

---

[7] I'm joking...it's not that good. I mean bad. Bad. Obviously bad.

[8] For an explanation see **https://www.youtube.com/watch?v=hB6u_prJY40&t=212s** One of the great giant killings (accessed 20/12/16)

for it can be as intense – and often more so – at Oakham United, Bishop's Stortford, Coventry City or Barnsley as it is supporting one of the bigger teams. Memories are no better or worse for having happened in the Premier League and indeed for some fans, the Premier league has diminished their experience and in some senses taken football away from them. So this history has been an opportunity to talk to fans and to reflect upon what these changes all add up to, not automatically to buy into the Sky self-myth of having created and/or saved the game. My thanks to all those who have helped; your names should appear next to your team below.

If I ever knew where this introduction was going I've long since forgotten. Perhaps it was that the 25th anniversary of the Premier League seems like a good point for reflection rather than celebration. You will now go on to read how the Premier League has taken football from the working class and money has changed its nature beyond all recognition. But after that, however we feel about these things, we are still drawn to it, so there is a section on the history of Premier League seasons, including each and every team that has competed. Even if our team will never win it, we might see our team beat the team that does and in any case the basic product is faster and more skilful than it's ever been.

Twenty Five Years of the Premier League

Winners with Total Premier League titles (to that date) in brackets

1992/93:	Manchester United	(1)
1993/94:	Manchester United	(2)
1994/95:	Blackburn Rovers	(1)
1995/96:	Manchester United	(3)
1996/97:	Manchester United	(4)
1997/98:	Arsenal	(1)
1998/99:	Manchester United	(5)
1999/2000:	Manchester United	(6)
2000/01:	Manchester United	(7)
2001/02:	Arsenal	(2)
2002/03:	Manchester United	(8)
2003/04:	Arsenal	(3)

2004/05:	Chelsea	(1)
2005/06:	Chelsea	(2)
2006/07:	Manchester United	(9)
2007/08:	Manchester United	(10)
2008/09:	Manchester United	(11)
2009/10:	Chelsea	(3)
2010/11:	Manchester United	(12)
2011/12:	Manchester City	(1)
2012/13:	Manchester United	(13)
2013/14:	Manchester City	(2)
2014/15:	Chelsea	(4)
2015/16:	Leicester City	(1)
2016/17:	Chelsea	(5)[9]

Roll of Honour

(those who have given of their time that their team should be represented in the best possible way)

Arsenal: Rob Cleary, Anthony Olivieri, Peter Wilkin, Paul Moore
Aston Villa: Claire Field
Barnsley: My family and other animals
Birmingham City: Stephen Hurt
Bishop's Stortford (eh?): Gareth Stephens, Lloyd Pettiford
Blackburn Rovers: Andy Watton,
Blackpool: Dave Ford, John Ford
Bolton Wanderers: Bolton Wanderers FC Supporters' Trust and their official, unofficial forum, Andy Gritt
Bournemouth: The terribly, terribly nice people in the club shop, I mean 'Superstore' (I'm not joking, your kindness when I burst in at closing time was much appreciated)
Bradford City: Keith Wildman of *The Record Cafe* http://therecordcafe.co.uk/
Brighton and Hove Albion (#48): Professor Peter Newell
Burnley: Gemma Avery
Cardiff City: The tweeters of #alwaysbeblue

---

[9] Yes Liverpool fans this is far fewer top flight titles than you have achieved and you are a great club.

Charlton Athletic: Rod Hammond

Chelsea: David 'Cardy' Harding

Coventry City: Sir Andrew Hamilton, Professor Murray Pratt, Ms Rachel 'Man-hater' Ward,[10] Mr Steve 'Oggy' Ogrizovic, Martin Mellet

Crystal Palace: Mark Newman

Derby County: Roland Fox

Everton: Andrew Taylor, Richard Griffith, Gareth Bell

Fulham: Dan Cordle, David Lloyd (*There's Only One F in Fulham fanzine*)

Hull City: Rich Cundill

Ipswich Town: Alan Leach

Leeds United: Terry Peer

Leicester City: Loren Price, Brendan Tyrell, Matt Merritt

Liverpool: David Knox, Tim 'the Anorak' Cunningham

Manchester City: Donna Lee, James Silvester

Manchester United: Heather Ann Pettiford (my own mother, a Man U fan, oh the shame!), Hansruedi Amsler (Swiss Devils), Ian Carey, Dean Hardman, Adam McLaughlin

Middlesbrough: Pete Hough

Newcastle United: Christina Philippou, Rob Enright

Norwich City: Rory Waterman, Peter Curtis

Nottingham Forest: Jim Tomlinson

Notts County: Billy Ivory, Martin Carnelly

Oldham Athletic: Steve Denton

Portsmouth: David Grover, Neil Hughes

Queens Park Rangers: Christian Wolmar author of *Are Trams Socialist? Why Britain has no Transport Policy*[11], David Baker

Reading: The Lucky Grandad and away fans at the City Ground

Sheffield United: Adrian Bell

Sheffield Wednesday: Edi Guinness, Martyn Ware, Tommy Craig

Southampton: Andy Bartlett, Steven Kneller, Fred (Family Cat front-man, aka Paul Frederick)

Stoke City: David Wild, Paul Lewis

Sunderland: Chris White, Martin Brown, Mark Bradley (Fan Experience Company), Jo McCormack

Swansea City: Cedric Rawlings

Swindon Town: Chris Merrifield

---

[10] Sorry, that should be Man U-hater

[11] Spoiler alert: Apparently they're not socialist.

Tottenham Hotspur: Professor Stephen Chan, Alan Shambrook, Jamie Garwood, Chris Baker, Rupert Smith
Watford: Ian Thorpe, James Crabtree
West Bromwich Albion: John Marks
West Ham: Julie Newman, Bob Duncan
Wigan Athletic: Liam Sephton (*All Gone Latics* fanzine)
Wimbledon: Geoff Hawley, Mike Fletcher
Wolverhampton Wanderers: Les Hurst

And those unaffiliated in Premier League terms or in need of thanks: Peter Hodgson and Gerry Goss (Toronto FC), Fito Alvarado (Olimpia, Honduras), Nathaniel Sikand-Youngs (cricket).

Finally, Matthew Smith whose passion for publishing has led to too many late nights and the occasional impulse to go with a very silly project.

Money

Billy Ivory concedes in his Foreword that Premier League football is faster and more skilful than ever, but suggests, perhaps counter-intuitively, that this doesn't make 'the football' any better. His theme - the increasing disconnections in the game - are explored further below by Peter Wilkin. Peter is described by some (well me anyway) as perhaps the brightest person they've ever met. On the other hand he's described in France (where he now resides) as 'un escargot short of un pique-nique'. So you make your own minds up, as he takes us on a journey which starts with small boys in the park, jumpers for goal-posts; enduring image, isn't it, hmmm?

The Perry and I...

When I was young I played football for Colchester Athletic, who morphed into Colchester Vikings. This was minor compensation for being re-located from London to what was then rural Essex at the tender age of 11. At the time they still had a cattle market in the town centre and it stank. I felt as though I'd moved not just 60 miles in space from London to Colchester but 400 years back in time to the middle ages. But despite being displaced in time and space I was convinced that I would be spotted by an Arsenal scout and fulfil my destiny as a star for the club in the years ahead.

At Colchester Athletic/Vikings our fiercest local rivals were a team called Cornard Dynamos (the 'Nard') who were famous for a number of things:

1. Having a female player who was very good.[1]

---

[1] According to my research...yeah I did some, I'm not just going to take Pete at his word, she was called Dawn Lawrence. Other teams – it does not specify who – tried to have her banned.

2. *Having the most ferocious and abusive parents, who would lambast their team from start to finish.*[2]

3. *Perry Groves.*

Of course, at the time only the first two of those points really registered with us. The 'Nard' were in the Suffolk league and we played in north-east Essex, so we only met in cup competitions that included teams from both leagues, often in the final. I'm happy to say that close though the matches were, we never lost. I'd like to say this was because of my contribution but from what I recall I usually underperformed in cup finals – clearly I never had the temperament for the big game. So I raise my hat to my most important team-mates who invariably made the difference in such games – Mitchell Springett, Christian Mclean, Chris Wheeler, Robert Conway, Gary Page and Leslie Marshall. It was them wot won it.

But Perry Groves is a wonderful figure who encapsulates perfectly the way the game has changed since football became a real commodity, rather than just the plaything of rich patrons. As we know, post-Sky it is a capitalist industry, big money, celebrities and 24/7 marketing and coverage. I can't help but think that Perry was not made for such an era. Instead he represents what I have loved about football in general and the Arse in particular. Here is a man that I played against, who through 99% perspiration and 1% inspiration clawed his way to play for the Arse, becoming a genuine club legend by arriving as part of the George Graham re-building of the club in 1986.

Let's be clear, Perry was a cult figure and the kind of player who, when things weren't going right, the fans turned upon as a scapegoat. Why? I suppose his limitations were apparent for all to see as well as his virtues. Plus, he was not the big money signing that Arsenal fans craved (how times don't change) and at a time when Spurs were still signing major players this probably rankled. But the fact is that Perry was part of one of the greatest Arsenal sides of all time and he has the medals to prove it. He also scored one of my favourite ever Arse goals in the final home game of the 1990-91 season against Coventry when, as my memory recalls, he made an inspired run to connect with a volley on the end of a cross from Winterburn to hammer the ball home from eight yards.

Best of all, as Perry acknowledges in his largely unreadable autobiography, even at the height of his fame he could still be found supping ale in the Hole in the Wall pub in Colchester, a favourite haunt for underage drinkers when I was at school. It is the

---

[2]   Their website makes them sound a far cuddlier bunch than this!

kind of thing that couldn't really happen now for Arsenal players I suspect. These days Perry would be thrown out of Annabel's at 3am with Jack Wilshire for vomiting on the shoes of a debutante from Knightsbridge, and then go home to tweet about it and send us all a picture of his cock. Or Jack's. Or make a video of it that would find its way into the Sun.

I love Perry and am not afraid to say it. If I ever meet him I'd tell him too. I doubt I will ever have the same sort of feelings for any current Arsenal player. They are from and live in a different planet and live like nouveaux aristocracy, sending their children to privileged public schools and generally living lives that have nothing in common with the supporters that made clubs what they are. To be clear, the gentrification of football is still a selective process; for every Arsenal, Chelsea, Manchester United etc. there are still a vast majority of teams, even in the Premier League, who provide an authentic football experience that connects with the past. Everton are a classic example of this; my favourite away ground and wonderful supporters. But for we disenchanted suckers who support one of footballs 'too big to fail' elite teams it is to enter the new football Disneyland: leave your soul and heart at the entrance door please, we will have no harsh language here.

To digress, when I was about 13 my cousin Andrew, still living in London, bought a house (or was it some land?) from Bobby Moore. Can you believe that? I couldn't. What is more (no pun) when my cousin got married, Bobby came to the wedding, dressed in his best dinner jacket. He danced with all of the swooning wives and gave autographs to gobsmacked kids. He danced with my aunt twice and she wouldn't let him go. I don't even know who the current England captain is – does anyone? – But I doubt Andrew could buy his house from him (or some land). I also doubt that he would attend Andrew's wedding. Not because he isn't an ok person but simply because elite football is now a different game and the culture that it once embraced has been replaced by the worship of people who are as removed from us as (thankfully) the Royal Family.

For a dozen years I lived in the far north and went to away games mainly, only occasionally going as far south as London and to Highbury. Away supporters are the hard-core of football fans I think and the away experience lulled me into a false sense of security. The emotion and feeling of being part of a persecuted minority, the noise that we made, all told me that nothing in the game had changed, Sky or not. Friends who went to Highbury told me otherwise but I chose not to believe them and by luck I got a season ticket for the Emirates and a new job in London at the same time in 2006. Like many gooners I grew nervously excited looking at online photos of the new ground as it was being built. Come the great day we entered a stadium that had all of the hallmarks of just about every other modern sporting venue of the past 20 years; functionally great but the aesthetic perhaps less catered for. Fantastic views, plenty of space, and look at those seats! They are more comfortable than chairs I have at home.[3] But it soon became apparent that this was a very different experience to the ones that I used to enjoy on the North Bank at Highbury. The middle-aged and fur coat wearing couple in front of us bought a picnic hamper and mulled wine to the game. This seemed odd. So much so that I thought it was a performance-art gesture ridiculing the modern bourgeois football fan. But it wasn't. And unlike the North Bank, I couldn't simply relocate next to some ugly ageing old git like myself. I bought the chair, I gotta sit there. Behind me was one of those people who are let out of institutions at the weekend and who foam and fleck saliva for 90 minutes, showering everyone in the area with globules of their DNA and taking any suggestion that they should keep their bodily fluids to themselves very badly. Strangely the stewards threw out anyone who was foolish enough to stand, wave a flag, or question the referee's parentage, but they never touched this guy. I don't blame them.

The strategy of the club has become clear, raise ticket prices, get rid of the local working class support that haven't got the disposable to spend £20 each game on a pint of beer (appalling choices) and overpriced food, and flood Arsenal with those that can afford to pay such prices. Over the course of a season or two it became clear that going to the Arsenal was more like visiting a multiplex cinema or a shopping mall, less like experiencing football as it had been at Highbury. And remember that Highbury itself had been nicknamed, 'the library', by cruel away fans in the 1990s.[4] So I should add that this piece is not meant as a contribution to the Wenger should go/stay debates that currently afflict the 'underperforming' Gunners. Wenger's management of the club in its transition to one of Europe's elite teams has been masterly and he remains the clubs most successful manager. All one can really say about the apparent 'crisis' gripping Arsenal was neatly summed up by Bill Hicks in a short skit about the Garden of Eden, and in a way this applies to followers of all elite clubs when they fall on hard times: 'Adam and Eve were in the Garden of Eden, and Adam said one day, "Wow, Eve, here we are, at one with nature, at one with God, we'll never age, we'll never die, and all our dreams come true the instant that we have them." And Eve said, "Yeah... it's just not enough is it?'

Despite my initial enthusiasm and excitement – a season ticket in a plush new ground – and much to my surprise, I soon found myself becoming more unmoved with the football as weeks went by. This was a shock but on reflection I think that there are a number of explanations. First, the game for the elite clubs at least has

---

[3] Although to be fair, French designers have always been totally uncompromising.

[4] By cruel he means 'accurate'.

moved on, changed and become something quite different than that which I grew up with. Those running clubs like Arsenal are looking ahead to the next 20 or 30 years when the customers will be of a generation for whom the experiences I had as youth will be as far removed as the Arsenal team of the Chapman era. Horrible though nostalgia is there is a sense in which it always lurking waiting to ensnare us with paeans about how things were better in my day etc. The idealised and distorted lens of nostalgia enables us to overlook the often grim matches we gooners watched in the 1970s and early 80s, my particular favourites being either the 1-0 home defeat by newly promoted Bristol City in 1976 or a 2-1 end of season home victory over just relegated Newcastle in 1978 in which absolutely nothing happened. Even the goals. So nostalgia is always a problem. After all, there must be some reason the Tories keep winning elections.

So the Sky revolution in football has profoundly changed the nature of the game in many ways: from what it means to be a supporter, the volume of money coming into the game, and the establishing of a new football aristocracy of celebrity players and clubs who will remain largely untouchable unless a benevolent dictator steps in to elevate another team to the upper tiers of the Premier League rapidly. It is hard in the current climate to see the elite clubs being removed from their places, and the thing that made the old First Division so exciting in the 1970s and even 1980s, the fact that unlikely clubs could be in serious contention for, or even win, the title has largely gone. Even Leicester's justly celebrated success comes on the back of a polo-playing Thai billionaire who didn't make his money by standing up for workers' rights (Arsenal don't stand up for them either as their refusal to pay the London living wage to its low paid staff under the guidance of the hideous Ivan Gazidis has shown). The football oligarchy of which Arsenal are a part will continue to provide us with over-hyped melodrama in order to try to create the sense in which we should all give a toss – 'will Jose transform Manchester United and make them champions? Who will replace Wenger when he retires? Can Pep make Manchester City kings of Europe etc.' Yawn… thanks for the money Mr Murdoch but can we have our game back please?

Peter Wilkin, January 2017

So there you have it; when your team is about to be relegated from the football league thank your lucky stars for the authenticity. But seriously, it is amazing how much fans just want their club back, and it's not just the obvious examples of Blackpool and Coventry (unsuccessful so far) and AFC Wimbledon and Portsmouth (successful); there are many ways in which the Premier League has taken football away from people – when it doesn't take your club it can still take the game.

Focus On: FC United of Manchester

As we shall see, even if you didn't know, Manchester United have done rather well in the Premier League. Nonetheless, even some of their fans wanted the game back after the Glazer take-over. Read more about FC United of Manchester at http://www.fc-utd.co.uk/index.php (accessed 17/1/17) from where I took the following introductory blurb:

Who Are We?

*FC United of Manchester is a **community** football club owned and democratically run by its members. Its corporate structure is a Community Benefit Society and membership is open to all, with everyone an equal co-owner, holding one voting share in the club.*

*The club was founded in 2005 by Manchester United fans following Malcolm Glazer's takeover of the Old Trafford club. This was seen as a catalyst and final straw by some, but it was not the sole reason for the formation of FC United. The club is semi-professional and currently plays in the National League North. The club regularly attracts crowds of more than 2,500 - several times the league average - and boasts many on and off the field **achievements** including three consecutive promotions and a number of trophies. It is unique at its level of English football in having its obligations to its fan communities and local communities written into its **Constitution**. The club was awarded Cooperative UK's Cooperative Excellence Award in 2009 for its cutting edge work with local communities.*

FC United seeks to change the way that football is owned and run, putting supporters at the heart of everything. It aims to show, by example, how this can work in practice by creating a sustainable, successful, fan-owned, democratic football club that creates real and lasting benefits to its members and local communities.

FC United is a development followed with interest by many. A different sort of fan ownership was attempted at Gravesend and Northfleet as they became Ebbsfleet United. However, perhaps because not backed by the biggest name in world football that had a much more difficult trajectory before the initial enthusiasm of fan ownership had to give way to foreign ownership. Read about it here: http://ebbsfleetunited.co.uk/club-history/

But we shall move on. Money has ruined clubs, saved clubs and made millionaires of young men. For every good billionaire like the saintly Markus Liebherr, still revered at Southampton, there are at least two reviled at other clubs. However, as well as those with talent, money has also attracted those of more dubious financial skills. Christina Philippou, author and academic, takes up the story...

Once upon a time, a company called The Football Association Premier League Ltd was set up. In 2005, it had income of almost £600 million and, by 2015 (latest available accounts at time of writing – any complaints to the auditors, please), they were bringing in almost £2 billion (the American billion, as this sounds more impressive than the British £2,000 million).

Then there's the clubs themselves. Previous Premier League winners brought in revenue to their clubs in 2015/16 of between £104 million (Leicester City) and £385 million (Arsenal). These are no small sums. Admittedly, the picture looks less rosy when you consider profit (what's left when you've paid all your footballers, managers, coaches, groundsmen, travel, other costs and tax), with losses of up to £82 million suddenly making appearances (I'm looking at you, Manchester United in 2016). But who cares about profit? When we talk about money, we care about the pot available. And that pot is income.

But why are we even talking about the clubs' and league's money? Surely all we want to do is grumble about overpaid footballers and underpaid grassroots volunteers? Well, no. We care about the club/league money because money, the theory goes, breeds corruption. And corruption, for all its faults and negative effects on victims (and I'm including fans here), is interesting. The rumours and whispers and missing money and scandals and court cases all make for great pub conversation (or wherever else you compete for superiority over your mates on footballing knowledge).

Corruption is an umbrella term, meaning it covers a lot of things, although the coverage is more like that of a golf umbrella than those cheap foldable ones that catch that singular gust of wind powered by a butterfly's wings and result in you poking your eye out and drenching your back when it snaps. Corruption includes the crimes of bribery, fund misappropriation (a posh term for 'stealing money'), fraud ('lying, normally about money'), money laundering ('making criminal money look legit'), and match-fixing (I'm hoping this one doesn't need a translation). Corruption also includes abuse of authority ('using your position in the club/organisation to get something you wouldn't otherwise get'), conflict of interest (where you have two jobs and can't do one without being tempted to act immorally when doing the other), doping ('using illegal or legal drugs when you're not supposed to'), and cheating (and yes, this does include diving).

The more money at stake, the more likely people that are given the opportunity to do something that may be corrupt are to actually do it. And this is how the rise of the money involved in football has led to instances of corruption ruining the beautiful game.

Bribery and match-fixing are both common accusations hurled at football matches (normally at the referee (more on them later) or under-performing players by the fans of the losing or under-performing team). There have been alleged cases of match-fixing for gambling syndicates involving referees, club officials, owners, and players. In other team sports, there has been a rise in allegations of spot-fixing (where a single event is fixed to happen at a particular moment in the match) as this generally requires fewer people to be bribed to ensure that the event happens. In football, this can be, for example, a corner, throw-in, yellow card, or free kick at a specified (sorry, magically coincidental with the bet placed) time. Spot-fixing is becoming more prevalent with the increase in gamblers' ability to 'bet-in-play'.

Fraud in football is also common. The Premier League provides useful advice to fans on its website on how to avoid and report counterfeit Premier League goods and merchandise (normally those that are cheaper, offered 'pre-release', and sold without official Premier League club clothing labels or packaging), how to buy tickets safely (generally, don't use ticket touts and/or avoid the sites listed on the website), and how to spot (3pm Saturday kick-offs shown in a pub, for example) and report illegal broadcasting of Premier League matches. Ticket sales are one of the most important sources of funds for clubs, so fraudulent ticket sales affect clubs' income. There have also been cases where officials or players are provided with tickets to high-profile matches that find their way (magically, of course) into the black market.

Fraud has also occurred at the expense of managers. There was one incident where a then Premier League manager received a phone-call from a former World Footballer of the Year asking whether the club would be interested in signing his cousin. Insufficient checks were done and when the cousin made a disastrous appearance for the club, it was revealed that the phone-call had been from the signing's mate and that the signing's CV was not what it had been made out to be. Evidently, lying on one's CV doesn't only happen on The Apprentice.[5]

Football agents have often come under the microscope when it comes to allegations

---

[5] No, this could never happen. What kind of idiotic club would fall for that kind of stunt?

of fraud in the Premier League. The role of agents is that of middlemen between the players and the clubs, but this has not always been regulated. The relevant regulations for proper behaviour by football agents are now set out clearly by the FA, and include being registered with the FA as an intermediary, not approaching players under 16, and avoiding conflict of interest (more on that later). These regulations attempt to stop issues where agents have requested (and allegedly received) cash in kind for contracts of employment or image rights negotiations with clubs. Players and managers have also allegedly been at the receiving end of illegal cash payments (or, from the receiver's point of view, unsolicited gifts that they decided to keep) in relation to player transfers.

Money laundering has been known to occur in the world of football, often combined with tax evasion (this is because laundered cash is not often declared and therefore not taxed). There have been cases where players have been bought and sold, or major building projects linked to clubs, that have allegedly involved money laundering. Given the large sums involved in transfers and the number of Premier League clubs based offshore, it is often hard to trace the sums or assess whether a seemingly under-valued (or indeed over-valued) player has been sold for the quoted price plus cash.

Cheating, too, is a form of corruption. While a debate over whether a single (being generous here) player dived or was fouled is often a healthy one to have with your mates, cheating can have serious repercussions on match outcomes (including future ones if, for example, a player is incorrectly carded and the card is not contested by the club and rescinded by the FA). We all know how it feels to be at the receiving end of an unfair loss.

Finally, conflict of interest is a common ethical issue that is often associated with corruption. This is not to say that conflict of interest always leads to corruption, merely that the existence of conflict of interest puts added pressures on individuals to make the right decisions if a conflict arises. For example, the Professional Game Match Officials Limited (which provides match officials for all the professional football matches played in England) had an income of £11 million in 2015, a good chunk of which was funded by the Premier League. The provider of referees also shares offices with the Premier League. Does it matter? Only if the match officials are faced with a dilemma between siding with the Premier League and siding with someone else and feeling pressured to take the Premier League's side...

Christina Philippou, March, 2017

(Christina originally submitted 75,000 words packed with allegation and evidence. This was what was left after we'd taken legal advice.)

THANK YOU FOR THE MUSIC?

Before we begin the grim business of analysing Manchester United's dominance of Premier League football, there was one more avenue of levity (*cul de sac* perhaps) that I wanted to take us down. Namely, is there, or has there ever been, any humour in singing at Premier League football matches?[1] If you compare English and European football atmospheres to those achieved at most (non-'soccer') sporting events in say the USA or Australia the difference is obvious. In the States, the best a basketball game will offer is orchestrated chanting of 'defence'. Meanwhile ice hockey (which is a great game) is riddled with tannoy-induced 'Go [insert team name or nickname] Go!' Rarely is there anything else. In Australia 'singing' seems alien, although ear-offending, tuneless 'chanting' can happen on occasion. Whilst the atmosphere in the Premier League is most often toxic, angry or drunk it is usually, at least, spontaneous and carries a tune.[2] Seeking out the smile in the bile is the task this chapter sets itself.

Gershon Portnoi is a fine name; I wish he'd gone to my school, as my own name might have got less 'teasing'. Anyway, whilst I think his attempt to write a book about hilarious football songs is a valiant one, he should surely have decided early on that there was insufficient material to merit such an enterprise. I don't want to 'diss' his efforts unduly; as a detailed chronicling of the pathetic-ness which constitutes the efforts of most teams' supporters it is a sound historical document. However, even the title of his book ('Who are ya?') suggests a less than rich comedy seam to be

---

[1] The answer is either, no, or yes, but it's very rare indeed. It is usually vitriol which gets in the way.

[2] I asked former goal-keeper Steve Ogrizovic if he had memories of anything funny coming from the terraces; his reply was that he was a focussed keeper, so didn't really engage in banter but that really the only thing you could be sure of were abuse, spit and coins. The latter may now be rarer, but the first is still a certainty.

mined here. At the end of the book (pp. 161-174), Portnoi attempts to sum up the book's 'hilarity' by providing a helpful 'Chants Directory' and the author, it has to be said, does his best with the dire material. For instance, I found the following on p.163 quite drôle as a description of surely one of football's more puerile songs ever.

> " 'Oh [insert city/team name] is wonderful'...The reasons given are usually threefold. One it contains ladies' breasts. Two, it contains ladies' sexual reproductive organs. Three, it contains the team they support."

But the dry description really serves to emphasise all the more that most football songs are *not*, in fact, funny at all. Often they are just supportive (C'mon [team name]), but when they try to be funny, collective drunken irresponsibility ensures that they are more often puerile, banal and pathetic, and regrettably the latter bleeds into plain offensiveness.[3] For the most part, unless you are extremely drunk, and possibly even drunkerer than that, there are many songs you'd never admit to singing. I mean: "Let him die" and "Let's all have a disco" (p.162)?! "Let's go f***ing mental" (p.163)? "Here we go"; "Olé"; "Shit ground, no fans". And so it goes on. "Your support is f***ing shit"; "When I was just a little boy" etc. To be fair, Portnoi approaches this with a wry smile and wit, but the material is, err, frankly...f***ing shit.[4]

Having said that Portnoi does his best ('Portnoi does his best') it has to noted that he really does go over the top in trying to make his case, claiming ridiculously for instance that 'everything within a chant, including truth and justice, is sacrificed to wit' (p.6). As if this doesn't already overstate an already overstated case, he later claims that football provides verses 'which Noel Coward or even Oscar Wilde would have been proud to have penned.' (p.18). Really Gershon? Obviously not! A possible answer for such hyperbole appears at the front of his book where the author urges us to buy his book on the grounds that 'I have a family to support.' (p.6). Apparently, this is an argument that writers of football books are prone to stoop to, usually – and in my case very definitely - out of economic necessity.

[Apology: I like to think I'm the sort of man who will admit his mistakes; and after writing that last paragraph I did have my nagging doubts as to whether I'd been entirely fair. So, I dug out a dusty copy of Oscar Wilde's *The Importance of Being*

---

[3] Sadly this offensiveness has included, and in certain eras even concentrated on, racist abuse; David Goldblatt documents to our society's shame the abuse meted out to Ruud Gullit at Everton in 1996 for instance. Shocking, nasty and extraordinary in equal measure. And even if attitudes, legislation and CCTV have seen this decline over the Premier League years, it has often been replaced with other bigotry, for instance homophobia and misogyny.

[4] I don't even want to dignify this with a place in the main text, but whilst every now and again Portnoi's book might make me grin – to be reminded of 'That's Amore' to the words 'When you're sat in row Z and the ball hits your head that's Zamora' (p.32) for instance. On the other hand 'With a packet of sweets, and a cheeky smile, [insert name] is a f***ing paedophile' (p.35) is just pathetic; a level which few songs in the book raised above.

Earnest and this is what I found in Act 2:

Cecily: Uncle Jack, do be nice. There is some good in every one. Ernest has just been telling me about his poor invalid friend Mr. Bunbury whom he goes to visit so often. And surely there must be much good in one who is kind to an invalid, and leaves the pleasures of London to sit by a bed of pain.[5]

Jack. Oh! He has been talking about the pleasures of London has he? Apparently, as I have heard him say repeatedly after a fine port or two, London Town is most assuredly full of fun! Oh yes it's full of fun; being as it is not only full of 'tits', and he most affably assures me, 'fanny', but also 'Ar-se-nal'.

So there you have it. Wildian wit that lives on to this very day on the (former) terraces. How could I have doubted you Gershon?]

Now, don't get me wrong, this is not simply a highbrow critique of terrace banter. I just think big crowds (such as inhabit the Premier League for the most part) make humour difficult *en masse*. The lowest common denominator and the big mouth always win out. Funny singing can work, as the cricket Barmy Army have proved; but those guys often meet in the pub the night before, have self-deprecation and irony uppermost in their minds (rather than superiority and venom) *and* produce song sheets. Funny songs may also be heard at lower footballing levels and especially at non-league football; here you can at least explain 'the joke' to your 10 mates before you start. However, with big crowds, the sledgehammer of insult and lowest common denominator usually wins out over the subtlety of wit. And it is possibly for the general lack of humour in football singing that the publisher and other enthusiasts for this project overall, looked at me when I suggested this chapter in a way which seemed to say both 'you're not very good' and 'you fat bastard' all rolled into one.

To be fair, I didn't start with a lot of evidence for a chapter on funny football songs. Probably the only laugh out loud moments I'd ever had with football singing at Premier League level were when my eight year old daughter (note the age of the laugher) 'lolled' extensively at 'is there a fire-drill' when home fans at Reading trudged out at 0-2 down in the 85th minute. The other time was a small attempt to sing 'Is this a pharmacy?' after drug allegations aimed at some Leicester players – the song, like the allegations, came to nought. But I felt that singing could make some contribution to this book. After all, if Gershon's book (I'm hoping use of his first name will soften the criticism) more often made me smile for his words than the allegedly 'Wilde-like' songs he reported, it did occasionally mention a song which seemed genuinely amusing.

---

[5] No, seriously, this really is from the play; well Cecily's bit anyway.

For instance, though not Premier League, I must admit, I liked the idea of the Tartan Army in Italy singing 'Deep fry your pizzas, we're gonna deep fry your pizzas' however pointless – the song not Scotland, of course. I can also not help be tickled by those apparently non-sensical songs that clubs adopt - like Notts County's 'I had a wheelbarrow, the wheel fell off' which has become the 'other Kop's'[6] equivalent of 'You'll never walk alone'. And also, though I'm sure by now you have me marked down as thoroughly erudite and sophisticated, I do have a puerile side and couldn't help but laugh at the inventiveness of Oldham Athletic's:

Give us a T (T)

Give us an I (I)

Give us a T (T)

Give us an S (S)

What do you do with them?

Oldham! Oldham![7]

I don't know if Oldham's brief stint in the Premier League was long enough ago that Lancashire's 'new man' had already evolved beyond this chant or not, but it made me snigger, probably against my better judgement.[8]

Another one which raised a smile for inventiveness (not least because it is apparently sung by people who don't seem terribly well heeled) is this from fans of AFC Wimbledon. It follows on from, with the same tune as, 'we are wombles, we are wombles, super wombles from the lane'

We drink champagne

We snort cocaine

We've got ladies over here

You've got shit jobs

You shag your dogs

and your wife is on the game

[More 'We are wombles' and then...]

---

[6] The city end of Meadow Lane.

[7] Portnoi, p.22.

[8] I have since conferred with Steve Denton, the very epitome of a Lancashire new man, who confirms that this song is and was sung by Latics' fans and that it makes him, err, titter too.

We drink Campari

We drive Ferraris

We've got wombles in our lives

You've got bus stops, second hand shops

And your mum's in readers wives.[9]

But despite such moments, I cannot really support the arguments made by Portnoi, even if you should buy the book to support his family.[10] No, more often, if I am impressed by football singing, it is around its volume, its bloody-minded determination in the face of adversity or simply its cruelty to ex-players and opposing fans, rather than for its comedy value *per se*. Nonetheless, I persisted in the belief that there *were* some nuggets out there to be picked up, if not for a book, then for a shortish chapter in one. And this is what I found.

Premier League Top 10 Songs

I'm going to include here those songs actually supplied to me by fans in the writing of this book, without any further pinching from the pages of Portnoi, so you've only yourselves to blame. If there are enough for more than a top ten I will subtly weave these within other sections of the book. So, in classic radio fashion:

At 10: Well this proves my point really. Peter Kay sang Tony Christie's *Amarillo* for Comic Relief (2005). Portsmouth beat Southampton 4-1 at Fratton Park and to this tune their fans sang 'La la la la la la la la (repeat twice more) - We're gonna send the scummers down'. Saints did go down. Ha ha! 'The Skates' presumably found this a jolly wheeze. However, eventually the universe righted itself again in terms of the footballing balance of power on the south coast. At which point Saints fans started singing to the same Amarillo tune (when winning or bored, if on TV or in need of cheering up) 'La la la la la la la la, Who the f*** is laughing now?' It's not terribly hilarious – unless you support Southampton. Makes me smile broadly just writing about it, but I'm whacking it in at 10 to give some semblance of impartiality and to amplify the point about lack of humour.

---

[9] Recommended by a serious poet, who wishes to remain anonymous.

[10] I really tried to be polite about this book, but then on p.41 Andy Goram's mild schizophrenia is discussed. The song 'Two Andy Gorams' is described as the 'cruellest-yet-funniest chant of all time' If one thought that perhaps the author didn't know what he was doing in mocking mental illness, he titles the section 'Andy-Capped'. Sad.

At 9: Rob Cleary has been watching Arsenal for nearly 60 years, man and boy (he still looks like the latter incidentally). His fondest memories pre-date the Premier League and are about the excitement felt by a young child. Nonetheless he concedes that the EPL has brought genuinely world class players to the club: 'Bergkamp was the first superstar' he says, 'but others followed, Henry, Vieira, Fabregas and latterly Sanchez and Ozil, not forgetting Pascal Cygan'. That last one is a joke, as was his very own song: 'He's bald, he's shit, he plays when no one's fit, Cygan, Cygan' There always seems more class in laughing at your own weaknesses rather than targeting the opposition.[11]

At 8: If poor Pascal Cygan got a rather raw deal from Arsenal fans, Liverpool fans were somewhat kinder to Peter Crouch to the same tune: 'He's big, he's red, his feet stick out the bed, Peter Crouch'

At 7: Proving that it's not only Arsenal who can serenade players who aren't especially good, Chris Baker (Spurs) suggests: 'What's that coming over the hill? Pascal Chimbonda! Pascal Chimbonda!' to the tune of the Monster by the band The Automatic.

(I was getting a bit desperate by this point and resorted to 'Best Football Chants' on YouTube and discovered that humour and abuse are inextricably linked in the football fan's psyche. Very often the latter is used interchangeably and mistakenly with the former.[12] Although based on physical characteristic, at the least offensive end of the range, I did smirk at a couple of protuberance based songs and wondered what might stick out of certain players to make them offside – nose, chin, eyes, gut, nob etc – but in the end it was still just abuse, so Chimbonda got in instead.)

At 6: Self (and team) deprecation is still a winner from my point of view, and it's good to see it occasionally in the Premier League, although the stock in trade of non-league teams for many a year. Honourable mentions go to:

- Tottenham fans losing 4-0 at Liverpool with 'Let's pretend we've scored a goal' with a celebration to match at the end of it.
- Various teams when losing: 'You're nothing special, we lose every week.'
- Southampton fans losing to European Champions Chelsea who were doing the whole 'Champions of Europe' thing: 'Johnstones' Paint Trophy, you'll never win that'

---

[11] Don't want to fill this with half-amusing Saints' songs, but in a similar self-deprecating vein, Southampton's once record signing was damned with exceedingly faint praise: 'Rory Delap, Rory Delap, sometimes he's good, sometimes he's crap'.

[12] For example, what is funny about saying Adebayor has a father who washes elephants and a mother who is a whore? Exactly. Nothing.

At 5: Here's one which is not so much the contemporary wit I was looking for, but one which can be laughed at as much as it is actually amusing. To a vaguely recognisable tune, Norwich City claim this as the longest existing, still sung, football song. It dates from around 1890. Enjoy!

Kick it off, throw it in, have a little scrimmage,

Keep it low, splendid rush, bravo, win or die,

On the ball, City,

Never mind the danger,

Steady on, now's your chance,

Hurrah! We've scored a goal.

At 4: 'Azpilicueta, we'll just call you Dave' isn't that funny, but even though it still betrays the little Englander inside, we should encourage Chelsea fans when they sing something which isn't simply rude and vitriolic.

At 3: Sometimes fans sing songs just because they do. That would seem to be the rationale behind Wigan Athletic's self-styled Banana Army's 'We all live in a tub of margarine.' I believe those were, in fact, the original Beatles' lyrics before drugs intervened.

At 2: Well, they just missed out on the Premier League in 1992/93 and constantly struggle even to keep their crown as 'Oldest Football League Club in the World'... so for apt bizarreness, and even though it is unlikely ever to be sung in the Premier League, Notts County's 'I had a wheel-barrow, the wheel fell off' gets second prize, even though it doesn't qualify and is very dark comedy indeed.

And officially the funniest Premier League football song ever, according to this book, so unofficially...

At number 1 it is: Well maybe my standards just slipped, I don't know, but given that they never win anything else, I thought I'd go for a clever and inventive song from Newcastle fans which has no swearing and doesn't abuse anyone. It is from a time when they had both Demba Ba and Papiss Demba Cisse playing up front, and is to the tune of that 'Knick knack paddy whack' children's song.

'Demba One. Demba Two. We've got more Demba's than you.

With a knick knack, paddywack, both can score a goal.

Geordie Boys from Senegal!'

Silly, but I like it. And I checked there was nothing offensive about the original children's rhyme too.

Exceptional Schadenfreude

Possibly the exception to the 'not really being that funny' rule is if you are a fan of Germany's substitute for comedy,[13] *schadenfreude*. At Goodison Park in 1992/93 for instance, Liverpool were getting the better of their Merseyside rivals yet again. At 0-1 up the Liverpool fans taunted Everton fans with chants of 'going down'. Not only did Everton recover to win 2-1 (and stay up eventually in miraculous fashion), but such was the poor season for Liverpool under Graeme Souness that there was even talk of the R word at Liverpool for one of the few times in their Premier League history. That's quite funny.

In fact gloating is a dangerous game; s/he who laughs last and all that. How often does your taunted former striker (who's not scored for 10 games) respond to the taunts with an outrageous winner? (rhetorical). Again in 1992/93 Oldham (needing to win to stay up) responded to their 4th goal (to lead 4-1) by goading the Southampton fans with 'Easy! Easy!' only to find themselves a few minutes later leading only 4-3 and enduring goal mouth scrambles to stay up. And as for the non-Saints fans who ever sang 'He's got a f***ing big nose' at Matt Le Tiss, that didn't work out well now did it West Ham?

A few seasons later, an already apparently doomed Leicester City side were nonetheless enjoying an afternoon cruising to a 4-1 victory against the very same Southampton and taunting the travelling support mercilessly. But when Saints pulled it back to 4-3 with a few minutes to play, the tables were turned; away fans, who had been placid and fatalistic, suddenly sprang to life so that the only song sung for the final five minutes was a rousing and spiteful chorus of 'you're s*** and you're going down' to those oh so lovely Leicester fans. But of course *shadenfreude* isn't really humour is it? Unless you were robbed of a World Cup 50 years ago and have been having the better of things ever since.

The karma police of football can be swift to punish the malicious football song. David Knox, like many Liverpool fans born in the 1970s is from nearby Norwich, but has moved to Nottingham to be closer to his beloved team. He remembers the scream

---

[13] Except for you Henning mate; you're one of us now!

from Djbril Cisse breaking his shin at Ewood Park in the mid noughties; under Mark Hughes the place was like a scene from *Casualty* at the time. Coincidentally, Cisse's first game back was at home to Blackburn, whose fans took great delight in singing 'Cisse, how's your leg?'. Visibly angered by such a nasty reaction, Cisse took great delight upon blasting a late free-kick to win the match 1-0.

Oddly, even without schadenfreude there is something about German crowds that I find curiously amusing, notwithstanding that kind of knee-jerk nervousness we all have about large crowds of shouting Germans. I love the goal announcements for a start (I've translated that which needs translating for you):

Announcer: Goal in the 67th minute for Werder Bremen scored by number 9, Rudi…

Crowd shouts: Völler

[I know that bit happens at some English grounds already, but the Germans don't leave it there…]

Announcer: The score is now Werder Bremen…

Crowd shouts: Three! (For instance)

Announcer: Cologne

Crowd shouts: Nil ('nul' I think, but even if the actual answer is two)

[And then my very favourite bit, which I'll even do in German for you]

Announcer: Danke

Crowd shouts: Bitte!

There is something quite hilarious about 30,000 or so mostly deep male voices being so polite. Other German songs sound quiet menacing and terrifying until translated. For instance the antipathy between north German Werder Bremen and Bavarian Bayern Munich is palpable, but not possible to take fully seriously when translated:

Bayern taunt: What is green and smells of fish? Werder Bremen!

Werder riposte: Get those little leather shorts off!

A chapter on funny Bundesliga songs would have been so much easier.

Soundtrack to the Book

(often, but not always, from round about the relevant season)

1992/93: Vic Reeves and the Wonderstuff – *Dizzy https://www.youtube.com/watch?v=BZzsi1y82Y8 (accessed 11/4/17)*

1993/94: Soul Asylum – *Runaway Train https://www.youtube.com/watch?v=NRtvqT_wMeY (accessed 11/4/17)*

1994/95: Red Hot Chilli Peppers – *Give it Away https://www.youtube.com/watch?v=Mr_uHJPUlO8 (accessed 11/4/17)*

1995/96: Oasis – *Wonderwall https://www.youtube.com/watch?v=6hzrDeceEKc (accessed 11/4/17)*

1996/97: The Verve – *Bitter Sweet Symphony https://www.youtube.com/watch?v=1lyu1KKwC74 (accessed 11/4/17)*

1997/98: The Cardigans – *My Favourite Game https://www.youtube.com/watch?v=u9WgtlgGAgs (accessed 11/4/17)*

1998/99: Shania Twain – *That Don't Impress Me Much https://www.youtube.com/watch?v=mqFLXayD6e8 (accessed 11/4/17)*

1999/2000: The Family Cat – *Bring Me The Head of Michael Portillo https://www.youtube.com/watch?v=0Zkr0DLtlwQ (accessed 11/4/17)*

2000/01: Linkin Park – *In the End https://www.youtube.com/watch?v=eVTXPUF4Oz4 (accessed 11/4/17)*

2001/02: Nirvana – *Smells Like Teen Spirit https://www.youtube.com/watch?v=hTWKbfoikeg (accessed 11/4/17)*

2002/03: The White Stripes – *Seven Nation Army https://www.youtube.com/watch?v=0J2QdDbelmY (accessed 11/4/17)*

2003/04: The Killers – *Mr Brightside https://www.youtube.com/watch?v=gGdGFtwCNBE (accessed 11/4/17)*

2004/05: Green Day – *Boulevard of Broken Dreams https://www.youtube.com/watch?v=Soa3gO7tL-c (accessed 11/4/17)*

2005/06: The Fratellis – *Chelsea Dagger https://www.youtube.com/*

watch?v=sEXHeTcxQy4 (accessed 11/4/17)

2006/07: The Kooks – *She Moves in Her Own Way https://www.youtube.com/ watch?v=pquhYpGHrlw (accessed 11/4/17)*

2007/08: Snow Patrol – *Chasing Cars https://www.youtube.com/ watch?v=GemKqzILV4w (accessed 11/4/17)*

2008/09: Paramore – *Brick by Boring Brick https://www.youtube.com/ watch?v=A63VwWz1ij0 (accessed 11/4/17)*

2009/10: The Libertines – *Don't Look Back Into The Sun https://www.youtube.com/ watch?v=jLYsIESNtUc (accessed 11/4/17)*

2010/11: The Hives – *Main Offender/Hate to Say I Told You So https://www. youtube.com/watch?v=C_Ue3PVB4tw&spfreload=10 / https://www.youtube.com/ watch?v=Uz1Jwyxd4tE (accessed 11/4/17)*

2011/12: Radiohead – *Karma Police https://www.youtube.com/ watch?v=1uYWYWPc9HU (accessed 11/4/17)*

2012/13: The Vaccines – *I Always Knew https://www.youtube.com/watch?v=84no_ HITKFo (accessed 11/4/17)*

2013/14: The Smiths – *This Charming Man https://www.youtube.com/ watch?v=cJRP3LRcUFg (accessed 11/4/17)*

2014/15: The Strumbellas – *Spirits https://www.youtube.com/watch?v=F9kXstb9FF4 (accessed 11/4/17)*

2015/16: Mumford and Sons – *Believe https://www.youtube.com/ watch?v=dW6SkvErFEE (accessed 11/4/17)*

2016/17: Viola Beach – *Boys That Sing https://www.youtube.com/ watch?v=dW6SkvErFEE (accessed 11/4/17)*

DIZZY (1992-93)

Champions:	Manchester United
Relegated:	Crystal Palace, Middlesbrough, Nottingham Forest
Unbelievable Relegation Escape:	Oldham Athletic

Sky declared themselves ready to change the face of football with the slogan 'it's a whole new ball game' and, to the tune of Vic Reeves and the Wonderstuff, the whole dizzying spectacle got underway. Watching the early coverage makes it abundantly clear that things are slowly changing, partly – indeed mostly - in the wake of the terrible events at Hillsborough, but also because of the money. Building work and crumbling terraces are the backdrops to Sky's coverage in 1992/93 rather than the completed soulless stadia we see today.

The attempt to bring a little US-style glitz and razzle-dazzle to the Premier League had an awkward start. Too many cheer-leaders are commented upon too creepily by old men – including Richard Keys and Andy Gray. Parachutists enter the unfinished stadia before kick-off for no apparently good reason. New bands (Curiosity Killed the Cat for instance) produce their latest hit with appalling sound quality and celebrities are wheeled out to add glamour. For the first Sky-styled 'Super Sunday', 'Canadian' boxer Lennox Lewis is at the City Ground for Nottingham Forest v Liverpool telling the viewers that 'yeah I like soccer' and that his favourite teams are Arsenal *and* West Ham *and* Crystal Palace.

No one seems really comfortable on camera; it is definitely a work in progress and a far cry from the situation a quarter of a century later. For the record, Nottingham Forest beat Liverpool 1-0, and as Sky extended our weekends into Monday, the first Monday Night Football saw Manchester City and QPR draw one a-piece. If one thing really helped Sky it was the change in the back-pass rule – henceforth football would have had to become more exciting regardless of who was filming it and whatever circus they tried to involve it in.

Creeping commercialism had already by that time begun to cash in on the replica shirt market, although only numbers featured on players' backs rather than names in 1992/93. Even as fleecing the fan for expensive odd-coloured nylon was becoming rife, Arsenal's 'curtain inspired' yellow away kit was still a wholly unacceptable step. I was relieved to discover none were available for purchase on Ebay.

Apart from the silly kits, some now unfamiliar factors were crucial that season in deciding the inaugural winners of the Premier League. First there was no board to tell you how long was left i.e. added on time was an entirely unknown quantity and the supporters of the team in the lead would be baying for the whistle from the end of 90 minutes without heed of injury or time-wasting. Referees could thus be encouraged to blow, but we had no idea what was in their heads. In a key end of season match, Manchester United trailed Sheffield Wednesday 0-1 in the second half of a 'must win' match. Although a Steve Bruce header in front of the Stretford End made it 1-1 it looked like the game was heading for a draw. In retrospect United didn't need the points (winning the league by ten after an extraordinary Villa collapse, which would also help Oldham Athletic survive), but at the time the race with Villa was very close and defeat (or even a draw) would have handed the initiative to United's former boss Ron Atkinson and his Aston Villa team. And so 'Fergie Time' was born – or as the rest of us know it, 'shall we just play on until United win time' – as another Bruce header (in the 7th minute of injury time) eased nerves at a league title starved Man U, leading to wild celebrations.[1]

Perhaps an even more important difference that season was the transfer window – which didn't exist and wouldn't for a time to come. Eric Cantona started the season with last First Division Champions, Leeds United, and continued his fine form, even as the team as a whole did not. Dion Dublin arrived at Old Trafford and despite scoring a winner at Southampton, promptly got injured. He was, in any case, a poor substitute for Alan Shearer who chose big-spending Blackburn Rovers instead of United; how differently things might have turned out if he'd moved to Manchester proper. And

---

[1] My sources tell me that Man Utd fans were well aware of the pressure Fergie's watch tapping had on officials and the favourable treatment that this brought them.

while United started with defeat to Sheffield United and only a point from their first three games, others looked good. Blackburn and Aston Villa (whose Paul McGrath won PFA Player of the Year and for whom now sadly departed Dalian Atkinson made a fine start) had invested money and Norwich – whose 'Amoeba Squad'[2] forward line of Ruel Fox and Mark Robins impressed - were the season's surprise package (ultimately finishing 3rd).

By November it hardly looked like we were witnessing the start of a 20 year period of United domination, but we were. With no transfer window, Neil Webb returned from Manchester to Nottingham Forest (to oversee their relegation) and Eric Cantona moved across the Pennines to Old Trafford. Those of us with ABU tendencies are utterly sick of the fawning adoration shown at United for this brilliant yet flawed loony, but it is impossible to deny his impact on English football and the destination of the Premier League title for a long half-decade to come.

Focus on: Manchester United

Given their utterly tedious domination of the Premier League era,[3] it is easy to forget that the inaugural Premier League season of 1992/93 was Manchester United's first title in 26 years. In the subsequent 26 years they will have won at least one title every two years. In assessing Manchester United's extraordinary contribution to the Premier League I wanted to dispel the ridiculous idea that all of their fans come from miles away rather than Manchester itself. So here with his take is Hansruedi Amsler based in Basel and Chair of the Swiss Devils assisted by Adam McLaughlin from Edinburgh.[4] But seriously, these individuals have offered in good faith their thoughts, so despite trying to get a cheap laugh, the point here is not really about the remote, glory-huntingness of Man U fans (I'd have brought you one from Basildon if I wanted to do that) but

---

[2] No one called Norwich's forward line 'the amoeba squad', this being a term invented for Tiny Flynn and other ineffectual small people at Bishop's Stortford FC in the mid 1980s.

[3] One man's tedious domination has admittedly been a remarkable achievement.

[4] As it turned out, all I could get from Adam was 'oh, aye, Man U are brulyant'.

about the status of Manchester United as the global brand whose reach crosses national frontiers.

Although living in Switzerland and supporting Man U, Hansruedi is not completely barking mad, so only gets to watch his team at the stadium a couple of times a season. It may be this, or perhaps the Swiss passion for time-keeping that makes his most treasured moment the two headed goals by Steve Bruce in injury time referred to above; the premiere appearance of Fergie time.

Like many of us, what he actually remembers and cherishes can be a mixed bag of stuff. He says his favourite song was 'Ryan Giggs, Ryan Giggs, running down the wing'. Maybe he didn't have many to choose from or perhaps it gets funnier in the second verse? Amazingly that's not in my top 10 of best Premier League songs. He also remembers Kleberson (an unknown Brazilian) producing the worst cross in history, and an unknown Portuguese coming on for half an hour v Bolton in Aug 2003 and producing a man of the match performance. (Cristiano Ronaldo by the way!)

Strangely as a foreign import himself, Hansruedi shows most emotion when complaining about the fact that *too many foreign average players are bought by the clubs* and demanding *more English home-grown talent please!* And although clearly with some money himself from one of the world's richest countries he also bemoans the fact that the *atmosphere has disappeared somewhat, due to all-seaterdom and high prices keeping average supporters away.*

Overall Hansruedi, a fan of English football for 40+ years, regrets what money has done to the game. Although clouds have silver linings; for a Swiss fan of the team that always seems to be on TV the glut of TV football that's grown along with the money has been a godsend.

Focus on: Oldham Athletic

Even though Oldham's incredible escape necessarily involved winning at Villa, it still rankles with Steve Denton that this win handed the title to Manchester United. An attitude which does him credit and ensured we hit it off famously.

He has to look back further than most fans to remember the Premier League years; a realistic man, he sees no prospect of a return, was glad he got a chance to visit the great stadia – Highbury, The Dell, Maine Road etc – and agrees that he got the chance to watch Latics in the Premier League before it ruined much of the ritual which goes along with the same Saturday afternoon routine.

Like many men of a certain age, when asked about the Premier League he immediately jumps to the pre-Premier League era and Oldham's extraordinary winning of what is now the Championship in 1990/91. Losing 0-2 to Sheffield Wednesday and needing a win, Oldham won with an injury time penalty. 'It couldn't have been stage-managed any better' says the commentator.[5] This was only possible because West Ham lost at home to Notts County; if that sounds careless, County ended up promoted through the play-offs and had a fine team. Anyway, according to Steve, West Ham were presented with the trophy for winning the old second division only to find out about Oldham's late winner. How he knows this I don't know, because I'm guessing he was one of the multitudes constantly invading the super-bouncy plastic pitch at Boundary Park and causing the delay which made West Ham suppose they'd won it. No smart phones then. If this happened, and I have no reason to doubt Steve, West Ham judiciously edited it out of their end of season video.

Of Oldham's incredible survival in 1992/93 Steve says little, but goes a bit misty eyed. Oldham needed to win their last 3 games and hope Palace got no more than a point from their last two games. After Oldham won at title chasing Villa and at home to Liverpool, they still needed Palace to lose whilst they beat Southampton on the final day. And that's what happened, although Oldham had a late scare as Saints recovered from 4-1 to lose by only a single goal. Palace lost 3-0 and went down on goal difference; if they'd lost 1-0 they'd have gone down on goals scored. Other things which Steve went misty eyed over were 'Mouldy Old Dough' by Lieutenant Pigeon, 'Boys in Blue' by Cannon and Ball and 'Meat Pie, Sausage Roll, C'Mon Oldham Give Us a Goal.' In case you are worried, this footnote doesn't offer a link to any of them.[6]

---

[5] See the overly-dramatic, yet dour and northern commentator here: **https://www.youtube.com/watch?v=S2rfnLRb36k** (accessed 26/1/17)

[6] I don't think it happened in the Premier League, but Steve also describes the day when police got tired of Man City fans chucking things over a fence and so literally released the hounds on them; only for an Alsatian to suddenly get lobbed over too.

Focus on: Norwich City

Rory Waterman, offers some snippets from the Canaries' time in (and around) the Premier League:

3 November 1993, in Norwich, UEFA Cup second round, second leg. A school night, and my first ever evening kick off. From my seat in the back row of the Geoffrey Watling City Stand, not very high above the pitch and about level with the penalty spot, my eyes dart around the huge swathe of German menace opposite, then the 'Canaries Welcome…' pages of the programme. Matthäus, Valencia, Nerlinger, Jorghino…. Daryl Sutch, warming up, misplaces a pass to Mark Bowen, which ricochets off an advertising hoarding. I bite my little fingers off and we draw 1-1, beating Bayern Munich 3-2 on aggregate. As we drive home, an Ipswich fan on the radio is keen to point out that they'd beaten us home and away in the Premier League the previous year, and my dad's friend Chris jokes that it is a bit like the Scottish rabble claiming they were the 'real' world champions when they beat England in 1967.

1 October 1996, in Grimsby, behind a goal and a pillar at Blundell Park. I wear my t-shirt that says 'NCFC – ON LOAN TO THE ENDSLEIGH FOOTBALL LEAGUE'. two goals from Darren Eadie and one from Keith O'Neil (our Ravanelli) push us on to a 1-4 win and top of the league. There is a pitch invasion, but I am too much of a wimp to join it – which isn't what I tell my mates at school. By May, we will be in the bottom half of the table.

15 May 2005, in the doorway to a sports hall at Leicester University. All we have to do is win our first away game of the season at the last possible attempt, at functional Fulham, and we stay up. I get out of an exam to learn from my mate Adam, who is

grinning his fat face off, that we've lost 6-0. I don't even entertain the possibility that he's winding me up.

19 March 2016, in scenic West Bromwich. A rare moment of levity that I don't dare to enjoy properly; a late high point in a doomed season. After being something close to cavity-searched at the turnstiles (they've recently had an 'incident') I pass into the Smethwick End ('HOME FANS ONLY') and sit on my hands as Robbie Brady does something useful for once by giving us a 1-0 lead early in the second half. 'Wey're aaawful, we are', I occasionally say, in my best undercover, hangdog, Frank-Skinnery voice, as the game dwindles away to a delightful nothing else. Opposite me, a big square of bouncing and coruscating yellow and green points its 2,000 pairs of hands in my direction and bellows songs of derision.

10 December 2016, Oakwell. Perhaps not.

Season's Awards

Silly hair: Neil Poynton and Ian Marshall (both Oldham Athletic) – I mean nothing like you see today from Borini or Pogba (for instance) just good old fashioned long 'Timotei' locks.

Miss of the season (possibly century): Ronnie Rosenthal for Liverpool at Villa, confidently rounding the keeper and hitting the cross-bar for no apparent reason. https://www.youtube.com/watch?v=kiVq5-u7MH0 (accessed 12/5/17)

Crazy But True Facts and Statistics

- Norwich finished 3rd but with a negative goal difference of minus four.

- Leeds (the 1991/92 league champions) took only 7 points from 21 away games, winning precisely none.

- Of 6 London teams in the top flight it was QPR who finished highest (5th).

- This isn't crazy as such, but as a reminder the Premier League started with 22 teams.

- Of those teams, Coventry were the only ones to win more points away from home than at home, and even dallied with the idea of a top half finish, before fading to their natural 'teen' level.

- Matt Le Tissier became the first player to score a Premier League hat-trick and still be on the losing side (4-3 v Oldham Athletic). He later became the second player to perform this feat at home to Nottingham Forest, a couple of years later.

- Brian Clough made it into the Premier League era but only just, retiring at the end of a difficult season looking as ragged as his team.

- Sky introduced the now traditional feature of showing Manchester City highlights to an Oasis soundtrack.

- Oldham had to remove their plastic pitch to play in the top flight, along with the massive tubs of Vaseline along the touchline that it necessitated. No, really! They replaced the flesh removing vinyl with rolled mud which they continue to use to this day.

Up Next

Newcastle won what people were probably calling 'the old second division' to ensure continued North East representation in the Premier League. West Ham pipped Portsmouth for the second automatic promotion place to keep the number of top-flight London teams at six. Swindon won the play-offs which was probably the day on which most Swindon fans would have chosen to stop time.

RUNAWAY TRAIN (1993-94)

Champions:	Manchester United
Relegated:	Sheffield United, Oldham Athletic, Swindon Town
Unbelievable Relegation Escape:	Everton

The runaway train had finally been released from the siding where it had long rusted, and if we did not begrudge Manchester United one championship in 26 years in 1992/93, so many of 'them' (I hesitate to say 'fans' in some cases) came out of the woodwork (in Essex, in Cornwall, in Gothenburg, in Bangkok...etc) that we quickly became bored. So, Manchester United repeated their inaugural triumph, this time allowing the older money of Manchester to triumph over Jack Walker's industrialist newly splashed cash at Blackburn.

It is unlikely that the second Premier League season will live long in the memory, yielding the same result as the first and many to follow, although once again the winning margin of 8 points doesn't quite reflect how close it was. Jack Walker's millions (you only needed millions in those days) took Blackburn Rovers even closer to the title than their faltering bid the previous season. It is a season perhaps most notable for nearly claiming the scalp of one of the self-elected 'big five' Everton.

Focus on: Everton

I've encouraged fans to make their own contribution to this book, rather than asking for a formula of favourite player, best win, most hated rival etc. Andrew Taylor chose to go with the stadium itself (which may not be around for that much longer) and to get all poetical into the bargain. Thanks Andrew.

Goodison Park, home to Everton FC, is the Grand Old Lady of football grounds. Not stadia, grounds. It is one of the world's oldest and has hosted more Premier League games than any other. It also hosted games in the 1966 World Cup, including the semi-final where Germany beat the Soviet Union to progress to the final at Wembley. It is, as my 1970s badge bought outside the ground says, 'God's Little Acre'.

Surrounded by terraced housing and narrow residential streets, Goodison Park is also home to a church. The Gwladys Street stand and Goodison Road stand (the Main stand) box in St Luke's, Walton. The 'God's Little Acre' badge clearly had a purpose in 1977. St. Luke's opens its doors pre-match for the Everton faithful to seek shelter and perhaps a place to pray before the game. It's more likely than for the memorabilia that is for sale upstairs and the cups of tea that are on offer. The church maintains a good relationship with the club.

Since the Premier League formed and the commercialising of the game of football, Goodison has hosted international football. In 1995, I was witness, alongside 29,326 others, who saw Brazil beat Japan in the Umbro Cup. Strangely, only 21,142 saw the national team play Japan at Wembley during the same tournament.

For many, the Premier League has introduced change into the national game. The TV deal that persuaded the Premier League to break away from the Football League in 1992, has meant the top tier has become awash with money. Goodison Park has tried to keep up with the times. As well as becoming all-seater, it has redeveloped the Park End stand or rather The Sir Philip Carter Park Stand (though the city council refused permission to use a slither of Stanley Park to extend the ground, while giving permission to our loveable neighbours to build there).

Goodison Park, to Evertonians really is a home from home. A poem that I wrote about what it is to be an Evertonian was published in the Everton fanzine When Skies Are Grey in 2000:

It's Enough To Make Your Heart Go...

*Woah. A rush usually reserved
for those on the dance floor at
Cream. The roar, the Z-Cars
theme and the inevitable loo
roll thrown onto the pitch.*

*Previously. The solitary march
around the ground. Gwladys St
to Bullens Rd, and through past
the Park End Box Office. Dodging
Police horses and kids asking
'Any spares mate?'*

*Now. With a dodgy colour photocopy
of the prototype Puma strip on my desk,
I realise that the tower, the laurel and the
badge itself, have come to mean
much more than most people would
ever understand. It's enough to make
your heart go...*

My favourite Premier League moment at Goodison was during the 1993/94 season. Final game of the season, May 7th 1994 and a packed Goodison witnessed Everton's survival by beating Wimbledon 3-2. 2-0 down after 20 minutes all looked doomed until Graham Stuart's winner nine minutes from time.

Goodison's capacity is currently 39, 572. There is talk of moving the club elsewhere. I'm not sure what I feel about this. Is it to merely accommodate more corporate seating? Make the game more of a spectacle? I hope not. As I said, Goodison Park is a part of me. It's enough to make your heart go...

Like it or not, there will be no further poetry. Finally on Everton, Gareth Bell nominates them as the team with the most bizarre list of possible PL era take-overs. These have included Sir Paul McCartney, The Sultan of Brunei, Chris Evans, Red Bull drinks and Sylvester Stallone, two of which had no chance simply on account of the 'red'. *Sly has readily admitted that not buying Everton in 2007 is one of his life's greatest regrets, presumably along with the film 'Stop! Or my Mom will shoot!*

Focus on: Swindon Town

The Premier League hasn't always been appreciated by the brief visitors, and for Bradford and Blackpool for instance, initiated a dangerous disequilibrium. However, for Swindon's Chris Merrifield it was splendid adventure to treasure. Here he describes the journey, and for once I resist the opportunity to interrupt his reverie in search of cheap laughs.

After 112 years, Swindon Town finally made it to the Premier League. They had beaten Leicester City 4-3 in the Play-off Final on 31 May, 1993, a match which is still regarded as one of the best Play-off Finals ever. Swindon took the lead just before half-time through their player/manager Glenn Hoddle, and early in the second half added two more, only for Leicester to come back with three goals in 12 minutes. With only five minutes to go, Chalkie White went over in the penalty area and Paul Bodin scored from the spot. Personally I thought the penalty award was a bit soft, particularly at such a vital time in such a vital match. Coming out of Wembley, we met several Leicester City supporters, who to a man offered us their congratulations and wished us well for next season. I was amazed at their generosity and sportsmanship, especially as Leicester had also lost the previous season's play-off, to Blackburn Rovers, so must have been hugely disappointed. Never mind. Their day would come.

Swindon thought that they had made it through to the top division three years earlier, when they beat Sunderland 1-0 in the play-off Final. But financial irregularities meant that the Football League decided to demote Swindon back to Division 2. Our chairman, Brian Hillier, was sent to prison for six months. Several years later, similar accusations were levelled at Chelsea and Tottenham Hotspur, but they only received a fine. Swindon fans have always felt aggrieved at the double standards, but then Chelsea and Spurs had friends in high places and we didn't.

Our euphoria at being promoted was soon dissipated, when Glenn Hoddle decided that greener pastures lay at Stamford Bridge, while our club captain Colin Calderwood, who had led us right through from the bottom to the top divisions in his eight years at the club, but whose contract was up, left us for Tottenham Hotspur. But he had been such a loyal servant and a brilliant captain, and we didn't begrudge him his chance with a big club.[1]

John Gorman, Hoddle's assistant, announced that he would stay, and the Directors gave him the manager's job. I was relieved at the time. John knew our players and our club, and what we desperately needed was some stability and continuity. The club invested some of Calderwood's transfer fee in a new striker, Jan Aage Fjortoft[2] *coming from Rapid Vienna for £500,000, and we started the season with a great sense of excitement.*

But foreboding soon replaced it, as our first two matches, against Sheffield United and Oldham, perceived to be two of the weakest teams in the league, were both lost, and these were followed by a home fixture with Liverpool in which we were thumped 5-0. Southampton also scored five against us at which point we realised how bleak things were. Premier League strikers could be lethal. If the defence made a mistake in the lower divisions they were quite likely to get away with it, but not in the top division.

We gained our first point after five matches, with a scoreless draw at Norwich. Congregated in one section of the Carrow Road ground, the away supporters picked on Robert Fleck after an incident on the pitch, and he responded by pretending to adjust his boot while pointing his backside at us. All great fun.

A month later came our much anticipated visit to Old Trafford. We lost 4-2, but to score twice against the mighty Manchester United gave us much pleasure and a bit of self-respect. Further draws against Everton and Spurs started to give us a little hope, though we were still bottom of the league and our main striker Fjortoft had yet to score. We bought Keith Scott from Wycombe, and he scored in his first match, away to Ipswich Town in a 2-2 draw.

Our next opponents were QPR and we finally managed a 1-0 win, Scott again being the scorer. We invaded the pitch in ecstacy, and were starting to dream that we might after all crawl away from the bottom spot in the league. An amazing point in a 2-2 draw at Anfield, followed by a revengeful home win against Southampton brought us in touch with the other strugglers. One more win and we could be out of the bottom three. But Arsenal visited the County Ground over Christmas and thrashed us 4-0, memorable for a fantastic goal by Ian Wright. Shortly afterwards, Glenn Hoddle brought his Chelsea team, and left with a 3-1 victory. Then came a 6-2 thrashing at Goodison Park. Our destiny seemed sealed. We were becoming the laughing stock, derided by both the opposition and their supporters, and it hurt.

---

[1] I thought he went to Tottenham? Ed.

[2] His name does have all sorts of foreign accents, but we'll go with his Twitter name I think.

Andy Mutch had been sent off against Everton, and his suspension meant that John Gorman was forced to bring bach Fjortoft. Amazingly he started scoring, firstly in a cup match against Ipswich and then in the following two league matches, against Spurs and Coventry, which brought us two wins on the trot. Fjortoft had developed a perfectly legal way of shielding the ball when receiving a pass, and his goal celebration – arms outstretched like an aeroplane – was quickly taken up by the Swindon fans who naturally christened him Jan the Man. Were our fortunes going to change after all? Were we somehow going to climb out of the relegation zone? We really did begin to wonder.

But a visit to Newcastle in March, where we were thumped 7-1, brought us back down to earth, and next up were Manchester United. The County Ground was bulging to see Alex Ferguson's stars, and amazingly we earned a 2-2 draw. Eric Cantona got sent off for stamping on a prone Johnny Moncur.³ Little Swindon had over the course of both matches scored four times against the mighty champions. Did anyone else do that in that season? I don't think so.⁴

After that, however, we gathered very few points, though did manage our only away win of the season against QPR at Loftus Road. We away supporters, who surmised quite early on that this was going to be our one and only season in the Premier League and were determined to visit as many famous grounds while we could, were finally rewarded with a victory.

Our final match of the season was at home to Leeds United, where we suffered another heavy defeat, losing 5-0. This took our goals conceded total to 100. We had 30 points and scored 47. Howard Wilkinson, the Leeds manager, said afterwards that we didn't deserve to be in the Premier League, a comment that did not endear him to the Swindon fans. We had after all rightly earned our place, but were totally unprepared for the challenge. As is usual with all teams that are relegated, we were left wondering what might have been. Would we have done any better if Glenn Hoddle or Colin Calderwood had not left, if Fjortoft had started scoring earlier, or if we had somehow strengthened the defence?

In the end I was relieved in some ways that the season was over, as I was fed up with being trounced every week. It would be nice to get back among teams that we stood a chance of beating. But it was an unforgettable experience, and one of the highlights of 60 years of following my beloved Swindon Town.

---

³ *Plus ça change*

⁴ Curiously, although Liverpool did score 3 in one match (a 3-3 draw at Anfield) only also relegated Oldham Athletic matched Swindon's total of 4 goals. However, Oldham lost twice, so Swindon's one point and 4 goals is more impressive.

Focus on: Coventry City

It would be difficult to imagine a worse move to a new stadium, than Coventry City's move to the Ricoh Arena in 2005, unless perhaps you are a Darlington fan. The Ricoh was once filled for an England under-21 international I believe, and may have been by Wasps rugby more recently, or Davis Cup tennis for all I know or care, but has not yet been brimming to capacity for its intended tenants. Coventry have just been relegated to the fourth tier. But it was not always so bleak for the sky blues.

In 1999 Randy Hamilton (as no-one except me calls Sir Andrew) wrote a piece for The Independent called *The unpredictability that keeps City alive*. Alas it is perhaps the predictability of terminal decline which has killed the passion of even serious devotees like Randy. At that time however, basking in the glow of an unusual 1-4 victory at Villa Park (and predicting defeat in the next match at home to Charlton), he concludes by suggesting that:

> "Nobody loves us but Coventry City will line up in the Premiership once again in five months' time – *you can bet on that!* (emphasis added)"

'His Randyness' (as even I daren't call him) might be interested to know that Coventry in fact beat Charlton in that next match, 2-1. I mention this because although he was correct that Coventry stayed up that season, if that result were reversed (and other things being equal) it would have been Coventry relegated, by a single goal, instead of Charlton. It is a sign of the increasing difficulty Coventry had in maintaining their top flight status; and once it was gone they did not look like making a quick/slow/ever return.

But it wasn't so very long ago that Coventry City looked like a permanent fixture in the Premier League, even if the unpredictability noted by Hamilton was almost part of their DNA. In 1992/93, 6 wins in the first 8 games put them in a very strong position which they threw away by gaining just 3 points and no wins in the next 11. Thereafter, 20 points from 12 games nonetheless offered the prospect of a top half finish, then wasted by just one win in the final 11 games of the season.

When 1993/94 dawned the sky blues were playing their 27th consecutive season in the top flight, and like the previous season it started brightly. The light of FA Cup glory against Spurs in 1987 had not fully dimmed either. And Micky Quinn scored a hat-trick in a 0-3 victory at Highbury against Arsenal on the opening day. That was 20% of the goals Arsenal conceded at home all season! After seven more games, including 5 draws, City were still undefeated. Playing in a sky blue version of the 1992/93 Arsenal away 'curtain' Ndlovu, Quinn and Wegerle were a potent attack. Chris Marsden football genius came on loan and claimed the assist in a Sky win over Swindon. Micky Quinn provided my own personal highlight by celebrating a goal with the 'Rimmer salute' from Red Dwarf. City won away at Newcastle and in the final game of the season were unlucky only to leave Old Trafford with a single point in a 0-0 draw. Unpredictability still defined Coventry but this time it all added up to 11th place. If that doesn't sound anything special, then let me be clear: there were still 22 teams in the Premier League at that time so that 11th constituted a *top half finish*.

This is the only time Coventry City have ever finished in the top half of the Premier League. As we shall see, their supporters have more often got their excitement by defying the relegation odds.

PS I asked another Coventry fan to name good Premier League memories and he suggested Viorel Moldovan; I was surprised when I learned that the Romanian Moldovan had only played 10 games for Coventry City despite being a record signing. I then discovered the probable explanation; he had scored the winner at Aston Villa in a 1998 FA Cup 5th round tie, thus breaking a supposed curse and 27 game non-winning streak at Villa Park just before Hamilton's excitement at a 1-4 thrashing at the same venue. For the record Coventry lost to Sheffield United in the quarter-final after scoring just one of their penalties in the deciding shoot-out.

Season's Awards

Painful Relegation: Sheffield United (and it doesn't get any better either)

Crazy But True Facts and Statistics

- Newcastle fans will be incredulous that Jo Kinnear won manager of the month in September that season.

- Newcastle fans *were* incredulous that season as they lost 2-1 at Southampton only because someone scored two of the best goals ever.

- You would never have had the chance to be incredulous at those 2 goals if Ian Branfoot had brought on Moody for Le Tissier which he was intending to do before the first of them.[5]

- All of us will be incredulous that Everton stole Norwich's manager in January, later being found guilty of poaching. At least they don't do that sort of thing now eh?

- Efan Ekoku became the first Premier League player to bag four goals in a single game in a 1-5 win for Norwich at Goodison.

Up Next

Palace and Forest bounced straight back. Tranmere missed out in the play-offs again and now struggle to be in the football league rather than the Premier League; you have to feel their chance has gone. Leicester came up through the play-offs and still had many years of yo-yoing to come before 'it' happened. That it did possibly still gives hope to Tranmere.

---

[5] Go on, educate yourself in 2 minutes. Even without the excited commentary these are special. The goals referred to are second and third on this: **https://www.youtube.com/watch?v=rp-XhGIyGdo** (re-accessed 12/5/17)

GIVE IT AWAY
(OR EVERYBODY WAS KUNG-FU FIGHTING)
(1994-95)

Champions:	Blackburn Rovers
Relegated:	Crystal Palace, Norwich City, Leicester City, Ipswich Town

When Derby County reigned supreme in English football (no really!) winning League titles in 1971/72 and 1974/75 and beating Real Madrid 4-1 at the Baseball Ground, they did so for long enough that you still come across the odd aged 50ish southerner (you will do in this book) who continued to support them beyond the playground. Such was the speed of Blackburn's rise and fall, however, that few outside the town claim allegiance...promoted to the inaugural Premier League, good the following season and then runners-up/winners/in decline in quick succession. But thank goodness they did win, if only to allay the nagging doubt that Manchester United might win it FOREVER and also because Jack Walker showed that money *can* buy you happiness.[1]

---

[1] Elsewhere I comment on the absurd claim that Premier League singing is infused with wit that Noel Coward would have been proud of; a good example of the spite that characterises PL singing was the charming 'You're f***ed when Walker dies'. They were though.

The fledgling Premier League was giving us two horse races and this season, like the previous one, saw Blackburn Rovers as Man United's sole realistic challengers. Despite twice losing to United, Rovers went to Anfield for the last game knowing that a win against Liverpool would give them the title, but anything less could open the door for Man U who could then take the title with victory at West Ham. As Blackburn took the lead at Anfield and West Ham did likewise at Upton Park[2] it looked like a nice celebration of an afternoon for Blackburn fans looking to win the league for the first time since before the First World War.

Oh, but the footballing Gods rarely make things *that* easy and both Liverpool and Manchester United equalised. This was in the days when transistor radio was the main medium of information and if you didn't have one you would look at the person who did, waiting and wondering if they would suddenly slump or jump, cheer or cry. (Younger readers should consult: https://en.wikipedia.org/wiki/Transistor_radio). So I'm guessing that as Jamie Redknapp's last minute free-kick for Liverpool ruled out any possibility of a Blackburn win, a few Blackburn fans were listening to radio reports from Upton Park (and the rest were watching those few) where Man Utd were battering Ludek Miklosko between the West Ham posts. Possible despair quickly turned to delight as the news was confirmed that Man Utd had failed to win. Liverpool fans had their cake (a win on the final day) and ate it (it didn't allow Man Utd to win the league).

Notwithstanding Blackburn's unlikely to be repeated achievement, and the closeness of the final day, you can't help feeling that the title was actually decided at Crystal Palace in March. That's when the somewhat hapless and subsequently vilified Matthew Simmons said some things which Eric Cantona took exception to. The Frenchman consequently aimed a 2 footed kung-fu kick at Simmons and then punched him. Perfectly reasonable those Man Utd players of course; it's why the rest of us loved them so much.[3] This is probably the stand-out moment of the season, unless you count *that* goal by Matt Le Tiss at Ewood Park, but I'm contractually forbidden from mentioning him too much.

Anyway...I'm no Quaker, but even so I'm pretty sure that karate-kicking someone is rarely a good idea, however much the verbal provocation. Having been instrumental in the destination of the last three league titles (once with Leeds), and destined to be so again in the next three, Eric decided to give it away with a moment of madness.

---

[2] The ground which suddenly became the Boleyn Ground 30 seconds before it was closed. Anyone know why?

[3] According to United's head of security at the time Cantona's reaction afterwards was to 'shrug' – quelle sur-effin-prise!

Blackburn admittedly did their best to give it away too, but somehow squeaked home to relieve the boredom which would become Man Utd titles.[4]

Focus on: Nottingham Forest

Being a football fan in Nottingham, on whichever side of the Trent, is all about the past. You can either approach it with 'pride and resignation' or 'pride and bitter, twisted resentment'. Jim falls solidly in the latter category. As he talks to me, he twitches and grits his teeth and looks at me suspiciously as I take notes. If you had only one word to describe football fans, while Bournemouth's are 'happy', Chelsea's 'cocky', Arsenal's 'ungrateful', Southampton's 'heroic' and Man Utd's 'smug', then Forest's are the epitome of 'frustration'. He has time for a short rant before we head to the pub.

I have a love/hate relationship with the Premier League; mostly hate, although to be fair I am a bit of a nihilist, however you pronounce it. Does anyone know? Does anything matter?[5] I love the fact that Direby County got the lowest ever points total. I hate the fact that Fester City won it. No, not so much that they won it, but that people seem to think that it's as much of an achievement as when we won the old first division and then the European Cup. And again. That's twice. I hate the fact that I was too young to really appreciate those days. I hate the fact that our owners

[4] It's worth reducing to a footnote here the obviously talented but loathsome Roy Keane. In this season he was sent off for stamping on Gareth Southgate. Another stamp, another season, allowed Southampton to beat Man Utd 6-3 which is possibly why he gloated openly on the day that a 1-2 defeat to Man Utd saw Saints' stay in the Premier League finally end. It probably says this in his autobiography (which I'll never read), along with an admission that a sickening attack in the Manchester derby was premeditated and that he has no remorse about it. For those who think it is remotely important whether this specific tackle ended Alf-Inge Haaland's career or not, I'd suggest you really are missing the point. As The Guardian put it: "It [was] an act of irredeemable brutality – a knee-capping the IRA would have been proud of. Keane should not have been merely sent off, he should have been imprisoned for assault." If you don't believe me, go to: **https://www.youtube.com/watch?v=kzrKTMSLcgQ** where it compares unfavourably with the worst of all time. Keane was, on occasion, an international standard player but never class.

[5] This is left comprehensively unresolved by beginning the word with both 'knee' and 'nigh' at: **https://www.youtube.com/watch?v=eJeQpdk-5IQ** (Accessed 22/2/17)

always seem to ask not what they can do for Forest, but what Forest can do for them. I hate the money, the cynicism. I hate Rupert Murdoch and phrases like the 'fan experience'. I hate that we're not there and I'd hate it if we were there again. I hate bloody football and I'll tell you what, I'll love it, I'll absolutely love it, if Leicester get relegated. Did I mention we won the European Cup twice?

Jim is currently residing at a safe distance from Nottingham and drinking to forget. If he watches football at all it is at a pub level and virtually indistinguishable from rugby, which he quite likes.

Focus on: Blackburn Rovers

Andy Watton seemed a very nice chap from the moment he got in touch and sent me a chunky set of ruminations on his beloved BRFC. They were headed with the words 'no review of the Premier League would be complete without a chunky section on Blackburn Rovers.' I felt my Liverpool supporting friends bristle at this idea, but who am I to choose between grim northern towns, even footballing enclaves in the egg-chasing wilderness. There, now you can all bristle together at the arrogant southerner.

By the time Andy's notes arrived, the rest of this chapter was already in place and I read through it quickly. My mention (above) of Jack Walker proving that money can buy you happiness jarred noticeably with a large section in Andy's notes which begins: *A personal bugbear of many a Rovers' supporter is the lazy suggestion that Blackburn Rovers 'bought' the Premier League title in 1995.* I will confess to being lazy like my hero, and occasionally provocative in search of a cheap laugh, but whatever it seems like, I really don't want to annoy anyone or for anyone to take any of it seriously. So how to deal with this conundrum or contradiction?

Let's look at the evidence provided. Andy's includes the fact that they broke the British transfer record to steal Alan Shearer from Southampton. Ah. And that they 'splashed the cash' to attract Tim Flowers...from the same Saints.

You're getting no sympathy from me mate! But seriously, he has a point. Rovers' title winning side also contained a 34-year-old free transfer from West Ham in Tony Gale and a £45k signing from Scunthorpe in midfielder, Mark Atkins. Others arrived for *comparative peanuts*. Le Saux from Chelsea's reserves for £700k; Henning Berg for £400k; Jason Wilcox from the youth team and Tim Sherwood for £400k. Man Utd spent considerably more, as they always do. *To put it all into perspective, Rovers entire back line cost less than the fee Newcastle paid for Darren Peacock and half of what Liverpool paid for their central defensive pairing of Phil Babb and John Scales.*

Andy concludes that it would be *unfair to overlook the team spirit, tactical and motivational aspects that King Kenny brought to the table*. Of course. But, on the other hand, if Rovers ever regain Premier League status, it will not be through astute signings and team spirit alone, but also money. In a sense, everyone - Leicester included – 'buys' the Premier League, but they also have to have that extra something special. If Rovers fans' bugbear is that people tend to overlook this extra special bit, then I am happy to concede the argument. It was a great achievement.

On the other hand, it does seem that Walker's money made Blackburn contenders in a way that subsequently happened for Chelsea and Manchester City. So, I used my private line to the footballing Gods to ask Jack Walker himself what he thought and he said:

> *I'm very happy to have contributed to Rovers' successes and that we had a manager in Kenny who didn't only rely on cash - because I'm not an oil tycoon you know. But if people think it was my money which bought Rovers the title then I'll die a happy man... What do you mean I'm already dead? Don't be soft lad, I just saw Rovers win the Premier League for the 20th consecutive season at our new 40 billion all-seater Pearly Gates Stadium. We're playing Bishop's Stortford in the FA Cup final next week, you should come.*

Being one of only six teams to win the Premier League which even giants like ~~Southampton~~ Liverpool have not managed, is a great achievement. Latterly, Rovers' time under the Venkys and Steve Kean barely intersected with the Premier League at all. Andy told me a lot about this time, but I cannot bear to repeat it or I'll cry like the soft southerner I am. Andy also reflected a lot on Shearer but if anyone leaves Saints for cash, then I'm leaving them out too.[6]

---

[6] Although Rovers clearly did not buy the title, this reminds me of the day a friend told me (pre-information overload age, unless you count obsessive teletext counting) that Blackburn had finally persuaded Le Tissier to leave The Dell, for £10m (about £200m in today's money). He was so convincing, it was awful. Still, at least you didn't get *one* of our players.

Season's Awards

Best Celebration: Jurgen Klinsmann gets the hang of English self-deprecation rather quickly by diving to celebrate his many goals in a season where he was Spurs player of the year.

Crazy But True Facts and Statistics:

- Everton having escaped on the last day of last season started with 8 points and only one win from their first 14 games.
- Joe Royle replaced Mike Walker and Everton not only stayed up, but also won the FA Cup.
- Man United thus did the double again; this time as runners up in both main competitions.
- Newcastle were the early pace–setters winning their first six games and not losing until their 12th (at Old Trafford); their decline was not as spectacular as one which was to follow and they gradually drifted downwards to finish in a season low 6th place.

Up Next

With the Premier League reducing from 22 to 20 teams only one automatic promotion place was up for grabs and went to Middlesbrough. Bolton finished 3rd in the regular season but beat 2nd placed Reading in the play-off final. Tranmere Rovers finished in the play-off places and with a home record better than anyone else's only need a moderately good away record to have gone up automatically; unfortunately, it wasn't as good as 20th placed Sunderland and they failed to make the Premier League yet again.

WONDERWALL (1995-96)

Champions:	Manchester United
Relegated:	Manchester City, Queens Park Rangers, Bolton Wanderers
Unbelievable Relegation Escape:	Coventry City and Southampton

"Maybe, you're gonna be the one that saves me, and after all, you're my Alan Ball"

(Man City fans, 1995-96)

But before we get to that especially satisfying moment for all you *schadenfreude* fans (which I'm guessing City fans have recovered from), I think I should point out that you probably think writing this book was easy: access to the internet; nothing better to do; desire to write pro-Saints drivel until it comes out of my ears.; other peeps writing the good bits. But if you thought that, you're wrong. Not just for the effort, but for some of things I had to watch. Keane's assault on Haaland for one, for which he is apparently unrepentant. But worst of all was this (accessed 12/5/17): https://www. youtube.com/watch?v=_Yenzdq5g6o

'This', in case you've not time to type it into a search engine, is none other than Kevin Keegan's rant which effectively handed Man U all the ammunition they needed and conceded the title race. Ooh it is painful. In the full version of his 'I would love it' outburst (as famous now as 'I have a dream' but rather less dignified) he actually starts off quite calmly but quickly descends into foggy, stuttering rage. Perhaps it is so painful because it so perfectly expressed the thoughts of so many who witnessed another double winning season for Man Utd? We would have loved it not to happen too, but it did.

Anyway, having won nine of their first ten games, Newcastle led the other United by ten points at one stage. This was reduced following the return of 'King Eric' in October after his community service etc. The lead was then extended again to be twelve points in January, before being gradually squandered by a team weighed down by a mixture of inexperience and high expectation. Keegan pointed out that Manchester United needed to go to Middlesbrough and 'get something' which they duly did (although didn't actually *need* to because Newcastle failed to beat Spurs anyway). So, it was three of the first four Premier League titles to Manchester; the other to Greater Manchester.

No sign at all at this stage that Manchester City would attract first cash and then the finest players and managers available to humanity. Indeed, the other Manchester team failed to win any of their first 12 games. Although by the end of the season they had started to look a half-decent side, City were relegated ultimately on goal difference, on the final day of the season. In reviewing that final day, it seems incredible now that Tony Gubba on Match of the Day noted that Coventry – inevitably in the relegation mix - had 'no idea what was going on elsewhere' during their match. Mobile – though not smart - phones did exist, but were rare and the trouble with transistor radios is that only one person can hear them in a crowd and some people are quite mischievous; I can still remember the sinking feeling as Everton fans celebrated a phantom Charlton 'goal' on the last day of a later season, and it took ages for local transistor radio holders to deny the rumour.

Into this informational void (so last century) stepped Coventry City (goal difference -18), ahead of Southampton on goals scored (also -18) and Manchester City (-25); all on the same points total. All had home games; all looked nervous. It was likely, even for Man City, that a win would ensure survival as it was unlikely that both the others would. As it happened the Sky Blues (CCFC version) and Saints couldn't even manage a goal between them let alone a win, but they did both get a point. Coventry manager Ron Atkinson admitted that it was difficult to know whether they should try to win or simply not lose the game. Southampton also drew 0-0 against Wimbledon; it is an eerie feeling to stand in a silent stadium at the end of a match waiting for someone to tell you what's happened elsewhere, unsure whether that 0-0 was enough; it had certainly made the Saints vulnerable.

All the day's goal drama took place at Maine Road where Manchester City had the toughest fixture that day (Liverpool) but looked in excellent form; in fact, they battered Liverpool, who then took the lead against the run of play (Lomas o.g.). They then further battered Liverpool, missing when it looked easier to score – bad luck (Niall Quinn) and awful finishing (Uwe Rosler) prevented an equaliser. Ian Rush scored a deflected and undeserved 2nd for Liverpool before half time. But in the second half City continued to stream forward, scoring twice; the equaliser from Kit Symons.

And then the stranger than fiction bit. Alan Ball took off big striker Niall Quinn (when City had to score) and Steve Lomas started wasting time by the corner flag (when City had to score). The former may simply be that Bally decided not to go gung-ho for once when actually that was what was required; it may have been poor tactics in other words, and I wouldn't be the first to suggest that of him. But what was Lomas doing? The most likely explanation is that someone in the crowd, and who knows the reason why, made players on the pitch believe that either Southampton or Coventry were losing so that a team that had to score was wasting time in the belief they didn't. And so Alan Ball was not, in fact, the one to save them, and was sacked shortly afterwards. Another reprieve for Saints and Sky Blues this time, but dark days lay ahead for them both.

Focus on: Newcastle United

There is something about fans of say Manchester City or Newcastle; a kind of belief that their stoicism is exceptional. They should try supporting Frome Town or Frickley Athletic or any other place with a name. But with that caveat inserted, for a club of its size and support, Newcastle do seem quite exceptional in their support for a team that never wins anything. Rob Enright picks up the tale:

I have been a Newcastle United fan since 1995/96 and have endured a wonderful 20 years of severe ups and catastrophic downs. Whatever club could be 12 points clear and throw it away? Or get relegated with a team that had the likes of Michael

Owen, Damien Duff, Obafemi Martins and Mark Viduka? Have the greatest striker and all time record Premier League goal-scorer on its books for over a decade and not win a trophy? Appoint Joe Kinnear (twice)! Picking some of the best memories and moments and sloshing them in a cocktail with the worst is a tricky one. But let's give it a go.

We have to start with Shearer. The man embodies Newcastle. A true Geordie, he may not have had the silky skills of Thierry Henry, or the prodigy hype machine of Wayne Rooney, but still to this day, if you offered me a prime Shearer I would take him over any striker in the league. The man was both footed, scored as many screamers as he did tap-ins and was phenomenal in the air for a man of his height. Mike Ashley has ruined any chance of Shearer coming back to manage us properly (tacking him on the back end of our relegation season doesn't count.[1]) But the man will always be a legend.

Whilst we are talking about Newcastle legends, there are two names that need mentioning. In a time before the internet allowed you to know everything about an unknown player before the ink dries on his contract, it was genuinely intriguing for your club to sign players you had never heard of. Enter Nolberto Solano and Temuri Ketsbaia. Peruvian Solano was such a wonderful player to watch, his delivery was fantastic. I think consistently for a few seasons, he actually whipped in more successful crosses than Beckham. The man was just a lovely gem of a player, who scored some wonderful goals and is held in high esteem. As is Ketsbaia, the crazy, bald Georgian who went completely mental on an advertising hoarding. He didn't stick about for long but you should YouTube his best goals. Some of them were ridiculous!

Some of the goals and games that I have been subjected to following the Toon Army will never leave me. From the 4-3 epics vs Liverpool (two seasons running!), to the 8-0 spanking of Sheffield Wednesday in Bobby Robson's first match as manager, there are just so many. The one that will stick with me though was in the late 90s; we were at home to Leicester and a young striker named Emile Heskey put them 3-1 up. With 11 minutes left, Shearer scored the first of what would be a hat-trick, with the winner coming in stoppage time. It was an amazing moment.

Now lastly, before we talk about the dark times, I need to recommend making a cup of tea and YouTubing Laurent Robert and then Ben Arfa. Their highlights at Newcastle make them look like Messi. They were just so inconsistent, and I don't agree with their attitudes, but some of those moments of brilliance were amazing. As were the first six months of seeing Papiss Cisse in a Newcastle shirt. From his thumping

---

[1] He means 'one of' their relegation seasons.

winner on his debut, his dink against Swansea or his physics defying volley against Chelsea, those six months were unbelievable.

Not so cherished, however, are the years of poor ownership. Freddy Shepherd, apart from slagging off the Geordie public, heard a small minority of fans booing Bobby Robson after a poor start to the season and pulled the trigger. We sat 19th, above only Blackburn who were managed by Graeme Souness. So who did he appoint? Graeme Souness!! It was a bizarre decision and easily the worst made at the club for years....

....until Mike Ashley, of the zero hour contract and rapidly growing waist line, thought it was a good idea to hire Joe Kinnear. The club was flailing, Keegan had left after a second coming that never started, and we needed saving. We needed someone with the talent and record of survival. Someone relevant. We got Joe Kinnear. A man who called Charles N'Zogbia, our best player at the time, 'Insomnia' and referred to Yohan Cabaye, a French international and our player of the year, as 'Kebab'. The man was a disaster and his phone interview, where he made so many false claims is one of the most ridiculous things I have ever heard. Newcastle is not a club that needs help to be a laughing stock!

We went down, we romped the Championship when it looked more likely we would do a Leeds, and we beat our relegators, Aston Villa, 6-0 in our first home game back. It was going well. Carroll was looking like the next Shearer, Nolan was rolling back the years and Coloccini was looking a class act. Then a crazy few months saw Hughton sacked, Pardew hired and Carroll sold (wisely I must add) for a ridiculous fee. Now Pardew did alright to begin with. Our season finishing 5th was brilliant. But there are a lot of issues we have with Pardew and I feel they need to be touched on.

He never took the blame for defeats, yet was happy to hype himself up when we won. In his final year in charge, where the press and everyone made out that we were hounding him out, was atrocious. In his final calendar year we lost 18 and drew four of our 28 games under him and I lost count of how many of those we lost by three or more goals. We lost six derby games, home and away, in a row.[2] He head-butted a player! It was truly awful and he should have been sacked. If he was likable in any way, then maybe he would have got some more support but the man just makes your skin crawl. Good luck to Palace – am pretty sure 2016 has been similar for them.[3]

So what's ahead? John Carver and Shteve McClaren have shown us new levels of

---

[2] Meaning Sunderland, not Middlesbrough

[3] Obviously replaced now by the loveable Allardyce. In fact it's likely that the players and managers you loved when you picked up this book have now been sacked and replaced by others that you then hated then and now love. Probably since you started reading this footnote in fact.

ineptitude and we returned to the second tier. However things have never looked brighter as we have Rafa Benitez, easily the best manager we have had since Bobby Robson. Ashley has finally scrapped his undeserved faith in his 'football men' and has asked a real football manager to fix his club. He certainly seems to be doing it. If we can keep him and Ashley keeps his nose out of it, the future certainly looks bright on the Toon.

Season's Awards

Schadenfreude: Alan Ball left Southampton to join Manchester City at the start of the season; City were relegated on goal difference behind Southampton having wasted time when they needed to score. Priceless.

Crazy But True Facts and Statistics:

- Juninho, one of the most highly rated Brazilian players at the time signed for Middlesbrough.
- This is the season when Manchester United played a game in two different kits. Was this 'colour me grey' incident a foray into obscene marketing? Partially yes, as they played the first half at The Dell in their marketable grey leisure-wear and the second in blue and white. They claimed they couldn't see each other in

grey, going down 3-0 by the break; the change led to a minor recovery and 3-1 defeat, their last of the season. The grey kit was discontinued, with little regard for those who'd forked out for it. Southampton's own 'beige-gate' got much less publicity despite a higher level of hideosity.[4]

- If I had a pound for everyone that mixes up the grey shirt game with the '6-3' game I'd have £34 by now. That comes later.

Up Next

It was all the yo-yo teams this season...Sunderland won the league having only narrowly avoided relegation the season before. They were followed up automatically by Derby County. Tranmere did not qualify for the play-offs but having finished 5th, Leicester City won them and seemed destined to do nothing but follow a cycle of endless promotions and relegations forever without ever threatening to win other than the League Cup. No, wait, that's not right...

---

[4] A new word but I like it.

BITTER SWEET SYMPHONY (1996-97)

Champions:	Manchester United
Relegated:	Sunderland, Middlesbrough, Nottingham Forest
Unbelievable Relegation Escape:	Coventry City

Imagine this: Your little Brazilian starlet is nutmegging people all over the place and jinking his tiny frame around the opposition at will. Your robust silver-haired skinhead Italian striker has a shot which threatens to break the net every time and bangs in more than 30 goals in all competitions, including an opening day hat-trick at home to Liverpool. Why did these exotic players come to your team and your grey, post-industrial wilderness? Who knows, but with their help, you reach the League Cup final (and you lose). You also reach the FA Cup final (and you lose, conceding the quickest ever Cup Final goal). In the league you do just enough to stay up, or at least you would have done, but you have 3 points deducted for failing to fulfil a fixture when your entire squad had the flu. And so you are relegated. That's what happened to Middlesbrough this season, allowing Coventry City to find another way to maintain their tenuous grip on top flight status yet again. This time it wasn't only the 3 point deduction that helped, but that other results went their way on the final day as they were posting an unlikely 1-2 win at White Hart Lane.

This season saw the lowest points total for champions since three points for a win was introduced in 1981-82 and suggests we finally had more than a two-horse race; and in fact this turned into a three-horse race. Initially this was between Man Utd, Newcastle and Liverpool for the title. But there was to be no photo finish, and ultimately the 3 horses competing – for the runners up spot – were Newcastle, Arsenal and Liverpool who were separated only by goal difference, all seven points behind Manchester United.

Liverpool in fact looked destined for glory (with the so called 'Spice Boys' of Fowler, Redknapp, McManaman, McAteer et al) but fell away at the crucial time and, with Fowler absent (suspended), even let runners-up spot slip away too on the final day. The consolation prize for not getting the consolation prize (that Newcastle took again) was that they qualified for the newly expanded European Cup. The European Cup was now called the Champions League, obviously, because it now allowed non-Champions to enter as opposed to when it was only for Champions when it was called the European Cup). As for the other United, they may have previously been in the wilderness for 26 years, but their dominance was becoming a drag, although an impressive drag you have to confess. To be fair, it wasn't United's best season, but they battled through a bad spell, including a 5-0 thrashing at St James' Park, and a 6-3 savaging at The Dell (not wearing grey) to emerge as true champions.

Focus on: Middlesbrough

Pete Hough's contribution acknowledges two truths of supporting Middlesbrough. First the yo-yo nature of their existence (pre and during the Premier League). Second that they are sustained by Newcastle's inability to win anything. He supplied me with a string of un-publishable, expletive laden songs to express this hatred which - like Bournemouth's for Southampton, Leicester's for Forest and West Brom's for Villa - isn't fully requited.

The early 1990s stand as a watershed for Middlesbrough FC in terms of progressing from being a solid, consistent but ultimately unsuccessful and ignored club to a much more high-profile and- relatively- high-achieving outfit. While League placings in the last quarter-century have not bettered those of the late 1970s or in the run up the two World Wars (when, on both occasions, we became less heralded victims of German aggression) Boro have certainly entered a new era.

Jack Charlton's over-achievers of the 1970s were moulded from local talent and low-money transfers from the lower leagues or players surplus to requirement at bigger clubs; but the 1990s suddenly saw us signing big name internationals, of a calibre previously barely dreamed of. The purchases of Juninho and Ravanelli were the most obvious symbols of this new status but the less heralded signings of Nick Barmby and Massimo Maccarone actually stand out more as markers of us entering the 'big time'. Barmby was a 21 year old Spurs regular and England international who they desperately tried to hold on to. Maccarone was the hottest young talent in Italy and his departure to Teesside rather than Milan or Turin was described as a 'black day' in the Gazetta dello Sport. As a fan it was joyous to stick two fingers up at the London media as they sneered at players moving to the frozen, polluted North East (as though living in Teesdale or the Cleveland Hills was less desirable than non-descript South-Eastern suburbia).

The undoubted low point of the Premier era was, of course, the surreal climax to the 1996-7 season which saw us beaten in both cup finals and also relegated after a dubious points' deduction by the FA. Boro were not only docked points for postponing a fixture at Blackburn but were additionally compelled to replay the game later in the season, contributing to a fixture pile up that saw us playing 3 matches a week in the run in. Had the punishment simply been to forfeit the game (which, in itself, would have been a harsh judgement) Boro would never have gone down. All of this, remember, was for having the temerity to have too few players available to field due to a virus suddenly sweeping through the squad . 1996-7 thus represented a triple whammy of misery surely unparalleled by any club.[1] Nevertheless, the pain proved bearable to Boro fans able to draw on the perspective that, ten years previously, the club had been liquidated.

The most tangible successful legacies of the Premier-era for Boro have been away from the league in acquiring the club's first major honour (2004 League Cup) and the subsequent 'small town in Europe' adventure which culminated in the UEFA Cup final. True to form, this latest renaissance did not last and Boro have been down and up since then. However, added lustre to that sole piece of silverware comes from the fact that it has eclipsed the efforts of our local rivals in the modern era.

---

[1] Contain your anger fans of Coventry, Blackpool, Blackburn, Leyton Orient, York City etc etc.

Season's Awards

Good sport: Eric Cantona's shock retirement at the end of the season; would the talisman's departure give the others a chance? (err, no)

Scoring a hattrick against Man Utd: Egil Ostenstad (Southampton). If you give some people power they simply abuse it, and so it was with the dubious goals committee after Southampton beat the Champions 6-3. Take a bow Egil!

Flatter to deceive: David Pleat's Sheffield Wednesday; 5 points clear at the top after 4 consecutive wins, but only just stayed up.

Wonderful Excuse: Fringe spice boy David 'Calamity' James, though he didn't have a fringe unlike many of the non-fringe spice boys who did, blames his erratic blunders on playing computer games affecting his concentration.

Who Are Ya?: Mickey Evans...a fleeting presence in the Premier league, won player of the month in April I think and then disappeared having kept Saints up. Truly an angel of the footballing Gods.

Crazy But True Facts and Statistics[2]

- Southampton conceded the most goals by an away team in a single match (7 at Everton) and scored the most by a home team (6 v Manchester United)

---

[2] 'SportsMole' website please note: Wimbledon, NOT MK Dons, finished 8th.

- Sunderland said 'goodbye' to Roker Park after 99 years.

- Arsenal said 'hello' to Arsene Wenger – he's working on the 99 years.

- The first foreign (non-British) manager to win a major trophy with an English club? Ruud Gullit as Chelsea won the FA Cup.

- This would probably have been 'the Leicester season' (9th and first trophy in 33 years – League Cup) if it weren't for more recent events.

- Beckham scored *that* goal from the half way line (57 yards) against Wimbledon https://www.youtube.com/watch?v=u4tVnpwp8d4 (accessed 12/5/17)

- This was the second of seven consecutive seasons in which Manchester United were top scorers; they never reached 100 though, a feat achieved only by Chelsea and Manchester City.

- Robbie Fowler hurdles David Seaman (rather than being tripped) and gets up to indicate that it's no penalty – but the referee gave it anyway. They really *never* change their minds (except at Fulham, see Focus on Fulham).

Up Next

Bolton are back again, stronger and wiser but with less luck, whilst Barnsley are about to get their first (and possibly last) taste of top flight football. Crystal Palace yo-yo again, this time winning the play-offs from 6th; they said it'll never last and it didn't.

SEASON 6

MY FAVOURITE GAME (1997-98)

Champions:	Arsenal
Relegated:	**Bolton Wandererers, Barnsley and Crystal Palace** (in the order they were promoted the previous season)
Unbelievable Relegation Escape:	**Everton**

Replacing Bruce Rioch towards the start of 1996-97, Arsene Wenger's 99 year reign as Arsenal manager began reasonably well, with the team ending up 3rd. But his first full season ended in spectacular triumph; his new fangled training ways (water instead of beer!) and management style (talk don't shout!) combined with Eric's surprise departure from the champions, combined to just give Arsene's Arsenal[1] the edge and saw Manchester United lose their favourite game – the two-horse race.

Actually, at the start of March 1998, Manchester United led the league by 11 points and one Manchester bookie called Fred Done (amazingly not bust but a billionaire) paid out on bets for United to win the title once more. However, thereafter Arsenal won game after game, including those in hand over United and at Old Trafford (0-1).[2]

---

[1] I mean what are the chances of Arsenal having a manager whose name, if said quickly and drunk, sounds just like 'Arsenal wanker'?

[2] If you have Sky you will be regularly treated to the Arsenal fan with the curly dark hair screaming like an extra from *Braveheart* at this victory - or was that 2001/02?

Combined with a narrow win at Highbury when the teams had met in November (David Platt's last minute header to make the score 3-2) and injuries to key United players during the season and everything conspired to just give Arsenal the title by a single point.

Arsenal fans will have enjoyed the season even more given events at White Hart Lane, although that goes for a great many Premier League seasons where Arsenal have one way or another bettered their old rivals. With Spurs in crisis, disciplinarian Christian Gros was drafted in and seriously misjudged the dressing room; he famously expected David 'because I'm worth it' Ginola to cut his flowing locks. Indeed the dressing room was lost from the off as the Gros 'era' began with a 1-6 home pasting by Chelsea. Chelsea themselves had a strange managerial change when Ruud Gullit left. Fell out with Ken Bates – you're nothing special Ruud. Vialli took over and led Chelsea to the Cup Winners Cup.

A change is said to be as good as a rest, though I suspect being runners up in the cup rather than league did not leave Geordies feeling refreshed. The most memorable aspect of the cup this year (though not strictly the subject of this book) was the 4th round tie between (then) non-league Stevenage and Newcastle. Stevenage were said to have disrespected their superstar opponents and at the end of the 1-1 draw none of the United players would swap shirts with the impudent part-timers. The replay at St James' Park was hardly comfortable, but Newcastle did take it 2-1 and from there went all the way to the final, where they helped Arsenal achieve the double. If you can find it, do watch Paxman savage Dalglish on Newsnight over Newcastle's generally churlish behaviour, including moaning about the bounciness of the ball; 'Are you a big girl's blouse?' Jeremy famously inquired.[3]

Other notables: If it wasn't the end of Blackburn's time, it was the beginning of the end as they managed 6th. Everton's survival may have been to do with goal-line technology after Bolton had a perfectly good goal against them not given despite TV showing it was over the line. As it was, Everton survived on goal-difference ahead of Notlob (for Python fans). Southampton and Coventry seemed habitually one place apart in the league, but on this occasion it was 11th and 12th rather than the two places above the relegation zone.

---

[3] http://www.telegraph.co.uk/sport/football/teams/stevenage-borough/8247072/Stevenage-relive-the-day-they-gave-Alan-Shearer-and-Newcastle-United-a-shock-in-FA-Cup.html (accessed 23/4/17)

Focus on: Arsenal

Paul Moore is a big Arsenal fan. By which I mean both that he's supported them for several decades and is a season ticket holder, but also that he is a formidable brick wall of a man. I suppose that would work better if you knew him. Maybe you do? Nice chap. Anyway, he kindly shared some thoughts with me, initially emphasising his credentials by noting that: *I do know what life was like before Arsene Wenger.*

Paul told me that Arsene Wenger's first title was special and that Tony Adams goal against Everton in the final game of the season brought emotional scenes. I can prove that with this footnote.[4] He goes on:

> *After George Graham's sacking, and the brief reign of Bruce Rioch, we had been in transition and in a bit of a mess. To be fair to Rioch, he did start to change our style of football from the Graham years and had qualified us for the UEFA Cup the year before, but Wenger took that to a new level. I remember losing 3-1 at Highbury to Blackburn Rovers in Wenger's first season; Tony Adams had a stinker that day and I believe we were in sixth place after the game. But at the turn of the year we went on a 10 game winning run that led us not only to our first Premier League title but also to our second double. A back line of Seaman, Dixon, Adams, Bould and Winterburn coupled with a young Patrick Vieira and Emmanuel Petit, the mercurial Marc Overmars and Nicolas Anelka and of course our then record goal scorer Ian Wright had turned us into title winners. It was no longer boring, boring Arsenal but a side packed with power and pace and the only side to give Man Utd a run for their money in the years ahead.*

Paul kindly lists so many memories that he is worried my book will turn into *War and Peace*. Tolstoy is reputed to have said of his famous work, that it was

---

[4] Rob Cleary gets teary: This was so special, in so many ways for me. This was the last time I went to Highbury with my whole family, the first time I'd sat in the North Bank, where we sat in the middle of the blind supporters section. For our captain, a so called Donkey, to score such a good goal; in front of the loudest group of supporters; behind the blind section (therefore with a completely un-obscured view of Tony Adams with his arms spread wide (which is now a statue outside the new stadium); with my whole family shouting and crying together, still gives me goose bumps!

'not a novel, even less is it a poem, and still less a historical chronicle' which is exactly this book. Furthermore, an early reviewer of *War and Peace* said 'What could this possibly be? What kind of genre are we supposed to file it to?... Where is fiction in it, and where is real history?' Again, very much the effect I'm looking for. Nonetheless, I have ditched most of Paul's memories. Sorry.[5]

Focus on: Barnsley[6]

Barnsley have the proud boast of playing more seasons in the second tier of English football than any other, participating in well over 3000 'second division' games. To do so, and yet only achieve one season at the very highest level explains a win percentage of little over 30% and an air of dour resignation that settles over Oakwell. It is a place which feels shrouded in mist even on a bright day. Of course it still rankles in South Yorkshire that Barnsley had not already been in the top division before 1997/98. They finished 3rd in the last season before the First World War and when post-war football started again in 1919/20 they could reasonably have expected to be playing in a First division which was expanding from 20 to 22 teams. However the Arsenal chairman took advantage of the football league having a ballot on the subject to bribe his team a spot instead.[7] Still, Barnsley only had to wait a little under eight decades for their minute in the sun.

And so to the 1997/98 season. With fans sounding like those of Ripping Yarns' Barnstoneworth United, Barnsley excitedly played in the top flight for the first time, excitedly went 0-3 down to Chelsea and excitedly sang 'we're gonna win 4-3'. They didn't (that day at least), although the song apparently tickled Gianfranco Zola which is some consolation. There were good days, but Barnsley didn't often sneak out of the bottom 3 all season. The telling game

---

[5] Paul fans will find more of him in 2003/04.

[6] Originally Barnsley St Peters. So just as Southampton St Marys became 'the Saints' Barnsley became the...err, 'Tykes'.

[7] I've no proof of this but by all means sue me; that's the kind of Roger Cook style journalistic bravery you'll get from me – calling out a man in his 140s if he's a day.

was a 2-3 home defeat to Liverpool in which dubious refereeing led to them finishing the match with 8 players.[8]

If that Liverpool game was the first painful nail in Barnsley's Premier League coffin, the week before the patient was very much still alive. I know because I was there to see Southampton lose as always. Arriving early, given the reputation of Barnsley as being amongst the top 500 tourist attractions in South Yorkshire, we looked around in search of a pub. Somewhere to eat then? A chip van? A vending machine? In the end we asked some locals who enthusiastically told us to follow them, straight to a supporters' club in fact where the bouncer frowned at our shirts and shook his head. 'Never mind' we said and readied to leave. But our new friends launched into the most enthusiastic spiel of all time about how we were like family to them.[9] So, with shirts tucked in pockets we entered Barnsley supporters club, where our friends also destroyed the myth of Yorkshire meanness by refusing to let us buy drinks.

Suitably lubricated we watched Barnsley take the lead 3 times in a 4-3 win where the score was already 3-2 at half time. Such was the extraordinary warmth of that welcome that I hardly begrudged them the win and have held a soft-spot for Barnsley ever since. However, I do not know any Tykes fans myself, having lost touch with our family shortly before kick-off on that day. And so, having not received replies to email invites to the supporters club to participate in this book, I decided to return in search of supporter insight with which to enliven this section.

Never go back they say. We parked at the top of the car park that leads down to the away end. This was next to a place called 'Bleak House'; it looked it, though it could have been bleaker if it had any Oakwell facing windows I suppose. I tried to engage some of the locals in conversation about the book, but it seemed I had become the black sheep of the family. Every look seemed to say 'E's one o' them soft writin' types from t'south' and to date none of the flyers I handed out has led to contributions. Perhaps the pink paper was a mistake.

Anyway, we took an ale in The Dove, a public house which was refreshing in that there was no one on the door, the bar-staff were friendly and home and away fans mixed without problem. The wall was adorned with numerous scarves and photos, especially celebrating the one season when the Tykes joined the elite. I started a promising conversation with a chap who spoke Yorkshire

---

[8] In favour of the bigger team? Hard to credit I know.

[9] That goes summit like 'thur like famly t'us'

who looked old enough to have been a fan in 1997/98. However he turned out to be a Bradford fan, there – as was I – with a friend who supported the away team, Norwich City.[10] I should have stopped the man I saw wearing an official Barnsley FC flat cap; instead I went to the club shop to buy one. Sold out.

As on my previous visit, Barnsley won, but I left without much local comment and not even some bizarre local millenary. Perhaps my expectations were too high? My expectations were that the people who met me in 1997/98 would welcome our car with showers of petals, escort us to the pub and buy round after round, before getting my name announced on the tannoy at half-time, giving me the freedom of the town and then presenting me with a Christmas hamper. Still, even with those modest hopes unfulfilled, I'm glad Barnsley had their season in the sun.[11]

Season's Awards

Sensitivity to foreign pronunciations: Barry Davies may have sounded ridiculous but he was determined to stick with Wan-chop-ay (Paulo Wanchope) and Sol-shy-rer (Ole Gunnar Solskjaer) whatever anyone else said.

Top Goalscorers: All English. Michael Owen bursts onto the scene. Dion Dublin chips in a bit more than usual. Chris Sutton survives the departure of Alan Shearer under Woy of the Wovers. All netted 18 Premier league goals.

Silly Pillock: Teddy Sheringham of Man United (he played for all the popular teams didn't he eh?) badge kissing at Highbury after scoring twice as the champions recovered from 2-0 down to level things. Arsenal still won 3-2 with a late header and the league by a point. You went to Man Utd and you're still a...yes.

Silly Pollock: Jamie Pollock in fact. One of the finest goals of all-time as he clipped

---

[10] Rory Waterman, who you can find elsewhere in this tome waxing lyrical about his beloved Canaries.

[11] Well, grey drizzle really but...

the ball over the 'defence' Le Tissiesque-style before calmly heading the ball over the advancing keeper. Alas it was an own goal which condemned Manchester City to relegation to the third tier whilst simultaneously offering salvation to opponents QPR (OK, so it didn't happen in the Premier League, but it was certainly of the finest quality).[12]

Crazy But True Facts and Statistics:

- The first Premier League season is likely to remain the highest scoring one, being the highest scoring one with a 42 game season; but this was the first season of more than 1000 goals with a 38 game season.

- Chelsea's three draws is the lowest number of draws in a Premier League season.

- Despite finishing bottom, Palace qualified for the totally tonto Intertoto Cup, presumably via Fair Play on account of not making a tackle all season.

Up Next

With Tranmere now settling for mid-table, Nottingham Forest clambered back again and so did the previously unfortunate Middlesbrough. Charlton Athletic won the play-offs to ensure a new Premier League face.

---

[12] Around this event you can find some more and less believable stuff on the internet. Did Jamie turn down Take That to concentrate on football? (Doubtful). Does he now work as a personal trainer? (Given that he could now do justice to the song 'two Jamie Pollocks, there's only...' very doubtful) and did QPR fans vote him most influential man of the last 2000 years, just edging out Jesus Christ? Only the last seems plausible.

THAT DON'T IMPRESS
ME MUCH
(1998-99)

Champions: (including of Europe)	Manchester United
Relegated:	Charlton Athletic, Blackburn Rovers, Nottingham Forest
Unbelievable Relegation Escape:	Southampton

Manchester United won not only the Premier League, but also the FA Cup and European Cup. I suppose that ought to impress anyone, and probably merits another 'Focus on' thingy. Nonetheless, after Southampton spent the entire season in the relegation zone and then drew two and won three of their last five to stay up, my own personal tribute was to drink myself to death and sing 'who the f*** are Man United?' I know this underlines a previous argument about the lack of wit and subtlety in football singing, and lack of sophistication amongst its supporters, but anyway...it was an amazing hangover to be sure.

Focus on: Manchester United

The first English team to win the Champions League, isn't strictly I suppose the focus of this book. However I found myself supporting Manchester United that night, which is unusual in itself, and the sight of Lothar Matthaüs punching the turf in frustration made my decision so worthwhile. Weeping Germans; we should really try to see more of that.

The teams had met at the group stage, both qualifying (obviously) after drawing against each other twice and at the expense of Barcelona. Both teams had done the domestic double and so both were chasing a unique treble. These were truly the heavyweights of Europe, and on the 26 May 1999 it was always going to be close.

Sadly, Roy Keane was both suspended *and* injured so the prospect of a good old-fashioned maiming was reduced. Bayern were ahead after just 5 minutes, and although the shot count over a pulsating match was remarkably even, in the second half Munich produced great saves from Schmeichel as well as hitting both post and bar when it looked easier to score.

Even so, when a minimum of 3 minutes injury time is signalled and your goalie is running forwards for a corner, you'd have to believe there is nowhere to go. However, mis-hits and deflections and reflexes meant that Fergie's two substitutes – Sheringham and Solskjaer - each got on the score sheet following corners. Scoring two goals in injury time to win a major trophy...surely a Manchester club would never do that again? Unless the footballing Gods had a plan of course...

Pierluigi Colina, he of the polished bonce and maker of some of the finest refereeing decisions of all time, said this was one of the most special moments of his refereeing career, particularly that the roar at full time was so loud that it could almost be heard across the universe. Peter Schmeichel – in his last United match – did cartwheels.[1]

---

[1] One day someone will write a golden book about it surely.

If not quite so exciting, the League title had also been full of drama, even as told by Arnold Rimmer. After Arsenal lost to Leeds in their penultimate game, Man Utd failed to fully capitalise by drawing 0-0 at Ewood Park. Blackburn had needed to win to avoid relegation, although throwing away three points (having led 3-1) at The Dell two weeks previously had been their real downfall. What it all meant was that Man Utd needed to win their final game at home to Spurs to win another Premier League crown. Arsenal needed a favour from Spurs. Les Ferdinand's neat lob was greeted with wild celebration at Highbury it is true, but by the time Arsenal took the lead in their own game, Man Utd had scored twice to do likewise. Arsenal finished on the same points as the previous season; then a point more, now a point less than Manchester United.[2]

Focus on: Southampton

This was the season of the great escape – thanks to a man called Marian, the little Latvian – and one of the last at The Dell. This was before the turmoil and despair and at the very end of a period when we saw a world class player play his entire career with the Saints. But ask Midland Saint Andy Bartlett, who's seen almost every minute of the journey, what he thinks of the Premier League and these things are not the ones which leap to mind.

> It's great to be a member of the Premier League. Even if you are a supporter of a cannon fodder club like Southampton you know that as far as the media are concerned you have at least a grudging existence, unlike the now invisible 'other 72'. And the unparalleled riches that membership brings have granted us an almost surreal level of financial muscle against clubs outside our golden circle. There is something very strange when Saints are apparently more attractive to quality players than true giants of the game like Feyenoord and Celtic. The result is that we can enjoy players of a class we could only have dreamed of years ago. Although of course our betters still have players of even greater quality.

---

[2] The FA Cup was rather more routine; a goal in each half leading to an easy win over Runners Up par excellence, Newcastle United.

But if it's all so great, then why 25 years on does it still feel so wrong to me? The reason is that I just can't get over the deep sense of betrayal over the creation of the Premier League. And that betrayal is based on two reasons. First is that Saints who only came to the top table as recently as 1966 were so willing to stab our former lower division compatriots in the back. We were not the only ones; the 22 first division clubs who signed up included Coventry, Crystal Palace, Luton, Norwich, Oldham and Notts County who all should have known better. It is supremely ironic that having decided to cast the lower divisions adrift Luton and Notts County have never enjoyed the bounty they helped give birth to. Far from it.

Second, we were seduced by the creation myth widely espoused by David Dein, then Arsenal Vice-Chairman and his cronies. That myth is worth examining, because it seems to have been swept under the carpet of history. We were told that the breakaway league was needed because the go-ahead plans of the 'Big Five' (a self-elected group of Arsenal, Everton, Liverpool, Manchester United and Tottenham Hotspur) were constantly frustrated by being outvoted by the likes of Halifax. The facts show otherwise. Following previous sabre-rattling and talks of breaking away from the Football League, by 1992 all clubs in the First Division had rather incongruously been granted 1.5 votes each, while Second Division clubs had 1 vote each. The 48 Associate Members in Divisions Three and Four had just 8 votes between them. So rather than being held back by the Halifaxes of the world the Big Five had only to attract the votes of one more First Division club to blow them out of the water.

The Premier League has brought benefits, especially in financial terms, to the chosen few. I still do not see how those benefits could not have been achieved within part of a unified Football League and with a much greater trickle-down effect to reduce the gap between the haves and the have-nots. But at least as Southampton fans we eventually had to take our medicine for the betrayal in the form of two relegations that took us very close to going out of business. There are many, me included, that regard the later years of our time in exile as a golden age. That might be due to us suddenly being the big fish in a small pool and able to ride roughshod over the smaller sides, like Arsenal and Manchester United used to do to us. If the experience had lasted a few seasons longer the attraction might have palled.

But here we are, back and established in the big boys' league, although we should never forget that it is all too easy to suddenly slip from grace as Villa and Newcastle have shown. This season we have broken our transfer record twice, thanks in no small part to the largesse resulting from the Premier League. It does make you stop and think that as recently as 2009 the money spent on just one of those players could have bought our entire club.

Season's Awards

Best at coming second award: Newcastle United are destined to win bugger all, so I thought it would be nice to give them this.

Crazy But True Facts and Statistics:

- Southampton drew the biggest crowd of the season, with thousands flocking to Old Trafford for their visit (55,316). Well it's expensive and people like to get three points for their money.

- The previous season, Chelsea set a record for fewest draws in the Premier League which still stands (just 3); this season they had more draws than anyone else (15). Given a run of 21 matches undefeated at one point, and finishing only four points behind the champions, Chelsea actually came rather close to winning the big prize.

Up Next

With Tranmere's ambition apparently gone, it was Watford who won the play-offs and left another third place team disappointed. This time that team was Ipswich. Sunderland were like a steamroller, amassing 105 points and a whopping goal difference of +63. Bradford City pipped Ipswich to the second automatic spot, thus starting the craziest few years in their history.

SEASON 8

BRING ME THE HEAD OF MICHAEL PORTILLO[1] (1999-2000)

Champions:	Manchester United (what, really, not again!?)
Relegated:	Wimbledon, Sheffield Wednesday, Watford
Unbelievable Relegation Escape:	Bradford City

The champions of Europe were simply unstoppable and cruised to victory in the following Premier League season as if sitting upon Gabriel's wings. Although Leeds had topped the table going into what was generally being accepted as the new Millennium even though it was the last year of the old one (a false dawn if ever there was one) Man United's winning margin was 18 points, again over Arsenal. After 6 wins in 8 Premier League years, it looked like the Manchester club that everyone now loved to hate would carry on winning it forever.[2] That was unless foreign money (honestly acquired obviously) from the sale of various non-renewable, environmentally disastrous, fossil fuels allowed other teams to challenge and provided another Manchester team to dislike, though nowhere near as much obviously.

---

[1] No justification at all for this; just a great song title that needed to be crow-barred in somewhere. The Automatic 'Monster' was also considered. https://www.youtube.com/watch?v=cbfBzQWUE6Q (accessed 16/5/17)

[2] When did ABU start? Anyway, we're not alone. See: @AnyoneButUtd

Focus on: Wimbledon

The Dons were only promoted into the football league in 1977. Less than a dozen years later they beat the once mighty Liverpool in the FA Cup final, to become everybody's second team. Another 12 years later to the day and they were being relegated out of the Premier League. And as Dons fans sang – it seemed tragi-comic at the time - 'Womble till I die' in their last day defeat at Southampton (which condemned them to relegation), little did they know that the extraordinary part was still to come.

First somebody nicked their club and tried to plonk it in Dublin or Belfast and eventually settled on Milton Keynes. The tainted 'MK Dons' so went on to replace Man Utd as everybody's most hated team. Then AFC Wimbledon emerged; initially playing in something like the South London Cub Scout League, they eventually worked their way back to the football league – a new team, but very much the successor of the 1988 Cup Winners.[3] But in terms of the Premier League years, we should pay tribute to the mighty Wombles, the crazy gang and the inspiration they provide to almost any club that the very top is not an unattainable summit.

Of all the clubs once in the Premier League,[4] Wimbledon fans have perhaps the least reason to worry about the Premier League having played at so many other levels, creating so many other memories. The Premier League is but one part of a story which seriously threatened to deprive the fans of a team at all. This might explain the measured response of Geoff Hawley (whose commentaries are not always so measured!) part of the AFC media team.[5] Having acknowledged that he was there as the Sky-fuelled "revolution" began, he goes on to pick out players who exemplify the spirit shown by Wimbledon then and AFC now. One in particular:

---

[3] In 2016/17 back to being neck and neck with the MK franchise team.

[4] Although technically a new club, 'AFC' developed pretty much from the same fan base.

[5] I'm not sure if this was Geoff, but it is interesting: **https://www.youtube.com/watch?v=bQbUy3kPrvQ**

Robbie Earle, the most dynamic and effective of midfielders who didn't get the chance with England that he deserved. Their loss was Jamaica's gain and it was typically an Earle header that marked Jamaica's first goal in a World Cup Finals game. Robbie covered every blade of grass; never seen an engine like his on a player before. He personified the Wimbledon way, full of hard work and with real quality too. His late arrival in the box on the end of a cross brought so many celebrations.

It didn't take much thought over whose name and number went on the back of the new midnight blue shirt in 1993: 8 - Earle and chuck on some of those Premier League sleeve logos too. In any case, Robbie was significantly cheaper to honour on a shirt than Holdsworth or Leonhardsen. I really liked the darker blue scheme. It was a departure from the lighter shades previously worn but it looked right. Under floodlights it seemed even darker and somehow stronger.

The establishment of the Premier League had me thinking on how it'd affect the pyramid below that we'd risen through. It seemed alien to the feel of the Football League and it felt like a barrier was being put up to spare the top table from the masses below. I wondered also why we were so looked down on. With players like Robbie Earle, John Scales, Marcus Gayle, Chris Perry and Warren Barton, we had real quality in the side and it never felt like we got the recognition those players deserved. There was this Neal Ardley guy about then too. I wonder what became of him.[6]

Focus on: Bradford City

Keith Wildman, owner of the Record Cafe on North Parade,[7] is proud that Valley Parade is built on a slope. As I leave his cafe (driving alas, and so having been unable to sample more than his excellent coffee) I headed down the hill to examine the phenomenon. It is truly a splendid stadium and really is built on the side of a hill. There isn't much that Keith isn't proud of when it comes

---

[6] At the time of writing managing AFC to mid-table respectability in League One.

[7] A good javelin chuck from the football ground and a must visit for away (and home) fans before the game with a fine selection of quality meats, vinyl, beers and cheese.

to his city and 'home town' team; the way they've recovered from the Premier League; the cheapest season tickets in the football league; the bond between the fans and club, strengthened all the more by tragedy; and the way the fans kept singing when 5-0 down in the League Cup final of 2013 as a League Two side. Keith also talked with enthusiasm about the city's industrial heritage and wealth and the FA Cup Final triumph of 1911. Well, who could forget?

It is perhaps only with the mention of the Premier League that Keith looks slightly apologetic, not to be more enthusiastic. Was it worth it? Would he want it to happen again? He asks himself these questions and offers a reluctant yes, but mainly because you want your team to win and if they keep winning there are consequences. But actually he describes the Premier League as 'battery football' and 'not like going to the football at all'. Fans kept apart in home and away pubs to drink naff beer from plastic. New stadia in the middle of nowhere, unlike Valley Parade which takes you past pubs on any approach. Keith remembers the patronising features on 'plucky Bradford' and nearly always being last on Match of the Day.

All in all, the Premier League wasn't that much fun is what he seems to conclude. Of course the day they stayed up was special, but football is supposed to be played at 3pm on a Saturday. You have your routine. Same mates; same pub. But the Premier League wants games which can be watched at a suitable time in Malaysia; games which accommodate the Europa League schedule and so on. Keith only gets fired up again when talking about promotion games and winning 2-4 in the cup at invincible Chelsea and how near his big, big team were to exiting the football league completely. The Premier League is not a highlight.

Keith couldn't imagine a better team to support. The madness of the Premier League era when everything at Valley Parade was bought on the 'never never' and when Benito Carbone was on more dosh than Roy Keane, almost took that away. But it didn't and the future looks bright again without the need to hope for the Premier League. Tellingly, when he searches around for a highlight of the Premier League seasons it is nothing I mention in my analysis below, but how City snatched defeat from the jaws of victory in losing 5-4 at Upton Park. Just a great game of football and the lunatic antics of one Paolo Di Canio.

But as an outsider, Bradford provided the proverbial breath of fresh air and their survival for more than a solitary season was remarkable. At the end of 1999/2000, with a better goal difference than Bradford, all Wimbledon had needed was to match City's result and they'd stay up. And with Bradford hosting Champions League chasing Liverpool and Wimbledon travelling from the city to the sea to face hardly terrifying Southampton with nothing to play for, it looked to be advantage Dons. However, both the difficulty and integrity of the Premier League (at least on the field) was demonstrated by Liverpool's failure to seize the big prize and Southampton continuing to regard The Dell as a fortress. Bradford took the lead through a goal from David Wetherall and clung on. Top flight status which had taken a mere 77 years to win back was preserved. Insanity and oblivion were soon to arrive, but for that day at least it was party time.

Bradford had in fact been in the relegation places for virtually the entire second half of the season, and were still there on the morning of the last day. That they had any chance at all was down largely to their penultimate home match against a Wimbledon team who went down in their place. If a 3-0 win sounds comfortable, most observers feel that the Dons deserved a draw at the very least. But in a tale of 'all a season's bad luck in one game' they missed open goals, conceded a penalty that no one appealed for, saw the normally reliable Neil Sullivan make two howlers between the sticks and had a player sent off. There was still the small matter of the last day, but Bradford City stayed up and even qualified for the Totally Tonto Cup for having been such jolly good sports.[8]

That much luck cannot go on forever and in the following season despite a few good weeks, Bradford were propping up the rest for most of the season. It may not have helped that their manager walked out (provoked?) to one of their relegated rivals the season before (Sheffield Wednesday) but you have to feel it would have happened anyway. Well unless you were the Chairman Geoffrey Richmond who went totally intertoto with the cheque book (six weeks of madness he called it) and made the new millennium a serious challenge for the Bantams.

---

[8] Real name: Intertoto (RIP)

Season's Awards

- **Over-hype:** Sky broke all kinds of records for over-using the phrase 'best league in the world' in an effort to deflect us from the fact that one team kept winning it.

- **General deity like behaviour, though not alas 'diety' as I first typed:** Southampton's increasingly ample midfield genius (Matt Le Tissier) scored 6 goals to limp over the line of 100 Premier League goals; the first midfielder to reach the milestone.

- **Longevity:** Steve Ogrizovic retired, thus severing Coventry City's final link to the FA Cup winning team of 1987.

Crazy But True Facts and Statistics:

- Coventry/Southampton – same points, separated on goal difference (again!).

- Coventry failed to win a single away game; no doubt a karmic punishment for the goings on two seasons back at Spurs, they nonetheless won 12 at home to stay up comfortably.

- Vladimir Smicer was. Why?

- Kevin Phillips managed 30 goals in his first season in the Premier League to ensure that the Stadium of Light was finally lit up.

- The curious case of Esteban Fuertes. Whatever Derby fans may have thought of his potential, he only netted once for the Rams after signing for £2.3 million. A mid-season break put an end to his Premier League career anyway after he was refused re-entry to the UK on his forged Italian passport. (Derby may have got him 10 years too soon; in 2009 he made his debut for the Argentinian national side – at 36 the oldest player ever to do so).

- The possibly even more curious case of Milton Nunez. Sunderland paid £1.6 million for him but apparently he was the 'wrong Nunez' and made a single Premier League substitute appearance against Wimbledon in April 2000. Most of the rumours about the player proved untrue or even libellous, apart from that he also took part in a League Cup game at Luton. However, despite taking on a cult status at Sunderland because of a) hopelessness b) looking slightly like Mike Tyson, he does seem to have racked up nearly 500 appearances as a professional footballer and scored over 100 goals including many in international football for Honduras.[9]

Up Next

Tranmere Rovers avoided further play-off agonies with a mid table finish. Charlton bounced right back, followed by Manchester City. This time Ipswich did win the play-offs at least.

---

[9] I checked the 'truth' with a fully fledged Honduran football fan. Apparently Milton was 'not very good, but he try hard and have charisma.' From the horse's mouth. Thank you Fito. Surprised he didn't fit in with Sunderland then?

IN THE END
(2000-01)

Champions:	Manchester United (aghhhh!!!!)
Relegated:	The 'Cities' of Manchester, Coventry and Bradford
Unbelievable Relegation Escape:	Well no one really, although Leicester managed to be the sole City to stay up so worth a mention for that. And Derby, comfortably safe in the end, were looking vulnerable until a win at the already crowned champions.

The first full season of the millennium was won by...yes them again (yawn!). Rumours that several Manchester United fans had spontaneously combusted from over-gloating remain unsubstantiated, although it seems entirely possible. Rumours that I was as fed up as a specifically force fed goose are absolutely correct, and I was not the only one. As grudging admiration went it was right up there.

Actually, before continuing, my inner pedant is requiring the following statement to be made: According to the standard internationally accepted Christian era calendar, the year is now 2017.[1] The first year in this calendar was 1, or the first year, not 'zero'. This in turn means that the year 2000 was the 2000th year, and was thus the final year of the second millennium, rather than the first year of the third as it has been widely celebrated from London to Sydney and all points in between. The fact that none of us could wait to have a party (as well as worrying endlessly about what would happen to toasters and planes when that 1 changed to a 2) does not alter this fact. Accordingly, whilst 2000/01 is under-recognised as the only Premier League season

---

[1] In the Juche Calendar currently favoured by North Korea (aka DPRK) the year is currently 106, the same coincidentally as parts of rural Lincolnshire.

to be played across two millennia, it cannot be regarded as the first full PL season of the new millennium.

Whatever you say my inner pedant! The point was that Manchester United made it seven of nine PL titles. Coincidentally, 'Seven of Nine' is the moniker of a former Borg drone played by actress Jeri Ryan in the TV series *Star Trek: Voyager*. The tightness of her costume is, I think you'll find, entirely justified on artistic grounds and her catch-phrase 'resistance is futile' is completely non-sexual and anyone aroused by it, or her, is a total pedant...I mean pervert. Anyway, 'resistance is futile' seemed to sum up Manchester United quite well...now, what was I saying? I seem to have lost all focus. Ooh, I'm all of a tizzy.[2]

After Manchester United beat Arsenal 6-1 in March, Fergie and Wenger were in agreement that the title race was over, with a 16 point lead for United. Wenger actually congratulated his rivals as the better team. Nonetheless, it was a season of sadness for United as Roy Keane was running out of people to be angry with. Mid-season he turned on the teams own fans with his 'prawn-sandwich' rant; then when the season was over it was the turn of his own team, questioning whether the first and only team to win the Premier League three consecutive times were good enough and whether it was the end of the line for them – to be fair he was questioning their European abilities, but even so...Oh and he also beat Luke Chadwick to a pulp, leaving him hideously disfigured...ah, no...sorry! I'm just hearing that's what he looked like.

Focus on: Ipswich Town

Tipped to go down, they almost got into the Champions' League in 2000/01, eventually finishing 5th. UEFA Cup qualification brought George Burley the Manager of the Season award. But as Alan Leach recalls, these oddities were all preceded by:

> *Newly promoted Ipswich were there in the first Premier League season. All-seater Portman Road was the very first in the new league. I was stewarding under the rather extravagant job title of Senior Executive Crowd Safety Enforcement Monitor,[3] with*

---

[2] **https://en.wikipedia.org/wiki/Seven_of_Nine** (accessed an indecent number of times including 5/10/16)

[3] Actually only the third and last of these words, but that didn't seem to fit Alan's description of 'extravagant'

the aim of identifying any possible dangers or trouble. My job was to inform the police or chief steward. Ipswich v Crystal Palace was heading for a 2-2 draw when in the last minute a controversial penalty to the visitors was awarded causing ten or so Palace fans in the Ipswich end to celebrate, something they had avoided during the rest of the game. Their presence was duly noted by some more centrally seated town fans and fuelled by the poor refereeing decision to give Palace this glorious last minute opportunity a few fans headed towards the visitors and surrounded them in the empty seats. I duly noted this and informed the one remaining officer, others having left to police outside the ground, that trouble may be ahead.[4] He thanked me for my vigilance and then promptly left, as if to say 'if there's trouble in the offing I'll go and stand somewhere else leaving a few stewards to deal with it.' Fortunately up stepped Gareth Southgate…[Alan goes on to describe what happened next, but you already know that Gareth diffused the situation beautifully…although of course his previous spot-kick miss (v Germany in the Euros of 1996) saw an enraged nation setting fire to BMWs.]

That season too saw Brian Kidd and Peter Schmeichel come out for a pre match warm up; rare in those days. Sadly for them they came the full length of the pitch to the North Stand with only one ball. The stand was filling and some light hearted barracking took place and within a minute the ball was in the crowd and not being given back. Stewards in the stand tried to retrieve the ball but failed, with it being tossed away when approached. Kidd and Schmeichel were getting frustrated and approached me on the pitch to 'do my f***ing job and get the f***ing ball back.' Explaining that I thought it would be easier for them to get another ball I was met with a torrent of abuse that I was very proud of as a claim to fame. Hearing Peter Schmeichel's repetitive swearing with a Danish tone was quite interesting and it was enjoyable watching the pair trudge back the length of the pitch back to the tunnel being waved on their way. If they'd just asked nicely…

Focus on: Sunderland

Even with Phillips more than halving his tally from the previous season, Sunderland managed another seventh place finish in 2000/01, marking a high point in the club's often unhappy affair with the Premier League. When seeking

---

4   Alan fails to note whether he did this by bursting into song.

Sunderland fan input (which I got from Martin Brown and Chris White) I was initially offered an utterly incomprehensible rant. That turns out to be just how they speak apparently so I got them to write it doon like. They wade into me without hesitation.

If the purpose of the book is to celebrate the success of the Premier League, it will be paying homage to cash and greed over everyday supporters - so do it while you can, before it crumbles or transitions into a Chinese based industry (where gambling will be the centre of the business model), and all the Premier League stars in England jump ship for a 'new challenge' i.e. more money.

As I have come to expect from Chris, a 40-page Gramscian Marxist critique of markets and business followed and concluded with: *They kiss the badge on their strip one day and kiss the club goodbye the next (if the price is right).*

But as much as every Black Cat has every reason to have a chip on their shoulder about money and big club bias and a London bias and and and...they haven't been able to justify a near 50,000 capacity 'Stadium of Light' without people liking football to an almost obsessional level. And, having got some stuff off his chest, Martin continues:

I must also confess to having some great memories of supporting Sunderland in the Premier League. Going with my son...and under Peter Reid watching Sunderland was undoubtedly fantastic. The build up to the game, the atmosphere, expectation and the desire of both the team and the supporters were as one (for a time at least). We were a team that no one fancied playing and we revelled in it!

My best memory was seeing us play and beat Chelsea 4-1 in December 1999 at the newish Stadium of Light. We outplayed, outfought and ripped Chelsea apart, scoring 4 goals in an unforgettable first half (2 each from Niall Quinn and Kevin Phillips). One of the goals Phillips scored was a 25 yard volley - the crowd erupted and the noise was deafening. Phillips went on to be the Premier League Top Scorer with 30 goals and won the European Golden Boot. He also won 8 Full England Caps. We made Chelsea's so called world class super stars look like rabbits caught in headlights. The atmosphere was electric and will remain with me forever.

As with many sets of fans, Sunderland's share proud feelings of standing together in times of adversity...which is fortunate. Having taken 2 points from their first 10 games in 2016/17 everyone assumed Sunderland's luck had finally run out and it had. But Martin and Chris are as proud of the fans who will stick with them as they are despairing of the team which this time was finally not good enough.

Focus on: Borg drone Seven of Nine

At least that's what I'm doing and I should be writing. Resistance is futile.

Season's Awards

Insane optimist: The Coventry fan holding up his 'We'll be back' banner on the day City finally went. I wonder if he's still among the 2000 1000 500?

Challengers of stereotype (team): Both Bradford and Leeds were casting off the image that Yorkshire folk are careful with their money as both clubs set themselves up for potential destruction and years in the wilderness by recklessly spending to try and achieve glory.

Challengers of stereotype (individual): With an opportunity to score, controversial, alleged fascist Paolo di Canio caught the ball rather than try to score because of a serious injury to Everton's goalie. Round of applause from everyone. Not for Jose Mourinho such human and populist touches.

Best goal never scored? Danny Tiatto (Man City's Australian left full back) picked the ball up in his own half, drove forward, into the penalty area and unleashed a low left-foot drive into the corner. The goal-keeper stood no chance. 'Wizard of Oz!' cried the commentator. ..The 'goal' is disallowed for offside 'which is a very, *very* strange decision' he continued.

Crazy But True Facts and Statistics:

- Matthew Le Tissier waddled off the bench to score the last goal at The Dell.[5] It was to be his last goal too, and he only ever scored at St Mary's in his own testimonial, when he was out-scored by his son Mitchell.

- Ray Parlour though scored a hat-trick in a game against Newcastle. Interviewed about it he said 'Attles and pezz, I luv Lundun tarn' – at least that's what it sounded like. I'd love to put him in a room with some Sunderland fans.

- In the controversial decision-fest that was the Merseyside derby at Goodison, Jeff Winter set a new record for saying 'go away' (232) to players who simply wanted to know if he actually new the rules.

Up Next

Fulham arrived on the scene floating on a river of diamonds (well Al Fayed's dosh at least) amassing more than 100 points to be promoted as champions. Blackburn finished second, bemusing Burnley (who narrowly missed out on the play-offs) with bounce-back-ability, and for once the third place team (Bolton Wanderers) actually won the play-offs. This was the golden era of *Soccer AM* and their 'Save Chip' campaign featured on numerous flags, including behind Bolton as they lifted the play-off winner's trophy.

These three clubs would all survive in the top division the following season; the first time that had happened since the start of the Premier League.

---

[5] You may now buy a property in Le Tissier Court on the very site.

SMELLS LIKE TEEN SPIRIT (2001-02)

Champions:	Arsenal
Relegated:	Ipswich Town, Derby County and Leicester City (the grim reaper of 'City' teams sweeping up after getting the other three the season before)
Unbelievable Relegation Escape:	Sunderland were only confirmed on the last day, but without a huge amount of drama, and Bolton the week before.

Bolton won their first three games of the season, prompting manager Sam Allardyce to suggest they could win the league. He was joking, although Mohamed Al-Fayed wasn't when he suggested Fulham would. In the end both Bolton and Fulham were just pipped to it by more than 10 places and about 12 wins worth of points. As for Big Sam, didn't you just always get a good feeling about him? Honest as the day is long.[1] What a shame that he got caught...was what he seemed to say of the sting operation which ended his magnificent 100% winning record/reign as the England boss. This is before we even get into the 'style' he always brought to his teams, which caused me once to tweet: 'Turned on Sky and thought it was an Allardyce team defending... turned out to be Pro-Kabbadi...'

Even if Bolton's challenge faded, this was probably a more open Premier League than any previously, as sponsorship reflected nicely the nation by moving from beer

---

[1] Reyjkavik, 25th December

(Carling) to credit (Barclaycard). Liverpool were top in December, but after a bad run were replaced by Leeds and then before the new year, Newcastle United who came from behind frequently.[2]

In fact, with snow in the air, the game between Leeds and Newcastle Uniteds on 22 December was probably one of the games of the season, full of famous faces like Robbie Fowler (Leeds) and Craig Bellamy (Newcastle). It also contained people only now at the ends of their careers (Shay Given), the star imports (Viduka and Solano who both scored), the destined for greatness (Rio Ferdinand), the notorious (Lee Bowyer) and the sadly departed (Gary Speed). Together they produced a marvellous tussle, as Sky again proclaimed the best league in the world.

This isn't the time or place to go into the details of why Lee Bowyer was back in the Leeds team on that day, after a considerable absence, along with Jonathan Woodgate. He had been acquitted of racist assault in an incident which involves drinking, sense of entitlement and racism in football. David Goldblatt describes and analyses it well in his book and, though it may not fit within these pages of fact-based inanity, I commend it to you strongly.

Bowyer, who Martin Tyler notes got a mixed reaction from the Leeds fans, was presumably forgiven by those braying 'Yooork-shh' when he equalized Craig Bellamy's opener to send the teams in level at half time. Soon Leeds had built a healthy lead, with excellent strikes by Viduka (after a fine turn) and Harte (from distance). But after Elliott's diving header got Newcastle back into it at 3-2, referee Jeff Winter decided he was tired of not being centre stage, and awarded Newcastle a dubious penalty. Shearer scored, and we had the refreshing spectacle of both teams trying to win the game and no time wasting or settling for a point. It was Newcastle who took all three with a cool right-foot finish by Nolberto "Nobby" Solano in the last minute.

The 3-4 victory kept Newcastle top, but their arch-nemesoid[3] Manchester United were top by the end of January and Newcastle faded. However, in a season of ever changing leadership it was Wenger's Arsenal (not Allardyce's Bolton amazingly) who went on to win the first, proper full season of the millennium (not one straddling two millennia) by winning match after match in the run-in. Having famously 'won the league on Merseyside' in the *Fever Pitch* season of 1988/89, Arsenal now won it at Old Trafford, though much less dramatically. After Sylvain Wiltord gave them a 0-1 success in the season's penultimate game, manager Arsene Wenger is believed to

---

[2] Placeholder footnote in case we go with a more low-brow book

[3] Made up word. I like it.

have uttered the phrase 'err, look-uh, I fink we showed a trwemendous team spiwit' for the 463rd time of his reign to that point.[4]

Amazingly, Manchester United did not even finish second for the first time in the Premier League's short history, pipped to the post by Liverpool, who completed an 11-0 season aggregate over Ipswich by winning 5-0 at Anfield on the last day of the season. Still, since Manchester United's arch-nemesoid[5] have never bettered second in the Premier League, whilst United have so far bettered runners up more often than not, they can probably live with that I reckon.

Leicester's last season at Filbert Street (after a mere 111 years) ended in relegation. With a new stadium to pay for (The Crisp Bowl) they later went into administration. Surely they would never recover nor amount to any more than a tiny footnote in Premier League history.[6]

Focus on: Aston Villa

Oddly as Birmingham the City (not 'Birmingham City') struggled to re-develop and present a new face to the world over the past 30 or so years, presenting a contrasting image of such improvements were its historically most successful football team, Aston Villa FC. League champions in 1981, European Champions in 1982, they went on to finish runners-up in the inaugural Premier League season. Indeed in the first 10 years of the Premier League, Villa only finished outside the top half on one occasion. They had three top 5 finishes. The next 10 years may have seemed frustrating at the time; Villa didn't finish higher than 6th, but even so with more top half, than bottom half finishes. Since that point however they finished 15th, 15th, 17th and then 20th. This final relegation season saw them disprove the adage about there being no easy games in the Premier

---

4   The number is now 2976, with rumours that he will retire (the phrase) at 3000.

5   No, I really do like it, but perhaps it'll stay as a little 'Easter Egg' for those kind enough to read this chapter?

6   Tiny footnote: It's possible that someone may read this without knowing, so I thought I'd build up the suspense a little bit.

League; in the final 3 months of the season 7 teams travelled to Villa Park and only Newcastle didn't win (0-0 draw). The other 6 teams averaged 3.5 goals a game and all left with 3 points. The boos broke non-existent decibel-meters. Given all of this, it's not been easy to get Villa fans to reflect on what happened to them. There was a really posh chap called Wills who seemed quite keen to contribute at one point, but then he went off the idea saying 'Ma-ma's had a heavy cold at Christmas and anyway I've got to go and fly a helicopter or walk the corgis.' Something of that nature.[7]

Anyway, having just missed out on royal patronage, I was delighted to hear from Claire Field, who I suspect was much too young (if even born) to appreciate the real glory days, but old enough to suffer the slow slide described above. Nonetheless, she remains fiercely proud of her team. Her grandad spent 80 years watching Villa including the losing Cup Final of 2015 and the victorious one of 1957. 1957 may lie slightly outside the timeframe of this book, but it seemed worth a mention.

At the other end of the generational scale, Claire notes that:

It was a proud day for me in September 2015 taking my son James along to see his first Villa home match at the age of 8. He loved the atmosphere and was shocked at the size of the crowd. It was a beautiful sunny day and we walked past Aston Hall in its lovely park surroundings to get to the ground. It is always special when you walk in under the magnificent entrance. This ended in a draw with Sunderland I believe. Little did we know, this would be our last season in the Premier League, but hopefully we will bounce back soon, although it won't be easy.

Claire also adds a post-script since she wrote to me in the week that Graham Taylor died:

He was the man who rescued Villa and oversaw our transition to the new Premier League. Villa were struggling and Graham was just the man to steady the ship. I had the privilege of meeting him a few years ago.[8] He was only too happy to talk to me about the happy days at Villa and gave me his autograph which is treasured. He was a charming and genuine man, and I shall always remember him. Just one of my treasured memories following Villa.

---

[7] Villans can always compare their efforts to those of Coventry City for comfort, but with Leicester Champions, West Brom in the top half of the Premier League and even Birmingham above them, it was a grim Christmas indeed (2016).

[8] I met him at the same event and can confirm Claire's impression of him.

Season's Awards

The 'Paolo di Canio' Crazy Italian Award: Chelsea manager Claudio Ranieri – you'll never win anything with kids, or loopy Italians (maybe).

Crazy But True Facts and Statistics:

- The most goals in a game was 8, but made up of 4 different score-lines: there was a 7-1 (Blackburn beat Wham, presumably Andrew Ridgely with the consolation), a 6-2 (Newcastle trounced Everton), Manchester United had two 3-5 away wins in the capital (at Spurs and Wham) and Charlton and West Ham battled out a 4-4 draw.[9], [10]

---

[9] Bizarrely, Wikipedia – yes I did use it when my razor sharp mind deserted me – only covers 19 teams in this season, omitting 7th placed West Ham. Perhaps the author couldn't face thinking of that defence. Even the West Ham 2001/02 page contains no commentary except for noting the continued association with Fila. Although it did show me that 17 different nationalities were playing at Upton Park that season which gives me an idea for the next chapter.

[10] This is a footnote to the previous footnote to say that for some reason Upton Park changed its name to the Boleyn Ground just before it was demolished. If this was an effort to confuse the demolishers, it failed.

Up Next

The grim reaper had happily disposed of Manchester, Coventry and Bradford Cities the season before and mopped up Leicester City in this one, so must have been disappointed about Manchester City's prompt return. West Bromwich Albion took the second automatic promotion spot, narrowly edging out Wolverhampton Wanderers. And despite finishing 10 points clear of their near neighbours, Wolves also missed out in the play-offs with another City, Birmingham, going up instead.

SEVEN NATION ARMY
(2002-03)

Champions:	Manchester United (with Arsenal as Runners Up would you believe?)
Relegated:	The Wests – Ham United and Bromwich Albion, as well as Sunderland
Unbelievable Relegation Escape:	Bolton Wandererers

It has to be said, especially if you count the home nations and the Irish Republic separately, that no Premier League team by this time resembled a *mere* seven nation army. Most had seven or more non-English speaking nationalities represented. In random fashion I took 4 Premier League teams of that season (two blue, two claret and blue) and looked at their squad composition. The figures do include the home nations and Eire as separate nations.

Aston Villa: 14 different nationalities in the squad
Chelsea: 13 different nationalities in the squad
Everton: 12 different nationalities in the squad
West Ham United: 9 different nationalities in the squad

It is worth making the point that West Ham had 17 the season before, and in this season alone transferred out 12 different nationalities. Perhaps that is the reason for their relegation?

Oh, you want something about football then? Not happy with reflections on the effects of globalisation and the European single market? Oh go on then, but I had to crowbar the White Stripes into the sound track somewhere. Additionally, I have a problem a bit like Sky had at the time; the best league in the world it might be, but when the same team keeps winning it, it can be difficult to keep the enthusiasm and find something new to say.

But for now, things seemed never to change. For instance, a Manchester United fan's YouTube montage of the season showed Roy Keane pushing his own team mate (Phil Neville) and elbowing Jason McAteer in the face and getting sent off. Actually the elbow is clear, the McAteer not so much, but he elbowed someone McAteerish. So I would argue, however staggering were the achievements of Manchester United (jolly well played chaps!), some more genuine challenge was needed, since this seemed to be the era of teams good enough to be runners up: Arsenal, Newcastle United, Liverpool, Aston Villa.

At least this season *looked* to offer the possibility of back to back non-United titles. Defending champions Arsenal led by 8 points going into March. However, they still contrived to let Manchester United win their 8th Premier League title in 11 years. The problem for Arsenal was leads squandered against Villa, Manchester United and Bolton – all 3 points turned into draws. A 2-3 defeat at home to Leeds for Wenger's men confirmed Manchester United as champions. Arsenal did at least win the FA Cup despite being out-shot 12-14 by Southampton.[1]

This was a season, in sum, difficult to get enthusiastic about for anyone. Even Manchester United has twelve other victories to compare it to. Runners-up Arsenal had done, and would go on to do, better. So the choice of 'focus' teams may seem odd, but somebody had to fill the gaps.

Focus on: Leeds United

In 2000/01 three teams qualified for the Champions League; Leeds finished 4th. In 2001/02 four teams qualified for the Champions League; Leeds finished 5th. Three decades before this they were feared and Reviered across Europe. But

---

[1] It was 12-14 to Saints on shots; go on, look it up if you don't believe me.

by now having mortgaged their future against Champions League TV rights they faced a bleak future indeed; they sold Rio Ferdinand for £30 million; the training ground and the Elland Road stadium went too; the fixtures and fittings (loo roll holders, the lot) fetched f-all down the auction; and then Leeds got into bed with Ken Bates. It's been a very sad tale from which the recovery has been long and painful. Just a decade before Leeds had won the last proper First Division. Are we not known universally known as 'The Last Real Champions'? Terry Peer (long-suffering season ticket holder) asked me. I put it to him that it must have been a traumatic time?

When you say it's been traumatic, in fact it hasn't really been as I've largely been in denial! We are a club that doesn't do 'steady'! We are either exploding or imploding, and there have always been enough distractions for me not feel traumatised. I actually think that by calling each league The Premier League, The Championship, League 1 or even National League, it's pretty easy to convince yourself you are in the top league wherever you are (especially if you stop watching MOTD as I did!) Anyway we were winners of the last proper league before Sky got hold of it and spoilt it all by creating the cash rich cartel we see now. The rest doesn't count. Although we were top of the Premier League as we entered this century so that bit does count.

Terry helpfully searches the memory bank for trauma. *A brilliant performance in beating Arsenal at Highbury 3-2 in May 2003 to avoid relegation.* Why traumatic? *In so doing we handed the title to Man Utd!*[2] Anything else? *How rubbish Frank Strandli was. How we managed to turn a previous World Cup winner, Roque Junior, into such a shambles that his name became synonymous with having a nightmare. For every Tony Yeboah there was a Carlton Palmer. I've also just remembered Terry Vegetables had a stab at it as well – another memory I need to forget!*

And then that look came across Terry's face; a look previously reserved for men upon whose heads apples fall, or who note displaced water when sitting in baths. He has remembered the meaning of traumatic:

In the year we were relegated, one day in the summer after the end of the season, I went on to our teletext page, entering the memorised number. Somehow another team came up! Eventually I realised that relegation lost you your teletext page. That day still haunts me. But beyond that, denial and blind faith in a return to the land of filthy lucre has kept me safe.

---

[2] Terry, along with several other contributors, used the word 'Manure' but on balance I decided I'd had enough digs. This also happened to Oldham in 1992/93 and Steve Denton was equally grudging and scatological in his description.

Terry thereafter drifted off into a bit of a persecution complex, claiming that *everyone hates us and they can't even remember why*. It's simply not true, although it might be if and when you're back in the Premier League.

Lovers of a good story and/or Leeds may also be interested in PJ Whiteley's *Marching on Together*. Another thumping good read from Urbane with lots of references to United.

Focus on: West Ham United

A fascinating aspect to writing this book was that fans not only have very different experiences of the Premier League, but respond in very different ways to requests to tell you 'something' about their team. For instance, Julie Newman sent me a contribution entitled 'My Saddest Day as a Hammer' which shows that even in these days of habitual shots of sobbing, shirtless north-easterners (usually) at the season's end, it is possible to be very quickly brought back to how insignificant it really, is.

Being a Hammer is not for the faint hearted. Despite our wonderful history, in recent years very often a good season is floating above the relegation zone. 2002/03 was no exception; in fact it was worse as a disastrous run had seen us bottom at Christmas - the kiss of death! But like so many die-hard fans I hoped we could turn it around. After all, our squad at the time was full of talented players, many who would go on to wear an England shirt. Towards the latter half of the season we had an upturn which fuelled this hope, but then our manager, Glen Roeder fell ill with a brain tumour. This news put things into perspective for me and the most important thing was his recovery... but without a manager I accepted that relegation was likely. Then it was announced that Trevor Brooking would manage the side for our final games of the season and for me that was enough to ensure our Premier League status. The legend that is Sir Trev had been a player during our most successful times, so of course he would save us. And let's not forget we also had Paolo de Canio, a prolific goal scorer whose volleys were legendary (take a look at his goal against Wimbledon in 2000[3]). Brooking's first game in charge was Manchester City, away. We won 1-0. Next up Chelsea at home, another 1-0 win. Final game of the season was against Birmingham City, at St. Andrews, whose then owners now own West Ham! Despite a valiant effort the final score was 2-2; that coupled with Bolton winning saw us relegated. This for me still rates as my saddest day as a Hammer.

Season's Awards

Worst Sponsors: NTL. No seriously, did you have anything to do with those guys? An OFCOM case waiting to happen.

Crazy But True Facts and Statistics:

- The most goals in a match was tied on 8 again, this time with only two matches reaching that mark. They were Manchester United 5-3 Newcastle United (in November) and Newcastle United 2-6 Manchester United (in April).

---

[3] Julie has a point. This excellent strike **(https://www.youtube.com/watch?v=KTsq5ZlTTeQ** – accessed 11/1/17) was almost as good as half a dozen Matthew Le Tissier scored in the previous 5 or 6 years.

- If anyone else was bored with Manchester United's success, their own fans certainly weren't; they had now won the Premier League more times (8) than they had ever won the old Football League (7) and were closing in slowly but surely on Liverpool's overall record.

- Football attendances continued to rise. Only Fulham did not have a highest attendance of more than 20,000, being able to squeeze only 19,000+ in Craven Cottage. Otherwise, only Bolton, Charlton and West Brom had a highest attendance of less than 30,000, each in the high 20,000s.

Up Next

Portsmouth won by a distance, managed by the entirely honest and dependable Harry Redknapp. Leicester City yo-yoing fortunes continued as they took the second automatic spot. This time Wolves achieved a more modest points total and entered by the play-off back door, thus ensuring a Premier League fixture that I don't think anyone has ever called the Wandererers derby versus Bolton.

Mr Brightside
(2003-04)

Champions:	Arsenal's Invincibles, without losing a single match (26 wins, 12 draws)
Relegated:	Wolverhampton Wandererers, Leicester City, Leeds United
Unbelievable Relegation Escape:	Too easy for the rest

The publisher advises me (on pain of non-publication) to tone down certain of my prejudices, especially the pro-Saints bit. Well with or without that encouragement, and in a season in which Arsenal didn't lose a single league match, I shall start this chapter instead by praising fans of Portsmouth FC whose story serves as hope to fans everywhere. It also exemplifies the point about the dangers of gloaty singing.

So clearly Pompey fans have had it tough. Their rivals are called The Saints and so obviously have a special relationship with the other worldly higher authorities. Accordingly, in early 2003/04 the side of truth, justice and all that is good in football (i.e. SFC) was riding high. It got better. The first ever Premier League derby between SFC and PFC took place at St Mary's on 21 December 2003. I remember it, because I forgot it. Having vowed never to attend another such match (following Alan Knight's testimonial on my solitary visit to Fratton Park) I forgot that it was a 12 o'clock kick off and was calmly writing a book about Le Tiss (available from Urbane) oblivious to a game where everything went right for the home team.

- Longest serving player Jason Dodd scores direct from a corner
- 'Injured a year' hero Marians Pahars returns to add a second
- James Beattie adds a third with a 'flying Houchen' deep into stoppage time

Southampton rose to 4th as a result of this win and a newly promoted Pompey looked in serious danger of relegation. But sometime in the second half, Saints fans started singing 'Premier League you're having a laugh' and I sensed profound irritation amongst the footballing Gods.

And every now and then, the football office of Heaven PLC decides to do something to ensure that English football doesn't look as fixed as Serie A. By the end of the season SFC had lost at Fratton Park and finished in 12th only 2 points above their neighbours. Strachan left, and after Sturrock the double disaster that was Wigley and then Redknapp arrived.[1] After relegating the Saints Harry then sodded off back down the M27 and led Pompey to the FA Cup. Of course, the footballing Gods have since returned the universe to normal, but I had learned my lesson and it'll be your turn again one day oh long suffering Pompey fans. I'm sure it will. Leeds relegation in this season, so few seasons after a Champions League semi-final and after 14 years in the top flight, shows how easily it can all go wrong...and even right again.

Focus on: Arsenal

As for Arsenal's amazing (and last) Premier League triumph...well it might be another example of footballing God ficklety![2] Don't lose a game all season, then don't win it again (ever? yet?). It wasn't as easy as it seems, especially as quite a few away draws kept Chelsea (and to a lesser extent Manchester United) interested for at least some of the season. I was going to write a play about it, but the script failed to grip me:

COMMENTATOR: Henry! Henry! Henry! Henry! Henry!!

---

[1] Redknapp claimed the following season that it would be difficult to keep Saints up even though they were not in the relegation zone when he took over.

[2] Ficklety™ is not a word, but like 'nemesoid'™ I claim it. © LLP

He ended up with 30 in the league. It was an amazing achievement...and although a couple of teams managed late equalisers against Arsenal, Arsenal themselves didn't need any injury time heroics to preserve their record. In fact their supporters only had to take care of half time business when losing on 3 occasions and were behind at all in only 10 games. Amazing achievement; difficult to dramatise![3]

Paul Moore does suggest, however, that there was some drama.

We were within sight of the unbeaten season. After losing the FA Cup semi-final and crashing out of the Champions league quarter-final within the space of four days, we were 1-2 down to Liverpool at half time. However, a second half hat-trick from Thierry Henry secured the win and Highbury breathed again; the upper tier of the North Bank was quite literally rocking up and down at the final whistle. Arsenal also nearly lost the *Battle of Old Trafford II* early in the season, but Ruud Van Nistelrooy missed the penalty. *Subsequent retrospective bans could not de-rail us, but had that penalty gone in there would be no 'invincibles'.[4]*

Apart from Middlesbrough winning something (League Cup), and yes, well, Arsenal being undefeated, the season was perhaps most notable for unfashionable Champions League place challenges. However, Birmingham City (1 point off 4th with 8 games to go) faded to 10th. Charlton Athletic meanwhile slumped less radically than in previous seasons, but still only managed 7th.

Focus on: Charlton Athletic

You have to salute a man who arranges to be married on a Friday to avoid football, and then insists on a pre-nup specifying that if there's a Charlton home fixture on the Saturday afterwards the honeymoon must be delayed too. So Rod

---

[3] That exclamation mark is my best attempt to do so.

[4] Paul also makes me feel better about my own sense of humour. *We used to have a fanzine called the Arsenal Echo ... A guy selling them used to say 'get your Arsenal Echo Echo' ... a fellow supporter asked me one day 'why does that guy say echo twice'...you probably had had to be there, but it still makes me chuckle.*

Hammond I salute you here. In fact Rod was very happy to relive the good times, what with Charlton being one of the many ex-Premier League teams where the current ownership has managed a complete disconnection with the fans and left a sour taste and bad feeling. Given that Rod was kind enough to send me a whole book of notes on his beloved CAFC, here are the highlights:

1. Celebration

Charlton earned the right to play in the Premier League for the first time after a monumental play-off final battle with Sunderland at the old Wembley. (Despite taking the lead, Charlton trailed 3 times before forcing a 4-4 draw in extra time. They then took the lead seven times in the penalty shootout, before finally winning 7-6 on penalties!) *It's a day I will never forget and it still sends shivers down my spine. I lived every emotion possible and then Charlton was in the Premier League! It took weeks to sink in. I would be in Tesco's getting milk, driving to work or out running and a little voice in my head would say "Arsenal and Man United at The Valley. Spurs and Chelsea. Liverpool..." and a huge grin would stretch across my face. It was surreal.*

2. Like a Virgin

For Charlton's first home game in the Premier League in August 1998 I was 1300 miles away in the Costa del Sol with my future wife and in-laws! Knowing I wasn't able to be at The Valley hurt so deep inside it felt like I'd been kicked repeatedly in the stomach. For which Rod wins the award for the most overly dramatic comment I received when producing this book – although to be fair I'm just bitter because I was at the game, supporting the Saints team Charlton clobbered 5-0 to go top of the league.

Charlton's season only got worse however and relegation looked increasingly likely. *By May we gave ourselves a glimmer of hope with a 4-3 victory at Villa* says Rod. Again whilst Rod gets glassy eyed remembering it at great length, I was at Wimbledon where I would have been saved a week's worry if Danny Mills (almost as irritating then as he is now on the radio) hadn't scored a late free kick winner for Charlton. But, relegated that season, Charlton were back for a much more successful spell.

3. Into the Groove

Rod tells me that he could go on forever about Charlton...and then tries to prove it. A 4-4 draw v West Ham (Johansson overhead kick seals a point). Sleeping with his wife at the valley the day after their wedding (as per the pre-nup above) – no I mean, they were so tired after the, err, 'exertions' of the wedding that they actually fell asleep; well it was the Saints again. Beating Chelsea 4-2 at home, Arsenal 2-4 at Highbury. And so on and so forth…

4. I'm Addic(k)ted/The Power of Goodbye

Charlton's last Premier League home game was Monday May 7th 2007 against Spurs. Before the game there was still the very faintest chance we could have stayed up if an unlikely series of results went for us, but not even the most optimistic believed it would happen. I can remember tears rolling down my cheeks as I drove to The Valley. I'd never taken our Premier League status for granted but it still hurt like hell facing up to the reality it was coming to an end. We lost 0-2. I remember little about the game other than the moments straight after Spurs' second when the entire Valley stood as one, to sing 'Valley Floyd Road' with every ounce of passion they had. As much as you brace yourself for relegation, as much as you know it's going to happen, when it finally hits it hurts like hell. Needless to say I cried all the way back home again… And to think I saluted you, you soppy, daft sod!

Unlike our first relegation I knew we wouldn't bounce back. The club was already in serious decline. 10 years on from then and Charlton's demise, save for a brief period under Chris Powell, still continues. I miss those days! Every goal meant absolutely everything to me back then. The club cared about its community and fans and there was a genuine 'togetherness' as we punched well above our weight. Breaks my heart to contrast it with now under the current ownership.

Season's Awards

Tina Turner "Simply the Best" Award: Hardly anybody this season thought that Thierry Henry wasn't the best at everything.

Best Fans: As well as the League, Arsenal also won the Fair Play league and its supporters the award for best public behaviour. This seems to conclusively prove the old hooly-era song 'we're the best behaved supporters in the land – when we win!'

Crazy But True Facts and Statistics:

- Southampton were again the prime draw; attracting a season high 67,758 for their visit to Old Trafford.
- Manchester City finished 16th with just 41 points, although with a positive goal difference; despite this latter crumb of comfort, no sign yet that the footballing Gods wanted to even things up a bit in Manchester.

Up Next

No new boys this time, with Norwich City, West Bromwich Albion and Crystal Palace promoted. The latter's home record included only as many wins as 21st placed Gillingham, and did not bode well for the following season.

BOULEVARD OF BROKEN DREAMS[1] (2004-05)

Champions:	Chelsea
Relegated:	Crystal Palace (almost inevitably), Norwich City and Southampton (finally, it happened, it was never supposed to happen, but as so often in life it needed to get worse so that it could get better again)
Unbelievable Relegation Escape:	West Bromwich Albion (with an assist from Portsmouth)

Chelsea (under not yet that irritating new boss Jose Mourinho from Porto) won with a massive 95 points. More to the point, clean sheets in nearly two thirds of games, including 10 in a row for the impressive Petr Cech were the foundation. The importance of good goalkeepers in winning titles (think Schmeichel x 2, Flowers, Seaman, Cech, Van der Sar) should not be underestimated. Manchester United not only failed to win for the second successive season but also missed out on runners up spot again, this time to Arsenal.

Although unlike Arsenal the previous season Chelsea did actually lose a game (to a

---

[1] This song just beat The Arctic Monkeys – *I Bet That You Look Good on the Dancefloor*, which as well as being a cracking tune is also what I imagine Jose Mourinho sings to himself in front of a full length mirror.

Nicolas Anelka penalty at Manchester City) they got more points and only conceded 15 goals – amazingly a third of these came against the bottom 4 with bottom of the table Southampton scoring as many as any other team (2). You're really struggling to pad when one team wins with ease; sorry. Fortunately, notwithstanding Chelsea's achievement, 2004/05 is probably the most exciting last day ever at the bottom of the table. The relegation battle was a corker with 4 teams clearly not good enough to be in the Premier League, though I wasn't able to enjoy it at the time.

The woeful quartet, with far fewer points than would usually permit survival, were (going into the final day) Norwich City (33), Southampton (32), Crystal Palace (32) and West Bromwich Albion (31). And yet one of them would survive. At kick-off, Norwich was the one which had their fate in their own hands, but quickly fell behind at Fulham. They ultimately lost 6-0 which seems to show a disappointing lack of spirit. Southampton were the first to climb above them in the 'as it stands' table by taking the lead at home to Manchester United. But Man Utd quickly equalised and took the lead as Saints also fluffed their lines in a 1-2 defeat. Crystal Palace, managed by Premier League poster boy Iain Dowie, went behind at Charlton as West Brom took the lead against Portsmouth whose fans were keen to avoid a derby the following year. But any hope of a comfortable afternoon for Baggies fans were erased as Palace turned things around to lead 1-2. However in the final twist, Charlton equalised and West Brom and Portsmouth fans were able to celebrate together. Bottom at Christmas and bottom on the start of the last day...probably the most miraculous escape of all time in a Premier League season when no team was already relegated going into the last match. Staying up with 34 points is going to be difficult to match.

Focus on: Bolton Wanderers.

Summary: Bolton were in the third tier of English football as the Premier League kicked off in 1992/93 and were back there again for its 25th season. In the interim they had a fine adventure and added to their record number of top flight seasons for a team that has never finished top. First promoted to the Premier League in 1995/96 and playing at their old Burnden Park ground, they yo-yoed between divisions until getting a toe hold at their new Reebok

Stadium; they survived the 2001/02 and 2002/03 seasons. That then laid the basis for four consecutive top 8 finishes and forays into Europe. By 2011/12, however, they were relegated and in 2015/16 went down to the third tier again as debts mounted. 2016/17 saw a successful promotion push in a very tight division.

Rivals: I just love the 'rivals' section for Bolton in Wikipedia. It goes something like...

Traditional rivals – Bury, but they don't play them very much any more

Historical (founder members of football league) and geographical (15 miles) rivals – Blackburn Rovers

Developing rivals – Wigan Athletic

Developing rivals?! And it then says, Bolton fans maintain a 'mutual dislike' with the fans of Tranmere Rovers, Burnley and Wolverhampton Wandererers.

The latter is possibly due to Wandererers bragging rights, or more likely when both were much bigger teams. Anyway, I wondered what would happen if you carried on down this list of 'rivalries' to its logical conclusion:

Bolton fans aren't on speaking terms with – Blackpool FC

Might manage to say hello to if they saw them in the street – Macclesfield Town

Would consider having a beer with – Manchester City

Send Christmas cards to – Fleetwood Town

Share a sense of humour with – Norwich City

Had a holiday snog with – AFC Bournemouth

Would spend a night of wild passion with...no this is getting too silly. Afterall, do laconic Boltonians do wild passion?

Best Moments: The very nice people at the Bolton Wanderers Football Club Supporters Trust helped me boost the word count with not only their name but by sending me a thread from the 'BWFC Forum – The Official Unofficial Forum for Bolton Wanderers Supporters'. The thread is called 'The 100 Most Memorable Bolton Moments of All Time'. Now I don't know about you, and I'm sure it's a faulty impression, but when I think of Bolton in the Premier League I think of Sam Allardyce getting his teams to clog their way to 1-0 victories. It seems I might be partially correct. Obviously some of Bolton's top 100 memories were outside the EPL, but here's a few that took place in the last 25 years.

1. 1997/98 Way before goal-line technology, Bolton drew 0-0 with Everton after having a perfectly good goal by Gerry Taggart – in the sense that it was a mile over the line - disallowed. This might not have stuck quite so long in the part of the brain reserved for 'bitter resentment' if Bolton hadn't got relegated on goal difference. Behind Everton.

2. 1997/98 Fast-forward to the season's end and Bolton would have still stayed up with a draw. But they trailed Chelsea 1-0 at Stamford Bridge late in the game. Football supporter dynamics are strange, but as Wanderers poured forward in search of a late equaliser, the whole of Stamford Bridge joined in, in baying for a Bolton goal. Alas, Jody Morris scored on the break for Chelsea, but having everybody behind you at an away game was a special and unusual moment.

3. 2003. Youri Djorkaeff was fouled in the dying seconds of a game versus Tottenham. Jay-Jay Okocha calmly slotted home the penalty. Bolton won 1-0. Crucial points, it turned out, come the end of the season.

4. 2003 (again) Jay-Jay (again) was famously 'so good they named him twice'. He was also called the African Maradona, although I assume he was insulted. Anyway he made a fine solo run from inside his own half against West Ham, shrugged off Joe Cole's 'challenge' and slammed the ball high into the net past Calamity James, who until then was having a good day.[2] *He produces another sublime goal, celebrates with another crazy dance and sends the Reebok into raptures.* Bolton won 1-0 and crucially stayed up, given the good times to follow. They were two points clear of...West Ham.

5. 2006. The good times had arrived at the Reebok and Ivan Campo (he of the silly hair) had given Bolton the lead against one of their multitudinous rivals, Blackburn Rovers. Disaster seemed to strike as Rovers were awarded a late penalty, but it was saved by Jussi Jaaskelainen whose name ought really to contain many umlaut type creatures. And then another even later penalty was awarded, taken by a different player but similarly stopped by the flying Finn. And, err, Bolton won, err, 1-0.

So, with 0.6 Bolton goals per memory, perhaps my feeling that Bolton often

---

[2] See it here: **https://www.youtube.com/watch?v=_6ahfnopd9I** (accessed 9/3/17)

won 1-0 was justified? In any case, there were other memories, most notably of beating Man Utd; though not stated as an official rival, it is probably considered automatic, especially in Lancashire. These memories also remind you of the players that Bolton managed to attract; rather like when Middlesbrough had Ravanelli and Juninho, Wanderers' fans probably had to pinch themselves to see the calibre of foreign player they could attract, not to mention the under-rated Kevin Davies.[3] Wanderers were relegated in 2011/12 but at least Fabrice Muamba was still alive.[4]

Focus on: Chelsea

David tends to look vaguely unimpressed when I ask how on earth he supports Chelsea when a) he was brought up on the outskirts of Southampton b) isn't a hugely objectionable 'Eng-er-land' chanting beer-swiller. However, it wouldn't be the first odd parallel in our lives that I was brought up on the outskirts of London and support the Saints. We also share a love of football, tinged with aging cynicism about aspects of it. Here's what he has to say about his 'beloved' Chelsea.

Yes, yes, yes, the Premier League has been wonderful for Chelsea. We've won it five times and finished runners-up another four times. When it started we were hated for being from London, now we are hated for being all that's wrong with football. And for being from London. Our top scorer then was Mick Harford now it's Diego Costa. Along the way I've watched Hoddle, Gullit, Zola, Vialli, Desailly, Terry, Carvalho, Robben, Lampard, Drogba, and my own cult heroes, David Lee, Eddie Newton, John Spencer, Jesper Gronkjaer and Eidur Gudjohnsen.

Personal highlights include: a huge row over a curry with a pwopah old skool Chelsea fan over the limitations of Celestine Babarayo; sitting with the away Coventry fans in

---

[3] Trouble is, to quote David Pleat, 'he literally had no left foot'.

[4] See: **https://en.wikipedia.org/wiki/Fabrice_Muamba** (accessed 9/3/17). His heart had 'only' stopped for 78 minutes.

1999 (if you ever want a strange insight into your club, sit once with the opposition[5]); and Jimmy Floyd Hasselbaink's 2002 'perfect' hat-trick v Spurs. And maybe the most satisfying of all in retrospect was being told in December 1995 by a Newcastle fan, who had just seen his all-stars lose 1-0 at the Bridge, that Chelsea 'weren't bad for a small club'. (Major trophies won since that conversation: Chelsea 18, Newcastle 0).

Yet, strangely if I think of 'Chelsea and the Premier League', I think of November 22, 1993. In the middle of a winless 10-game run, we played Manchester City at home on a Monday night. Just 10,128 people turned up for the privilege of watching Neil Shipperley, Jakob Kjeldbjerg, Steve Lomas and Michel Vonk run around. It finished, of course, 0-0. I wasn't even there.[6]

The reason I find it so memorable is because it was the first game I had ever watched on Sky. My friend Rakesh had bought a Sky TV package. Don't do it, I told him; it's a waste of money, I said; who wants to watch the likes of Sheffield United play Swindon on television, I sniffed; and, can I come round yours on Monday to watch Chelsea?

The game confirmed everything I thought about Sky, the EPL and football in the 1990s – it was a barren wasteland and that no amount of PR could polish up a game between Chelsea and Man City and anyway, who plays football on a Monday? It was dreadful, energy-sappingly dull. I left telling Rakesh that he really had wasted his money and probably something about Rupert Murdoch and that Chelsea and Man City would never win another trophy in my lifetime. I admit, I may have got some of that wrong.

Of course, the game fits a common narrative that Chelsea (and City) were utter crap before their respective sugar daddies came along. But, it's worth noting that in the decade between that game and when Roman Abramovich pitched up, Chelsea won two FA Cups, one League Cup, a European Cup Winners' Cup, finished in the top 4 three times, beat Real Madrid in a UEFA Super Cup final and were an extra-time loss to Barcelona away from getting through to a Champions League semi-final. Not bad for a small club.

---

[5] Also recommended by Andy Watton who watched with the 'toon army' during a crucial win for Blackburn in their title winning season, and Rory Waterman who practised his Frank Skinner impressions at the Hawthorns supporting Norwich.

[6] This answers the taunt 'where were you when you were s***?

Focus on: West Bromwich Albion

The Premier League looks unlikely ever to live up to John Marks' footballing 'gold standard' of the 1975/76 season, and particularly its culmination. To summarise for you: Johnny Giles arrived as player-manager-deity and took a club that had lost its way back into the old First Division; 20,000 Albion fans (so legend has it) went to the final crucial game at Oldham to see Tony 'Bomber' Brown score the only goal of the game. *It was the most exciting, nerve-wracking day I'd ever experienced and, it's the yardstick against which I measure everything in football. Behind the corporate gloss of the Premier League, the spirit of 1976 may still be there, somewhere, but I get no more than the occasional whiff. The days when Willie Johnston negotiated the purchase of a greenhouse from a fan whilst taking corners are long gone.*

I'm pleased John was able to contribute to this book because my plan B was Frank Skinner and I doubted I'd get past his agent. On the subject of Frank, John notes that his *unforced optimism is an admirable quality, but it's unusual to find an optimistic Baggie. Many of us are the football supporting equivalents of nervous flyers, convincing ourselves that we keep our club in the Premier League by a kind of sustained force of will/hope that keeps planes in the air. If we relaxed for a moment, who knows what would happen? More usual is this Adrian Chiles style pessimism which sees disaster around every corner – 2-0 up with 20 minutes to go makes us very nervous. I maintain this is the natural state of Albion supporting. It's an existential demeanour that runs very deep; a sense that the good times are probably in the past. That's what comes of being spoiled in your childhood with the likes of Regis, Batson and Cunningham.*

Albion first appeared in the Premier League in 2002/03 after 16 years away from the top flight. Scary Gary Megson was dour enough to get them out of the Championship, but not to keep them up. John maintains however *that if Albion had been awarded three of four of the penalties they should have had, they could have survived.* Welcome to the Premier League as a 'not big' club. John notes other signs of this, like not being mentioned in reports of matches you took part in; even if you win, the story is always Man Utd, Liverpool, Chelsea's failure. Also, *you find yourself going to quite a lot of matches that you realistically have very little hope of winning – unless you're Frank Skinner I suppose.* Finally, beware of big club cast offs.

A good case in point is Ronnie Wallwork. Apart from the intriguing issue of how a child born in 1977 came to be called Ronald (he always felt like something of a footballing throwback) Ronnie was symptomatic of Albion's experience of the Premier League in the 2000s. He was, I believe, the club's first signing after promotion in 2002, a free-transfer from Man Utd, referred to by Alex Ferguson as 'the best Bosman of the summer'. I think I naively expected that we were going to get a little bit of the Man Utd glamour. But he didn't have a galvanising effect on the team, and there was always the faint suspicion that he couldn't quite come to terms with leaving Man Utd for little Albion. (To be fair, in more recent times, Darren Fletcher and Jonny Evans have arrived from Man Utd to much better effect.) Ronnie's best period playing for Albion was the legendary/landmark/ludicrously lucky 'Great Escape' under Bryan Robson in 2005.

This particular relegation escape, being both personally painful and dealt with in detail elsewhere in this chapter, is not covered again here. However, as a special moment for John, here is how it happened for him:

I was sitting high up in the East Stand with my dad listening to Radio 5 live on my headphones. I had resigned myself to a return to the Championship – Charlton had little to play for and Palace would surely see out [their] game and win to stay up. I still maintain that I was the first person in the Hawthorns to react to Charlton's unexpected late equaliser. I remember standing up and seeing a wave of recognition going around the ground. There followed a strange interlude when the final whistle went and we had to wait for the Crystal Palace result to come: it duly did and wild celebrations ensued. Without doubt, it was a great day, and a memory I will always cherish: but, even so, it wasn't Oldham 1976 was it? It was, in short, a definitively Premier League experience. We were celebrating finishing 17th after all, and the reliance on other results and luck gave the whole day a strange dynamic, made even stranger by the fact that the travelling Portsmouth supporters clearly wanted Albion to win to see their arch rivals Southampton relegated. Yes, OK, that's quite enough.

Seriously, John was kind enough to give me much more than this, mainly concerning the dismal, or bewildering, selection of managers Albion have appointed over the years. But of course no one was ever going to live up to Johnny Giles were they? *He was a canny, tough, self-reliant individual, who knew his own mind and was ruthless when he needed to be. The achievements of Guardiola and Mourinho cannot be denied, but in comparison they seem to me a little like they are method-acting the part of the intense 21ˢᵗ century manager. We now have a somewhat old-fashioned manager. Tony Pulis wasn't always popular at the Hawthorns – and I can see how his tactics get up other fans' noses at times – but he is undeniably getting the most out of a team of seasoned pros, of which a few have been at Albion a good few years. Back to the future.*

Season's Awards

Golden Glove: Petr Cech for 24 clean sheets (no really that's actually an award)

Dixon of Dock Green meets Kevin Keegan: Delia's 'Let's be 'avin' you' rant.[7]

Crazy But True Facts and Statistics:

- It was the first time no team had been relegated prior to the final day.
- West Brom became the first team who having been bottom at Christmas managed to stay up.
- On the last day Norwich had their fate in their own hands. Just needed to win. Lost 6-0 at Fulham.
- Given that fact, Saints just needed to win and led 1-0 against Manchester United. Then lost 1-2.

---

[7] See **https://www.youtube.com/watch?v=Bop4rr6sUQo** (Accessed 24/4/17)

- Given that fact, Palace just needed to win and led 2-1 going into the final 10 minutes. They drew 2-2 with Charlton Athletic.

- Given that, West Brom (bottom at Christmas, and still bottom at the start of the final day in fact) stayed up by beating Portsmouth 2-0, giving both team's supporters something to celebrate.

- Everton managed a Premier League high 4th place with a negative goal difference.

Up Next

Sunderland, Wigan Athletic and for the second successive season, the 6th placed team with just 73 points via the play-offs (West Ham United).

CHELSEA DAGGER
(2005-06)

Champions:	Chelsea
Relegated:	Birmingham City, West Bromwich Albion, Sunderland
Unbelievable Relegation Escape:	The footballing Gods continued to protect Pompey as Harry Redknapp (grrrrr...) won Manager of the Month after 4 wins and 2 draws in April when they looked totally doomed at the end of February.

Chelsea are the only Premier League team so far to defend their title except Manchester United who have defended it a remarkable 6 times in total, managing 3 in a row twice.[1] So, after 50 years since their first top flight title, numbers 2 and 3 came along very quickly as Chelsea celebrated their centenary in style. At the time it felt like their money might make this as monotonous as Manchester United's dominance, although since then Chelsea have managed just three more titles, to United's five. Whilst not quoting Wikipedia very often, its assessment of this season opens up with: "Chelsea continued spending vast sums of money in their third season under the ownership of Roman Abramovich." What else is there to say about them? Highlight, winning the Premier League by 8 clear points. Lowlight losing to Fulham

---

[1] Original drafting suggested 'since Leicester look unlikely to do so' but by early March 2017 it had already become mathematically impossible.

thanks to a Luis Boa Morte goal. Arsenal, meanwhile, had a quiet final season at the Highbury library before moving to the fiery cauldron that is Airplane Gardens.[2]

Against the odds performers of the season were probably Wigan Athletic. After an opening day loss to Chelsea (champions to be) was followed up by defeat at Charlton, the pre-season relegation favourites seemed to be justifying the bookies' lack of confidence. However, before their next defeat to Arsenal, Wigan took 25 points from a possible 27, effectively ensuring Premier League survival before December. This included 6 consecutive wins at one point, meaning that Paul Jewell beat Jose Mourinho to the Manager of the Month award in both September and October. Thus Wigan's first Premier League season ended with a top half finish (10th) and an appearance in the league cup final, although they lost (4-0 to Man Utd).

Season's Awards

No one likes him, he don't care: Chelsea won 15 of their first 16 games *and* the league but O Senhor Mourinho didn't win manager of the month, not even once.

What a waste of talent: Joe Cole, one of Chelsea's best players this season, could surely have done so, so much more in the game.

---

2   A not very good anagram of 'fiery cauldron' is 'u fail, cry, drone' – which actually does sound a bit more like it really.

Crazy But True Facts and Statistics:

- Aston Villa drew 0-0 with Arsenal on New Year's Eve; nothing happened, but I thought you ought to know I watched that kind of rubbish just to ensure this book was comprehensive.

- All the coaching staff at Chelsea spoke Portuguese, except Steve Clarke who just sounds like he is if you're not really concentrating.

Up Next

Reading with 106 points and a positive goal difference of almost 1 and a half goals per match. Then the temporary resurrection of Sheffield United. For once the third place team won the playoffs: it was Watford FC.

Focus on: Watford FC

I've taken the step of including Watford in a season they were promoted to, rather than actually being in, the Premier League. Cynics might argue that this was simply because this chapter looked a bit thin otherwise and in order to balance the word count but...

Actually, OK, the cynics are right, but this was a fine season for Watford, promoted back to the Premier League via the play-offs beating Crystal Palace and then Leeds without conceding a goal. Probably lives longer in the memory than the 28 points they achieved next season on the way back down. Anyway, Ian Thorpe told me a little about his club.

Watford FC is the 'Family Club' with a proud history. Recently that has included being on the brink of administration, facing winding up orders and, latterly, being a surprise new force in the Premier League with two of Watford's four Premier League seasons being the 24th and 25th. Previously they'd appeared in 1999-2000, when Graham Taylor took the side from Division 2 (now League One!) straight to the Premier League, and when Aidy Boothroyd (in his first managerial job) won promotion via the 2005-2006 playoff final at the Millennium Stadium in Cardiff.

Both those initial appearances would result in Watford finishing in 20th place and outside of their two Premier League appearances Watford endured several years of selling its best players to keep the club afloat, fans raising money to keep the club playing at its home ground of Vicarage Road and a series of owners and board members who had interests other than football to think about. In 2012 ownership passed to the Pozzo family, who have owned Serie A side Udinese, their hometown club, since 1986. Over the course of four short years, they have transformed the club, whilst keeping its core community values.[3] The club's entire infrastructure has been completely re-developed, from the training pitch right the way through to the stadium. New stands have been built, the club's transfer record has been broken four times and the fans have never been so optimistic as a result.

The journey to the Premier League was an incredible one, filled with moments that football fans all over the world can enjoy. Watford's extraordinary 2013 play-off game v Leicester for instance; totally unforgettable.[4] It has also had its moments of controversy with loan rules being changed as a result of the high influx of international loan signings and a small matter of eight managers in four years and four managers in two months. The 'Watford FC Project' (as it is referred to by the club's management) is still in its infancy however, and it's becoming more and more evident that it is something special and unique within the English game.

---

[3] A conversation with another Watford fan indicated, however, that this aspect has, unsurprisingly, changed a little, with hard-nosed business practice winning out over sentiment. He meant at all levels of the club, though the change of manager at the end of 2015/16 and 2016/17 perhaps exemplifies the tendency.

[4] See it here: **https://www.youtube.com/watch?v=Pma5RDt6MRw** (accessed 15/1/17). In short Leicester get an undeserved penalty in added on time of added on time. Score and they win the tie. But Knockaert misses it and misses the rebound and Watford pop down the other end and win it instead. As you now know, the footballing Gods were just collecting down payment from Leicester City on a bigger project they had in mind.

Watford's time in England's top division has been brief. In their return to the Premier League the club (guided by the charming Quique Sanchez Flores) managed to comfortably retain their Premier League status by finishing in 13th place alongside a stunning FA cup run which ended Arsenal's 16 match unbeaten run in the competition. At the Emirates too. An equally impressive display against Liverpool in the league, resulting in a 3-0 win also sticks out in the memory. Having not entered the relegation zone all season, had it not been for the incredible feat of Leicester City, Watford would have been recognized more for their efforts.

Yet another change in manager and overhaul of the squad has occurred and still the club continues to thrive. They have already improved on the highlights of 2015/16 by beating Manchester United for the first time in 30 years and 2016/17 was another of comfortable survival. With the club's infrastructure in order and the calibre of players being brought to the club by the Pozzo's worldwide scouting network, the future of Watford FC is brighter than the yellow shirts they wear.

SHE MOVES IN HER OWN WAY (2006-07)

Champions:	Manchester United
Relegated:	Sheffield United in controversial fashion because West Ham won at Old Trafford on the last day with a goal from Carlos Tevez, Charlton Athletic, Watford
Unbelievable Relegation Escape:	Wigan Athletic because they won at Bramall Lane on the last day.

If you need to be sick, check out the incredibly cheesy YouTube video entitled 'We won our trophy back'. I'm not putting a link to it, because who does actually *need* to be sick. OK, someone who's accidentally drunk bleach or taken an overdose maybe, but I'm pretty sure the NHS isn't yet using Man Utd in such treatment. Although... maybe it could work? Anyway, I needed to find another way to start a chapter about Manchester United winning the Premier League again. 'Their trophy'? – barf, barf! Unless their pleasing trend of not winning continues, I hope the maker of that particular montage has gone onto other things by the time they next win it.

Focus on: Sheffield United

Supporting Sheffield United has made Adrian Bell the man he is today – bitter and defiant. But not too bitter to re-tell, or even 'retail', the story:

A down-market red-top, celebrating some Premier League anniversary or other, once stated that the first Premier League goal had been scored by Brian Deane 'of Leeds United'. I was incensed…I ask you! How could we be mistaken for one of Yorkshire's lesser lights? Deane was definitely wearing the red and white of Sheffield United on Saturday 15th August 1992 and despite the worst efforts of some lazy tabloid hack, nobody can take it away from us that we scored the first Premier League goal.

Alas, working in retail, I missed the momentous event. Not only was I careless enough to find myself employed in an industry that favours Saturday working, I was also daft enough to live over 100 miles from Sheffield. No nipping out to watch the game or even tuning in to Radio Sheffield. The best I could do was avoid lunch until 3pm and then take all my breaks at once from then until sometime after sports report had finished. Mind you, I did have a slack boss, being as I was the manager of a small convenience store in Brackley, Northants, where everybody knew me as 'that bloke who supports Sheffield United' or 'boss'. So I made my own rules up, and my staff were quite relaxed about my general absence from the shop-floor between the hours of 3 and 6 on a Saturday because they saw me busting a gut to catch up with my work later, although once I discovered Danny Baker on 6-0-6 straight after Sports Report they would see even less of me. At 3 o'clock then, I'd take my Daily Mirror into the office with a sandwich and a bottle of flavoured carbonated volcanic water and settle down to listen to the already-tuned-in-and-switched-on radio, only emerging at half-time to buy myself a Gino Ginelli ice-cream for pudding. My staff knew to only disturb me if it was an extreme emergency, so by and large my Saturday afternoons passed quietly, barring my own thumping of the table, kicking the change-safe or swearing very loudly. The staff could gain no insight from these sounds as my reactions would be the same regardless of whether we were winning or losing.

We were the focus of the Premier League in those early days. Dave Bassett held an early Christmas party at Bramall Lane <u>before</u> the start of the season. The previous *two years, in the old Division One, Sheffield United had only bothered to turn up in the New Year, escaping relegation with high winter to spring velocity. So the logic of an early party was sound, and with the Premier League being launched, and Man Utd our first opponents, the mainstream media picked up on the stunt too. Of course, there may be a modicum of interest in who is going to score the first goal of any season; but this time the media were positively agog with excitement over who would score first. Radio listeners enjoying a meal deal in the back office didn't have long to wait for Radio 5's tantalising news that we had that first goal, following that up with a quick 'over to Bramall Lane' - words which sent me all of a quiver and had my tummy doing somersaults. As soon as I heard the reporter describing Sheffield United's throw-in I knew it was us who had bagged it, and the celebrations started; thumping the table, kicking the change-safe and swearing very loudly, not to mention a rousing chorus of 'Deano! Deano! Deano!'*

It got better; Radio 5 announced that the match at Bramall Lane was to be the second-half commentary so now there would be no more holding of breath every time they said, 'Quickly back to Bramall Lane'. Instead I could go a bit mad when we won a penalty after 50 minutes, and then go off the scale with my celebrations when Deano stroked it casually home. Eleven minutes later Mark Hughes nicked a goal back, meaning I then had a full thirty minutes of sitting at the desk with my head in my hands, getting up to pace around a bit when my legs started to go all pins-and-needly. At last, the final whistle went – cue table-thumping, change-safe-kicking, loud-swearing celebrations followed by me emerging from the office grinning broadly to tell my largely uninterested staff that the original United had stuffed Newton Heath 2-1 and that Christmas had come early at Bramall Lane (credit where it's due, I nicked that one from the Radio 5 commentator).

Surely things couldn't get any better? Of course not. Both our controversial relegations from the Premier League have been witnessed by me first hand, at the ground, fittingly in the rain. Away at Stamford Bridge in 1994 (lost 3-2 to a last-minute Mark Stein goal) and in 2007 at Bramall Lane to Wigan (a 2-1 defeat whilst West Ham were getting out of jail with a 1-0 win across the Pennines against Newton Heath's reserves, with Tevez scoring the goal). Football is often as much about the suffering as the success, so it is rather appropriate that I've copped for the misery like a wet casey walloped full-pelt at your ear, and yet have been stuck over 100 miles away tuning in on a dodgy radio when Sheffield United have created history.[1]

---

[1] I'm not quite sure what this last bit means, not speaking York-shh as I don't. However, I think I get it from the context so it stays.

Focus on: Portsmouth FC

The season after this, Portsmouth were 8th in the League and FA Cup Winners; Southampton were nowhere to be seen. The season before Portsmouth had defied the odds to escape relegation. Southampton were nowhere to be seen. This season was PFC's first top half, top flight finish for a long time. Southampton were nowhere. It doesn't get any better than that – well not for Pompey it doesn't. Fortunately. In fact Pompey's Premier League era is perhaps the strangest of all in a kind of 'death or glory' way, and a reminder of how quickly things can swing around in sport, both one way and then the other.

As one of those formerly big clubs now doing moderately well, Portsmouth at one time seemed like Huddersfield Town or Wolverhampton Wandererers. Destined to do OK, but just to sit as a mediocre entity forever. But in the first season of the Premier League they were almost promoted to it; they lost out to West Ham on goal difference for promotion and then lost to Leicester in the play-offs.

Thereafter the occasional good season was not good enough. In 1994/95 they finished 18th in the second tier. In 1996/97 they just missed the play-offs (7th) but in 1998/99 they were 19th and survived only on goals scored.[2] This was also Pompey's centenary season and to celebrate they went into administration, saved by Milan Mandaric. Nonetheless by 2000/01 a glorious new millennium saw then finish 20th, surviving by just a point.

Alchemy then arrived at Fratton Park in the form of Mandaric's money and Redknapp's willingness to spend it.[3] Initially this saw promotion and survival, but the Redknapp era really got going after he and Milan had a tiff. Redknapp

---

[2] If surviving on goals scored sounds dramatic, this was the only football league season where goals scored actually took precedence over goal difference. Four teams finished on 47 points and Pompey were safe either way. But spare a thought for Bury; rarely in the second tier they would have stayed up instead of Port Vale if it had been, as in every other year, goal difference.

[3] Of course no suggestion here of any wrong doing on 'Arry's part, he was just a wheeler and dealer in the transfer market. I must remember to pay the royalties for this book to my pet vole Colin who currently resides for a majority of the year in the Cayman Islands.

pottered off to Southampton for a short while. He declared the task of saving Saints to be impossible and promptly took them from outside the relegation zone when he arrived to bottom by the end of the season. He was then able to return to Portsmouth a hero by saving them from a genuinely impossible looking situation.

Spending more money and absolutely not benefitting at all himself, in 2007/08 Harry led Portsmouth to an 8th place finish which was above both Manchester City and Spurs. It would have been higher but for end of season losses, including the one that helped Fulham stay up. Still, sides often have that lull as no-one wants to get injured for the cup final. Yes, Pompey made the cup final! And though the wins in the semi-final and final at Wembley might not seem spectacular (1-0 v West Brom and 1-0 v Cardiff, respectively) you can't say they did it the easy way with three away wins *en route* to the final: at Ipswich in the 3rd round (1-0), Preston North End in the 5th (1-0) and most amazingly of all at Old Trafford in the 6th round (err 1-0).[4]

This is a book about the Premier League after all, so much after this point does not concern us. Pompey did manage another, unsuccessful, cup final appearance, but someone had spent all the money and PFC might be summed up thereafter as: administration/relegation/administration/ relegation. They are currently supporter trust owned and constantly threatening to get out of League Two, which they finally did. The future may not be bright, but it seems assured at least. 15,000-20,000 loyal and deluded souls regularly pack into the living museum that is Fratton Park and, who knows, another thrashing at St Mary's may be just around the corner.

I wrote all of that assuming I'd struggle to get a Pompey fan to write for a Saints fan's book. But we're not all that petty (at either 'end' of the M27) and on the 10th day of Christmas my email brought to me, two Pompey fans. So here below, in much more balanced fashion I'm sure, Neil Hughes and David Grover. Neil wrote a lovely long piece and David's missed about five games in 40 years, so I've had to edit.[5]

---

[4] If I really really throw my weight behind a Man Utd win, *this* is what happens!

[5] Neil went to a lot of trouble for which I'm very grateful. These I found interesting for instance: The first Jamaican footballer to play in England Lindy Delapenha, plied his trade at Fratton Park; the first football match to gross over a £1000 was a game between Portsmouth and Manchester United in January 1907; the first floodlit match in the football league saw Pompey play Newcastle at home in February 1956; Portsmouth fans can also stake a legitimate claim to English, possibly even world, football's oldest chant still in use today - the Pompey Chimes that ring out across Fratton Park every match day. ('On the Ball City' still sung by Norwich City predates 'Pompey Chimes' but Portsmouth were singing their song before Norwich was formed (1902). 'On the Ball City' was apparently sung, however, by fans of one of the teams which formed Norwich City. Who knows? Neil uses the phrase 'legitimate claim' so let's just leave it as part of the mystery that is life).

It is bold to claim that Pompey is the south coast's most successful club when Bournemouth and Southampton and now Brighton are in the Premier League but by initial reference to the Roman military leader Pompey the Great (approx 50 BCE) and holding the FA Cup throughout World War 2, and referring back to titles won in the first half of the last century that is exactly what Neil Hughes is able to prove.

However, despite the continuity in name, Portsmouth FC today is very different and very much a forward looking club. Having 'recovered' from over exposure to money and the Premier League, Portsmouth is now owned by its supporters (PST) and Neil emphasises *its ambitious medium-term plans which include improving the stadium, developing a sustainable academy capable of producing high quality players, increasing both youth support and club membership and strengthening links with the community within which the club is embedded. The latter aim is central to the PST's mission. As part of its community work, the PST is reaching out to new groups not normally known for their interest in football such as Portsmouth's Lesbian, Gay, Bisexual and Trans (LBGT) community and striving to make Fratton Park more family friendly by creating a welcoming atmosphere and by stamping down on offensive chanting and behaviour. All of these actions mark Pompey out as a progressive force for good that the city of which it is an integral element should rightly be proud and that other clubs in England, and further afield, would do well to emulate.*[6]

How did we get to this point? The Premier League is crucial to the story. Over to Neil:

In the first decade of the new millennium, for six uninterrupted years, Portsmouth F.C. graced the Premier League with a team laced with players from the highest echelons of world football. Although it would end in acrimony and protest, this was a period in the club's history during which its long suffering supporters experienced those moments of football joy reserved for fans of provincial teams punching fleetingly above their weight. A literal high came early on - in August 2003 - when the recently promoted Pompey topped the Premier League table for the first and possibly only time in its history.

In 2006/7, despite being at the bottom of the table, eight points adrift with just ten games to go, Pompey managed to retain their top flight status. Other highlights include qualification for the 2008/9 UEFA Cup, two appearances in the FA Cup final - as winners against Cardiff City in 2008 and losers against Chelsea in 2010 - and the unforgettable 2007 victory over Liverpool in the Barclays Asia Trophy. For obvious

---

[6] Sadly, one team will not be enjoying this friendly new approach if we ever play you again.

reasons, the FA Cup figures prominently in Pompey fans' recollections of this time. In many ways it was a period book-ended by performances in one of world football's greatest knock-out competitions. Thus, whilst a shock third-round away win to Premier League Nottingham Forest in 1999 might, arguably, be seen as the start of Pompey's journey to the summit of English football, the 3-1 defeat to Chelsea in the 2010 final, just weeks after going into administration, marks the end.

But the club became synonymous with the worst excesses of the Premier League era, with many coming to see Portsmouth FC as an example of a failed model in which owners driven by the lure of fame and personal economic gain, with a total disregard for financial risk, and under the inept gaze of the footballing authorities, brought the club to, and over, the brink of disaster. It lured the top players sure enough: Teddy Sheringham, Andy Cole, Peter Crouch and Jermaine Defoe. Other players to play for England during this period include Glenn Johnson, Sol Campbell and David James.

In the new era of globalised football Pompey drew heavily upon new sources of both talent and finance to enhance its standing. Players such as Arjen de Zeeuw, Svetoslav Todorov, Shaka Hislop, Dejan Stefanovic, Nwankwo Kanu, Pedro Mendes (whose spectacular injury time winner against Manchester City started the 2006/7 'Great Escape') and Hermann Hreidarsson became firm favourites with the fans.

Whilst not in the same league as Kanu, several other African players would go on, after Portsmouth, to have impressive careers either in England or elsewhere in world football. Sulley Muntari, for example, who scored an FA Cup 6th round winner at Old Trafford, signed in 2009 for Inter Milan. Other renowned African imports include Kevin Prince Boateng, Diomansy Kamara, Armand Traore, Djimi Traore, Hassan Yebda, Papa Bouba Diop, Aaron Mokoena, Roudolphe Douala, Nadir Belhadj, Younes Kabul, Yakubu Aiyegbeni, Lomana LuaLua, Aruna Dindane, John Utaka and Benjani Mwarurari. Benjani figured in another of the highlights of Pompey's PL stay - an 11-goal thriller at home to Reading in which he scored a hat-trick. Another player worthy of mention in this context is the French-Ivorian, Lassana Diarra. Diarra's performances during his two seasons at Pompey brought him to the attention of one of European and world football's greatest club sides, Real Madrid, who would pay an eye-watering £22 million to secure his services.

The other region of the world to provide Pompey with a rich seam of talent is Eastern Europe. A particular favourite, signed from Liverpool in 2002, was the richly talented Czech, Patrick Berger, who memorably scored the only goal in the 2003 victory over his former Anfield teammates. Other stand-out names from countries that until the fall of the Berlin Wall in 1989 had been part of the Soviet sphere include

Robert Prosinecki, Svetoslav Todorov, Boris Zivkovic, Niko Kranjcar, Milan Baros, Dejan Stefanovic and Ivica Mornar, Of course, it was more than just football skill and talent originating in Eastern Europe that fuelled Pompey's progress in the first decade of the noughties. The club's unlikely purchase by the Serbian businessman, Milan Mandaric, in 1999 surely marked the beginning of a south coast debt bubble that would inflate to unsustainable levels under his successor as owner and chairman of the club Alexandre Gaydamak. Although their involvement hardly improved the situation, most of the financial damage had already been done by the time the likes of Sulamain al Fahim, Ali al Faraj, Balman Chanrai or Vladimir Antonov and Convers Sports Initiative (CSI) came onto the scene.

Despite the many footballing highs and undoubted lows experienced by fans in the period covered here, it is a move by supporters off the field that, ultimately, will go down in history as Pompey's greatest. There can be little doubt that without the courage, vision and originality of the fans that formed the Pompey Supporters' Trust (PST) that this great club would have disappeared from the English football scene. It is thanks to them that Portsmouth FC is now debt free, has made improvements to Fratton Park, has new training facilities and is building the foundations, from an admittedly lowly position, necessary for a more sustainable and successful future.

And really, not even a Saints fan would begrudge the South Coast's most successful club its dreams of former and future greatness.

Before we finish with PFC, I know David Grover and he has relished or suffered almost every game of the above. He's also not a gloater, or knee-jerk anti-Saint, but one of his memories is one particularly treasured at Fratton Park. Perhaps by others not with the same level of empathy David shows when asked about any extraordinary events at matches:

The nearest would have been on the day that Southampton visited Fratton Park and many of their fans were located on the uncovered Milton End Terrace. Unfortunately the heavens opened just before and during the match and those poor souls would have suffered quite a soaking! Hail I believe. *David says he cannot recall the date but Pompey won the match 1-0 with Yakubu netting the winner.* Definitely hail.

Focus on: Reading

The only Reading fan I ever knew would have been nearly 110 by now and is unavailable for comment. He took me to my first ever football match (Bishop's Stortford won 4-1 at Wembley in 1974) and I took him to his last one (Reading won 4-1 at Wembley in 1988). In between, we stood on the terrace at Reading's old Elm Park ground in 1982 and watched Bishop's Stortford get their only ever win against a football league team (FA Cup first round). In total, he accompanied me to 24 Bishop's Stortford away games and never saw us lose, leading to chants of 'there's only one lucky grandad'. As a tribute to him, I decided to cover Reading for this book by standing with their fans for the away match against Nottingham Forest on 22 April 2017. I started with a pie, large chips and a pint; well, it's what he would have wanted. No literally, he was a bit of a gannet too. Beef and onion probably.

Reading find themselves focussed on in this season, not only because 8th, including the double over Manchester City, is very good, but also because it's the only one of their three Premier League seasons so far in which they were weren't relegated. I say 'so far' because after poor seasons in 2014/15 and 2015/16, they once again have a team challenging for promotion in 2016/17. So, having taken more than 130 years to reach the top flight they now at least look like they are established in the top two tiers for a while. But having watched this match you have to wonder if it's all worth it.

To begin at the beginning. Forest had suddenly plummeted, just a point above the relegation zone. An argument could have been made before the match that Reading might make automatic promotion (as Newcastle faltered), or miss out on the play-offs altogether (as other teams started winning) – but neither argument was very strong with the play-offs looking the most likely scenario by far. I heard fans talking about how Jaap Stam had put out a weakened side. But whatever the reason (and I have no love of Notts Forest, as I've just demonstrated with that faux pas) the home team just looked far superior and at one stage it looked like Reading might mimic their recent 7-1 mauling by

Norwich. That defeat was at least explained by this performance. If Forest got the relegation jitters and made it a close finish (3-0 became 3-2) it could not disguise the fact that Reading look hopelessly unprepared if they think they'll cut it in the Premier League.

Amongst the fans (not enough to fill the smallish allocation) I sensed no real excitement. Or anger. Or fun. They sang about being on their way back and about hating Swindon and I genuinely found myself wondering if Reading wouldn't be happier being a 3rd tier team like back in grandad's day. Probably not, but I didn't find anyone to tell me that. A day to forget but the extra season in the Championship (after play-off final penalty agony) may not end up being such a bad thing. Oh and the front cover of this book looks just like a bloke with a Royals flag I saw.

Season's Awards

Inventive YouTube Clip: Adolf Hitler of all people captures the mood of the people of Sheffield (the red and white bit anyway): https://www.youtube.com/watch?v=cNDRt-Ze-yU (accessed 18/5/17)

Rahul Dravid Wall Award: In the PFA team of the year, Manchester United's 7 representatives included the goalkeeper and entire back four, despite not having the best defence. They also had no forwards despite scoring an official 'shed-load' (19) more than anyone else.

Crazy But True Facts and Statistics:

- Moritz Volz of Fulham scored the 15,000 Premier League goal and became nicknamed '15,000 Volz'. Ha ha!

Up Next

Sunderland, Birmingham City and Derby County (a second consecutive third place team to win the play-offs, after the increasingly tiresome footballing Gods allowed them to win a penalty shoot out against Southampton in the semi-finals and then gave us 'quite a soaking' the like of which we'd not seen since that Fratton Park incident above).[7]

---

[7] The Gods of course are forgiven for a) having a Swiss billionaire up their sleeves b) banishing Pompey to the fringes of the footballing universe c) relegating Derby the next season with fewer points than the UK usually makes in the Eurovision Song Contest.

CHASING CARS
(2007-08)

Champions:	Manchester United
Relegated:	Reading, Birmingham City and Derby County (11 points!)
Unbelievable Relegation Escape:	Fulham

'Let's waste time, chasing cars, around our heads.' So goes the Snow Patrol song, and whether in your head, or on a motorway, the futility of car chasing seemed somewhat akin to the efforts of 'the rest' to stop Ferguson's men. They didn't this season – again – and Manchester United got into double figures for Premier League titles (10 of 16 in fact; Seven of Nine's dumpy Borg sister). It will take another team a fair while to reach double figures, although at least the rate of winning for Man U was slowing somewhat by this stage.

Still, dear reader, have faith, for the footballing Gods are always just around the corner waiting for smugness to exceed acceptable levels. Verily did they smite Derby County this season for their goal-keeper's gloating in the previous season's play-off semi-final penalty shoot-out! And with certainty they were plotting a denouement for the 2011/12 season which would drain away all the colour from even the hardiest of Man U fans. More on that story later. Nothing more on this season though.

Focus on: Derby County.

Football supporters have that habit don't they? What if we'd held on in that game, or won that 6-pointer etc we might just have stayed up/won the league etc. But for Derby, this season, no amount of 'what if gymnastics' could have saved them. What if Gerrard had not scored a last minute winner for Liverpool? What if substitute Stokes hadn't netted late-on at the Stadium of Light? What if Giannok..Ginokopolou...Gianni...what if Stelios hadn't done the same for Bolton? The answer is that none of it would have been anywhere near enough.

Derby set records galore including 32 Premier League matches without a win, first Premier League team to be relegated by March, lowest points total under three for a win (11) fewest away points (3). Top scorer Kenny Miller's total is occasionally reached by players in a single match (4). The one bright spot of this season for Derby fans is that despite everything, the lowest crowd of the season didn't dip below 30,000. Have there been other Premier League highlights for a Derby fan? I met one in Diagon Alley (Mr Fox) and asked him:[1]

If you are looking for the footballing Pyrrhic victory, then look no further than Wembley, 28th May 2007, which presaged a season of misery for even the most positive-thinking Rams fan. How we chuckled at the bad loser attitude of Chris Perry of the defeated West Brom side who said something along the lines of 'that lot are absolute shite and will be straight back down with about eleven points if they are lucky'. It was fair to say we would need to spend to strengthen the squad but instead, Billy Davis big pre-season outlays were on Rob Earnshaw, who had previously proved himself not good enough for the top flight, and Claude Davis, who was more suited to league two, where he later ended up.

Still, we were back where those of us of a certain age think we belong. If you are a Rams' fan in your fifties there is every chance you have seen Derby play Real Madrid and Juventus at the Baseball Ground. Of course a decade later that was tempered by

---

[1] That place in London where they filmed it anyway.

league contests against Newport, Lincoln and York. Oh well, variety and all that... life as a Rams' fan is never dull!

Derby have spent a paltry seven of the twenty-five PL seasons in that hallowed company and whilst only that one season seems to live in the memory of non-Derby fans, there were a few seasons where we weren't a laughing-stock. We even knocked on Europe's door a couple of times. Out of duty I will touch on (gloss over) this dreadful 07/08 season. The highlights video would be shorter than an Undertones single.[2] A not-too-bad 2-2 home draw and a promising 1-0 defeat at Eastlands in the first two games gave us false hope that we might have something to build on. We signed Kenny Miller and his wonderful winner on his debut (I think) against Newcastle gave us a first win in September. Unfortunately around the same time, we were losing 0-4 (Spurs), 0-6 (Liverpool) and 0-5 (Arsenal). And we looked hopeless – really hopeless. The squad was nowhere near PL quality and we all knew it. Billy Davies went, Paul Jewell came in and nothing much changed. Other thumpings came and went and we were down before March was out. Unheard of. The stats say it all – Played 38 Wins 1 Goals for 20 Against 89. Fond memories – nah.

So let's rewind to the previous decade instead. We were promoted automatically – it can make a difference, believe me - in 95/96 with a squad far better prepared for life in the top flight than the team of Billy Davies and with a more experienced manager at that level. Igor Stimac had been signed during our promotion campaign and the Bald Eagle (Jim Smith) added his compatriot Aljosa Asanovic (gifted and on his day a world beater but in my view a bit of a footballing mercenary who could go missing when the going got tough), Jacob Laursen (solid, dependable and consistent) and the versatile Christian Dailly. All proved they were up to the task. Players from our promotion squad such as Gary Rowett, Chris Powell, Lee Carsley and to an extent Darryl Powell and Dean Sturridge adapted well to the higher tier. Along the way, Smith added Paul McGrath to shore up the defence. His knees were knackered, he couldn't run and he didn't train – but the brain was as sharp as ever. Just turned up for the game and read it as well as ever. And he had Stimac for company. Wanchope and Poom were added at the right time later in the season. In time in fact for that memorable win at Old Trafford and Wanchope's marvellous goal to introduce himself to us adoring faithful.

That first season in the Premier League will always be for me the most memorable one. I looked at the fixtures when they were published and wondered where our points would be coming from. The inferiority complex must afflict many a promoted

---

2   Presumably *Get Over You* rather than *Thrill Me*

supporter. One moment you're at Roots Hall and the next you find yourself at Old Trafford. But we needn't have worried too much. Although relegation was always a possibility going into April, survival was the catalyst for two more enjoyable years - and three where the spectre of relegation loomed ever larger and we seemed to be playing continual relegation six-pointers against Bradford City.

There were plenty of highlights from those years. The obvious ones: being there when we won at Old Trafford; beating champions-elect Arsenal 3-0; beating Liverpool home and away; being able to say good-bye to the Baseball Ground in its rightful place, the top tier of English football. And the more personal ones: watching us get battered for 90 minutes by Middlesbrough in a downpour one Sunday and winning 2-1; the first match in the Premier League (a 3-3 cracker in searing heat against Leeds with the realisation that man-made fibres in replica shirts of the period did not do a lot for personal hygiene); being 4-0 up against Bolton by half-time (if memory serves me correctly) and Horacio Carbonari's thunderbolt decider against the deadly enemy down the other end of Brian Clough Way. There were also some great away days – losing can almost be fun when it's a battling performance at Highbury as opposed to a lacklustre defeat at Blundell Park.

This was also the period of English football where overseas signings became the norm. The likes of Stimac, Stefano Eranio, Mart Poom, Francesco Baiano won our hearts. The likes of Mikkel Beck, Francois Grenet, Bjorn-Otto Bragstad and Vass Borbokis did not. And Fabrizio Ravanelli was paid a lot of money but I never felt his heart was in it.

And as for that play-off final and the losers that day? West Brom went up as champions the following season and but for one season have remained a top division side ever since. Is there such a thing as a Pyrrhic defeat? They regrouped and were ready. We went up with a mediocre side (at best) and were not. We haven't been back since in spite of some recent close calls. But, footballing Gods, we are ready now, honest.[3]

---

[3] This excellent summary by Roland Fox is generous in not mentioning Benito Carboni's dive sparking a 4-0 win against Southampton (it was 0-0 with 10 minutes to go) and the play-off semi-final when his beloved team was also out-classed.

Season's Awards

He Should Give Broadcasting Lessons To Danny Mills and Steve Claridge He Should: Jimmy Armfield received the PFA Merit Award for his services to the game. Nice man, not at all irritating.

Crazy But True Facts and Statistics:

- Derby were the first team in Premier League history to be mathematically doomed before the end of March.

- An 11-goal thriller is an oddity indeed, but it happened this season in the shape of Portsmouth 7-4 Reading.

- Another oddity is players on opposing sides scoring hat-tricks in the same match, but it also happened – for the first time in the Premier League - as Marcus Bent and Roque Santa Cruz did so during Wigan Athletic 5-3 Blackburn Rovers.

- Whatever he may claim Roquefort "Santa" Cruz (to give him his full name according to my text auto-correct) isn't the real Father Christmas.

Up Next

West Bromwich Albion boing boinged their way back once more, and Stoke City took the second automatic promotion spot. Hull City won the play-offs and entered the golden era of their history. Fourth in the table were Bristol City, who like Tranmere Rovers have had the odd near miss but never quite made the Premier League. Yet. I suppose the good news for them is that their near rivals, as opposed to Tranmere, have been much less successful than Liverpool and Everton.

BRICK BY BORING BRICK (2008-09)

Champions:	Manchester United (Yay!)
Relegated:	Newcastle United, Middlesbrough, West Bromwich Albion
Unbelievable Relegation Escape:	Hull City and Sunderland (not a great season for that north-east coast of 100 miles between Hull and Newcastle)

Ferguson continued to build his impressive legacy brick by boring brick, equalling with this success Liverpool's then record of 18 top flight titles. The success may have had something to do with Cristiano Ronaldo being named world player of the year, although Arsenal had the even better Nicklas Bendtner, so it's a mystery why they didn't challenge more strongly. Giggsy wiggsy (isn't it?) kept up his record of scoring in every Premier League season. Allegedly.

Liverpool had in fact been top at Christmas and Martin Tyler suggested that 'a title challenge is finally coming from Merseyside.' He didn't mean Everton, where Brazilian 'Jo' (who?) made an instant, but in the end not big, impact on loan from Manchester City, where his only impact was on the wage bill. Merseyside's challenge faded anyway after Liverpool manager Rafa Benitez launched a rant every bit as ill judged as Keegan's all those years previously, and Ferguson was handed the psychological edge (a-gain!). Van der Sar managed 11 clean sheets in a row, and United were five points clear at the end of January.

Nonetheless, although the inevitable inevitably happened as it invariably and inevitably does, Liverpool did win 1-4 at Old Trafford in March. When United then lost at Fulham, the title race opened up once more. But in the end Man Utd came from behind to win at both Villa and Wigan and just seemed to have that mental strength that made them almost everyone's 91st or 92nd favourite team.

At the other end of the table, by the last day, Middlesbrough had all but gone due to goal difference. One of the other north east teams (if we stretch that as far as Hull) would go with them. As you'd expect, with Premier League status on the line, all the teams gave it their very best. Hull lost. Sunderland lost. That left the way open for Shearer to save Newcastle, if only they didn't lose. They lost.

Focus on: Hull City

(Rich Cundill's eye-witness account from a rugby league town)

As I write this piece my team Hull City AFC has played 7 games in the 2016/17 Premier League season. They have amassed 7 points and sit 15th in the table. A more than decent start, despite latterly losing back to back games against Arsenal, Liverpool and Chelsea (by an aggregate score of 2-11, for the stattos out there). A run of games against some of the allegedly less strong teams is coming up and the possibility of achieving the season's aim of avoiding relegation looks more than reasonable at this stage.[1]

It is the club's 5th season in the top flight of English football. That is five seasons out of the most recent nine, and as such for many young City fans it has almost begun to feel like the norm. Which you can understand I guess. It wasn't always thus…24th May 2008 is a date you will find very close to the heart of any Hull City fan over the age of about 12. For me it was one of the greatest days of my life. I drunkenly bawled this fact down the phone to my wife as I left Wembley Stadium. Thoughts of our wedding day and the birth of our children seemed to have been obliterated from my mind such

---

[1] A well-known case of early season optimistic insanity syndrome.

was the euphoria. Only a matter of minutes earlier I was crying. Actual tears. The simple facts behind this sudden tide of emotion were as follows:-

- *Hull City had beaten Bristol City 1-0 in the Championship play-off final*

- *This meant they were promoted to the Premier League*

- *Hull City had never played in the Premier League before*

- *They hadn't even played in the top flight of English football before it was rebranded*

- *My Grandad and Dad, who had first taken me to Boothferry Park in the 1970/71 season when I was nine, were no longer around to see this most ridiculous feat that the club we all loved had achieved*

- *Things were going to be different from now on. Or so we assumed*

And so the wait for the start of the 2008/2009 season was one of extreme impatience combined with matching financial planning as the anticipation of travelling to watch our team play at Old Trafford, Anfield, The Emirates etc, in actual league games, not some cup competition where City would be the complete underdogs, kicked in.

The first few months of that season were absolutely amazing. A national newspaper even used the headline 'London 0 – Hull 4' (stolen from Hull's 4th best band The Housemartins). This starts to tell the tale of how we generally speaking got up a lot of people's noses. Beating Fulham (H), West Ham (H), Arsenal (A) and Spurs (A) in just a little over 2 months, with a manager in Phil Brown who (bless him) could barely control his delight (and his ego) at this unlikely turn of football events…just like the rest of us really. Surely it would never get better than that? It didn't.

Season's Awards

Dr Krippen Award for outstanding defence: Kevin Nolan protests his innocence after a ridiculous stamp on Everton's Anichebe. He was, however, rightly sent off.

Still not on the winning team!?: Arsenal were 0-1, 2-3 and 3-4 up at Anfield and the player the fans used to call 'Arse Shaving' (Andre Arshavin) scored 4 goals in a 4-4 draw.

Crazy But True Facts and Statistics:

- Gary Megson was caught smiling on the touchline. He did, I saw it on YouTube, though it's too gruesome to put a link to.

Up Next

A bumper year for very grim places to live as Wolverhampton Wanderers, Birmingham City and Burnley all made it.

DON'T LOOK BACK INTO THE SUN (2009-10)

Champions:	Chelsea
Relegated:	Burnley, Hull City and Portsmouth
Unbelievable Relegation Escape:	No, only mundane ones

Chelsea are not a popular team. I judge this by the lack of YouTube coverage of their triumphal seasons compared to other seasons/winners. That this was 'all about Mourinho' is disproved by this season at least, so it is best put down to the fact that many of their fans are pwopah knob-heads; this is a fact widely acknowledged by the many Chelsea fans who are not knob-heads, which might include you discerning reader. But it is well known that an identikit portrait of the stereotypical England hooligan of the 1980s would have CFC tattooed across his enormous flabby buttocks. Yeah...what has this got to do with the Premier League?

Focus on: Birmingham City

Who'd be a Birmingham fan? I can't say I would relish the prospect. This season's 9th place finish was their best in the top division for over half a century and that for a team whose name is also that of the 2nd largest city in England. The following season they upset the odds to win the League Cup against Arsenal, but also got relegated. And that was the golden age.

Birmingham has often received a bad press, most of which is entirely justified. I mean, no amount of surrounding it with even grimmer places usually, but not exclusively, beginning with 'W' can disguise its inadequacies. That said Telly Savalas (aka Kojak) loved the place.[1] His bizarre endorsement notes for instance that 'you can really eat in this town.' Eat? High praise indeed. For instance, you can 'ingest Indian.' Ingest? In jest? Anyway, Stephen Hurt, when he's not 'chewing Chinese', 'guzzling Greek', 'devouring Danish' etc loves the team and was glad of the opportunity (after the most bewildering managerial sacking of the year - Gary Rowett) to reflect upon the good (well reasonably average) old days. Steve started by answering my question...who *would* be a Birmingham fan?

I was born in Birmingham. Of course I was; why else would I be a Birmingham City fan! Us 'bluenoses' are a hardy bunch and there is always a sense that our expectations are set firmly in the realm of reality. I remember walking to a game at St Andrew's during our first season in the Premier League and spotting a fan in a replica shirt with the number 17; on the back, instead of his favourite player's name, simply the word 'FINISH'. Our ambitions encapsulated in nylon.

The 1980s and 1990s were barren even by our standards, but for a few years during the 2000s we enjoyed some very special times in the Premier League, bookended by finals at the Millennium and Wembley stadiums. In May 2002 we beat Norwich City via a penalty shoot-out to secure promotion to the Premier League. After sixteen years of obscurity, we were back . Three seasons followed in mid-table, which sounds

---

[1] Has to be seen to be believed: **https://www.youtube.com/watch?v=9EGWCG8fq9A** (accessed 22/2/17)

uneventful but these were very much halcyon days to be a 'bluenose'.

There is only one place to start in picking out the best of the average. September 2002 and the first Premier League local derby against Aston Villa. Blues romped to a 3-0 win but it was the 'Enckelman moment' which was the sweetest. A simple Aston Villa throw-in from Mellberg somehow ended up as an own goal after slipping under the keeper's foot. This is a favourite for me on YouTube even now![2]

Nonetheless, things were looking quite bleak come February when an amazing run of seven wins in nine games kept us up. This run involved a 2-0 win at Villa Park and the best game I have ever seen live at St Andrews. Christophe Dugarry, World-Cup winner, arrived on loan and in a crucial game against Southampton in April 2003 he scored two helping secure a 3-2 win. We had other top players during this period: Mikael Forssell, David Dunn, Matthew Upson and Robbie Savage. OK maybe not the latter, although he epitomised the work ethic of the team and also provided some amusing memories; like the time he scored a free-kick against Middlesbrough and then had a tantrum after losing his hair band during the celebrations.

All reasonably good things come to an end though, and in 2005-06 we were relegated. Promotion followed immediately as did another relegation and yet another promotion. Then, under the defence-minded management of Alex McLeish we reached the astounding heights of a 9th placed Premier League finish. Solid defence built around centre-back pairing, Roger Johnson and Scott Dann, made us hard to beat during that season. The following year was the epitome of life as a 'bluenose'. A League Cup run, including victory over Aston Villa, saw us reach a Wembley final against Arsenal. Against the odds Obafemi Martins scored the vital goal in a 2-1 win and his summersaults captured perfectly my own delight. At home with two newborns I was less acrobatic, equally ecstatic. However, these things shouldn't happen to Birmingham City, and sure enough a run of five defeats and a draw in the last six league games resulted in relegation. And now, in 2017, the Premier League looks and feels a long, long-way off. Our anthem 'Keep Right On to the End of the Road' has never seemed more apt.

---

[2] It looks like Enckelman missed the ball and so the correct decision should have been a corner to Birmingham, but he was one of many who didn't know the rules and assumed it was a goal anyway. Here it is: **https://www. youtube.com/watch?v=18QsjFUquD8** (accessed 18/5/17). The records note it as an 'Enckelman own goal' so the referee must have assumed a feint touch (or said he did afterwards perhaps?). I dare say Steve thinks it's a terrible shame as he watches the clip that the commentary, as the throw is taken, says 'there's so much more zest about Aston Villa now' with Birmingham just 1-0 up with 15 minutes to go.

Focus on Tottenham Hotspur

It's odd, that of the self-elected 'big five' who gave impetus to the Premier League idea, only two of them have actually won it. Spurs are not one. Arsenal, of course, are. This may be just one of the reasons why, along with Liverpool fans, Spurs supporters seemed the least keen to help with this book.

I'm putting Spurs in this season, because they qualified for the top European competition (now the Champions League) for the first time since 1961/62. They actually did pretty well, beating AC Milan on the way to a quarter-final. But during the domestic season itself, despite being joint top at the end of August they tailed off, never really threatening better than 4th and thus finishing below Arsenal yet again. Indeed, although the counter ticking up the time since Spurs last finished above Arsenal has finally been reset,[3] the fact that it surpassed 8000 PL days before it finally happened is the most likely explanation for Spurs' fans reticence.

Attempt One: I know that Professor Stephen Chan OBE, mentor and friend, supports Spurs because he once came to the Lane with me and saw a rare Saints victory. My invitation for him to write something for this book, however, was politely declined in that gentle but definitive way of his. Shame, the man can write. An invitation to lunch was more successful, although attempts to discuss football were deflected by observations about whether I'm getting to the gym as much as I ought to. It was a nice, large, lunch and he paid. Thanks. I suspect Stephen is bored by the whole moneyed circus rather than by Spurs themselves. Never mind, I know other Spurs fans...

Attempt Two: Alan Shambrook, defier of medical science and accomplished guitarist, accompanied me to a stodgy pub lunch. Professor Chan's right you know, I really do need to shift some weight. Anyway, we went to a pub

---

[3] **http://www.2atoms.com/time-since-spurs-finished-above-arsenal.htm** (accessed 7/3/17) When accessed again after the end of the season, I suspected some hilarious observation and the clock to have stopped...as of 31/5/17 it was still, illegitimately, ticking over however.

showing Spurs v Everton. I hoped the beer and football might loosen Al's tongue on a team he has supported nearly 50 years.

It soon becomes clear however that 'Sham' regards supporting Tottenham not so much as something to declare with pride, but more like a genetic disposition to illness. Inevitable, passed down and borne with stoicism it is, but scarcely a cause for celebration. He tells me the tale of a brother who opted to support Darlington instead (no really), seeking escape from the family illness. He has since been dragged back into the fold. Spurs beat Everton 3-2 playing some sparkling football and frankly I got more excited than my friend, possibly because I got confused when White Hart Lane nicked our song again. When the *Spurs* go marching in, indeed. Anyway, third time lucky?

Attempt Three: Ah ha, finally some enthusiasm about Spurs as Chris Baker and Jamie Garwood tell me what supporting Tottenham Hotspur means to them. *It's an addiction and obsession*, Chris began. Hmmm…perhaps Spurs really is an illness? A shameful secret? Fortunately for me though, Chris bares his tortured soul:

> *Three years ago, after 14 long years on the waiting list, I got a season ticket. It's an honour and a privilege to be able to go and see my beloved team play live on a regular basis. It's something I don't take for granted and I still get a buzz every time I see the hallowed turf on a match day.*

> *I've been going to White Hart Lane whenever I can since 1994 and it will be an incredibly emotional day when the place is torn down. Each visit this season has been tinged with a sadness because it means I'm a game closer to my final ever visit. Having said that, seeing the new stadium taking shape each week is really quite remarkable and I'm sure our new home will be an arena we can truly be proud of.[4] It's been a long time coming and I did have my doubts that it would ever happen. The fact that the club is staying in our spiritual home of N17 is really important not just to us as a fan base but to the local community as well.*

Some of my older contributors are quite grumpy about the Premier League. I am reminded of my grandad's angry nostalgia for the days when you could pick up the goalie and throw him into the net quite legitimately and that said goal-keepers would shrug off minor knocks like broken necks. But young Chris is much more upbeat:

---

[4] And an infinitesimally tiny bit larger than the Emirates probably.

The success of the competition/brand has not only fundamentally changed football in this country but it undoubtedly has had an impact all over the world. I sometimes forget going to games in North London that the matches are screened in every corner of the planet. Overall, I think you'd have to say that the Premier League has had a positive impact on English football if not on the English national football team. The introduction of all-seater stadia has made attending fixtures much safer and more women and families are attending matches than ever before. That said, I do think it's time for safe standing areas to be introduced, but that's a different matter altogether.

Spurs have always been an exciting team to watch and while it's not always been for the right reasons - it's never dull! Jurgen Klinsmann was my first idol and watching him in the flesh was a true joy. My first ever trip to White Hart Lane was a 0-0 draw v Crystal Palace in 1994. I can't recall much about the game other than Jurgen hit the cross bar and that the pitch looked amazing. By then it was far too late; I was totally hooked and Tottenham Hotspur were the drug of choice for my illness.

When Klinsmann left after just one season I was utterly heartbroken but then David Ginola came along and we had a new god to worship. Ginola is loved by Spurs fans for many reasons, not least of all his lovely hair.[5] But I believe the reason people have so much affection for him is because he played in some of the worst Tottenham teams in history. He was a shining light in a sea of darkness. He was the quintessential Spurs players; maverick and mercurial in equal measure. Every time he got the ball, people got off their seats. Although, on reflection it might have been sheer desperation on our part as we hoped he did something brilliant because none of his teammates were capable of anything at all.

When Ginola and Klinsmann were together that was a real treat. The highlight was a 6-2 demolition of Wimbledon at Selhurst Park which guaranteed Premier League status. Jurgen's place in Spurs folklore was assured.

Since those halcyon days we have been blessed with the likes of Robbie Keane, Dimitar Berbatov, Jermain Defoe, Gareth Bale and now Harry Kane/Dele Alli. I hesitate to list current players in the sense that while their progress and development has been nothing short of unbelievable, they are part of a much stronger collective these days rather than a team that relies on the individual brilliance of one outstanding player.

Our motto: 'to dare is to do'. We now dare to dream we might actually win the title some day. Or at least finish above 'them'. Please. It is done, but 'they' did win

---

[5] Yes, it originally said 'incredible skill'.

a trophy. Chris went on to list terrible Spurs players, but the word count wouldn't support them. Ho ho! [6], [7]

Focus on Fulham

David Lloyd, editor of *There's Only One F in Fulham* fanzine, ably assisted by similarly afflicted enthusiasts, says this.

Making it to the Premier League in 2001, we got a 'good luck' message from Bradford City supporters. Paraphrased it was: 'Best of luck in the top flight. Enjoy the big-game atmosphere, watching the big-name players and the increased attention via the TV companies and the media in general. But be prepared for the big clubs getting the big decisions, and for the genuine, 'home and away' fans to be well down the list of anyone's concerns.' In essence, those Bantams fans got it about right.

Under Jean Tigana, we had stormed through Division One, posting a record points haul of 101 in romping to the title. First up in the top flight was an easy one: Manchester United away. Two minutes in, Fulham took the lead through Saha (Fergie promptly made a note of his name for future reference!). With half an hour gone we could have been three-up but for Barthez; instead, a free-kick for a routine foul on Finnan by Giggs was awarded... to United! Up stepped Beckham: 1-1. A surprise away win now looked less likely; indeed, we lost 3-2. No points for the 'plucky losers'.

If that was irritating, Mark Halsey's interpretations of the rules in a home game with Arsenal in 2004 were bewildering, bordering on absurd. With the game goalless, the referee awarded Fulham a penalty for Ashley Cole's challenge on Andy Cole. On being harangued by Arsenal players, however, he changed his mind on the basis of 'player

---

[6] Jamie Garwood shares similar memories and listed some of the same favourites and terrible players. He also used the word 'privileged' in the context of supporting Spurs. Weird eh? Thanks for your input.

[7] Last word to Anthony Olivieri (Arsenal fan living among Spurs ones for a long time and so allowed a bit of a gloat): *They will finish above us sometime soon. Their improvement is undeniable and their training setup and facilities are second to none, like the Arsenal improvements of a decade ago. Their stadium looks like it will be impressive and it's no surprise they have decided to build it slightly bigger than The Emirates. When it happens, they will celebrate it like the moon landings or the World Cup win of '66. They'll finish above us one day..... but above or below, they are always in our shadow.*

reaction'. In retrospect (and applying the Corinthian spirit) he may have reached the correct decision. But just minutes later, Collins John looked to have headed Fulham into a deserved lead. It seemed a perfectly good goal – there was certainly no 'player reaction' to suggest otherwise – but Halsey chalked it off, for an apparent push. And guess what: Arsenal scored three unanswered goals after the break.

Don't worry, this isn't a whinge-fest, just acknowledging that there was substance to the Bradford City fans' warnings. We had other concerns, anyway.

Despite our magnificent rise through the divisions (having been 91st of 92 clubs in February 1996), Fulham's future at Craven Cottage remained unclear. We had special dispensation to retain the terracing for our first season 'up top', but then had to conform to the all-seater policy. So it was up-sticks to Loftus Road while a brand-new state-of-the-art stadium was constructed. Or not, as it turned out.

Final home game of the 2001-02 season was against Leicester, managed by Micky Adams – who'd masterminded Fulham's promotion from the basement division in 1997. The game was as drab as the 0-0 score-line suggests, but a fair few of us were melancholic, thinking it might well be our final game at Craven Cottage. FFC were actively pursuing other options, including a site at White City. Worried supporters formed a 'Back To The Cottage' group, with some fans sufficiently incensed to boycott the switch to QPR, believing the club was at best keeping them in the dark over future plans, and at worst preparing to sell its famous riverside ground. The underlying feelings of mistrust weren't helped by similar tensions between manager and owner. Mohamed Al Fayed fell out with Tigana, who was dismissed in April 2003, but not before winning the InterToto Cup, and with it a passage into the UEFA Cup.

New boss Chris Coleman inherited a talented squad and enjoyed an excellent debut season, finishing ninth. Even so, 'Cookie' learned the hard way that when Man United come a-calling, you do their bidding. His 'over my dead body' insistence that top scorer Saha was going nowhere counted for naught as the brilliant Frenchman switched for £12.4m midway through the season. Fulham, though, were mixing it with the big boys; our 3-1 win at Old Trafford in October, especially satisfying!

Fact is, we were doing more than okay. And, with a welcome return to a revamped Craven Cottage somehow secured for the 2004-05 season – spiralling costs put paid to the state-of-the-art project – our relative stability in the Premier League and being back at our historic home outweighed any negatives of being in the top flight. True, Saturday kick-offs at 3pm were fewer, and games were prone to fairly late switches on a whim. Also, the commercial aspects (plus the lack of a Supporters' Club bar) meant there were nowhere near the levels of camaraderie experienced in the lower divisions, either between groups of supporters or between managers and players.

Lawrie Sanchez and Fulham weren't a good fit. Having replaced Coleman, Sanchez took Fulham backwards in his eight months in charge, despite spending heavily. With Fulham in 18ᵗʰ in came Roy Hodgson. Although not apparent immediately, Hodgson and FFC became a near-perfect match. Relegation was all but nailed-on when two-down at Manchester City at half-time. The two remaining fixtures, Birmingham (home) and Portsmouth (away) were irrelevant. But remarkably, two goals from Kamara and one from captain Danny Murphy not only earned an unlikely win but pre-empted the greatest of escapes.

A 2-0 win against Birmingham meant a last-day decider on the south coast. Fulham had to win. Twelve minutes remained when Bullard sent a free-kick into the Pompey box where Murphy, that well-known target man, rose unchallenged to head home the winner. We stayed up on goal difference. Cue not only scenes of delirium among the travelling supporters but also, not that we knew it at the time, an incredible adventure under the wily Hodgson, ably assisted by FFC legend Ray Lewington. In 2008-09 we finished seventh – our best-ever league position. With it came a ticket for a European tour: the newly formed Europa League.

The first of 19 matches in that adventure kicked off in Lithuania in late July; astonishingly, we reached the final itself the following May when a patched-up Fulham side only succumbed to Atletico Madrid (De Gea, Forlan, Reyes, Aguero et al) seconds from the end of extra time. And to a deflected effort at that.

At this juncture, it's fair to say that 'little' Fulham were punching above their weight. But we were doing so, and continuing to improve, thanks to a fantastic work ethic on and off the field. We were an established top-flight club and had reached a major European final, deservedly so; what could possibly go wrong? Hodgson switched to Liverpool and his replacement Mark Hughes lasted just one season having decided, perhaps correctly, that we lacked ambition. Enter Martin Jol, seemingly a dream appointment as, for a while, we looked like a top-eight side, playing with more flair than the Hodgson set-up and, as with Hodgson, taking several notable scalps. But instead of galvanising, we sold instead; Chairman Al Fayed was preparing for a parting of the ways.

US tycoon Shahid Khan took over, promising 'a viable and sustainable Premier League future' and 'synergy' with his Jacksonville Jaguars. Our Premier League future promptly became our Premier League past, and the only telling synergy with the Jags was how terrible we both were.[8] Along the way, Jol lost interest, but was retained so as not to rock the sinking ship. That was ridiculous enough, but several

---

[8] And Khan's idea for a fanzine 'There's Only Two Syllables in Jaguar' was terrible too.

astonishingly inept decisions later (including the Meulensteen fiasco, Wilkins, Mitroglou, Magath, the turnover of players – 78 first-team players in three seasons) we not only plummeted through the Premier League trapdoor but then had to scrap for Championship survival. A self-inflicted disaster – one that no one was responsible for, apparently.

Just four seasons after being everyone's second-favourite team thanks to our stirring Europa League exploits and sitting more than comfortably in the top flight, we dipped out with barely a whimper. 'Omnishambles' roared the front cover of a certain fanzine. What a massive slap in the face to all those who'd worked so hard to get us there and who then oversaw our steady improvement. And what an almighty kick in the orange, maize-based cheesy-poof snacks[9] for the supporters.

There's a lot wrong with the Premier League, but it's the place to be. As I write, we're nudging ever closer to the play-off places under Slavisa Jokanovic and, as Paul Johnson's regular cartoon in TOOFIF reminds us, 'We Can Dream'. We crave success as much as any set of supporters but we don't demand or expect it; that's not a little Fulham thing, just a grounded approach. In fact, here's a recently heard aspiration from a Fulham fan: 'Not being shunned by that abysmal Channel 5 programme any more and going back to being last on Match of the Day!' I'm sure most Bradford City fans would say the same.

Season's Awards

Football Billiards: Darren Bent shoots low for Sunderland, hitting a red beach ball in the area which was knocked to Pepe Reyna's right while the ball deflected to his left and into the pocket, err, net.

---

9   This was originally 'Wotsits' but the publisher warned me against product placement.

Crazy But True Facts and Statistics:

- Portsmouth became the first Premier League team to go into administration which, despite the 'pay up Pompey' chants, pleased not even Saints fans; well not many anyway.

- Pompey also got to the cup final (losing to Chelsea) – a remarkable feat bettered by Wigan who won the cup and got relegated in the same season about 40 pages from now I'd guess.

- Roberto Martinez career as Wigan manager gets off to a dubious start as he describes one player thus: 'Technically it would be very difficult to find a better player at Premier League level, he's a magician, his first touch is out of this world.' The unmistakable Jason Koumas who went on to bag a whopping 2 goals in 54 Latics appearances.

Up Next

Newcastle recover from the Shearer era. The Baggies go boing boing again. There were not too many new faces arriving in the Premier League by this stage but Blackpool provided one by winning the play-offs from 6th. Surely their finest hour – apart from 1953 and all that, obviously.

MAIN OFFENDER/ HATE TO SAY I TOLD YOU SO (2010-11)

Champions:	Yes, them again obviously!	
Relegated:	Birmingham City, Blackpool, West Ham United	
Unbelievable Relegation Escape:	Wolverhampton Wandererers	

Manchester United won again. Where were the footballing Gods?[1] Frankly, contract or no contract, I refuse to do anymore bloody 'analysis' until some other bugger wins it. Simple as.

---

[1] I told you, they are ever vigilant, looking always for the appropriate punishment or reward! Patience.

Focus on: Blackpool[2]

Of all former Premier League teams, Blackpool competes with Coventry as the one to fall furthest from the sun. They held onto 6th place in the Championship the season before (2009/10) and came up via the play-offs. This not only kept up an extraordinary record of play-off victories (broken only when they tried to get back into the Premier League a second time) but also made them the first team to win promotion via the play-offs to all possible football league divisions. Alas they are one of the teams which appear where they do in this book by dint of it being their only Premier League season, rather than because of any other significance. They have, at the time of writing, slidden[3] all the way to the bottom, and this former giant shows few signs of repeating its Premier League heroics, notwithstanding another play-off win in 2016/17 this time minus thousands of protesting supporters.

Centenary seasons often offer up something interesting, and the centenary of continuous league football for Blackpool was certainly an eventful one. Those who saw all their games in the Premier League saw considerably more than 3 goals a game, and even the 0-0 draw against West Ham was a classic. Their own scoring approached 1.5 goals a game and was as good as, or better, than half the top ten. Alas, their goals conceded column was a less than impressive 78, a figure not got close to by other teams. As Dave Ford puts it, *there was no 'last on Match of the Day' for us that year.*

Typical were an opening day win over Wigan Athletic (4-0) which saw Blackpool technically top of the league for a short time, for the first time since Christians formed the staple diet of lions. But this was followed up by a painful and harsh loss to Arsenal (6-0). Things were never likely to be dull, or ultimately successful, with the volatile Ian Holloway in charge (bless) but it was certainly a roller-coaster. And like someone in an ill-fitting hat who has just

---

[2] Blackpool play in tangerine. Apparently it is important not to say 'orange' or 'blood orange' or any other shade in the red-yellow spectrum, though you'd think they had bigger things to worry about.

[3] Yes I know, not a word. Don't care.

had a big lunch, this was a ride Blackpool were just not properly prepared for. I don't know anyone, however, who didn't enjoy it in the end, and Blackpool won awards for fans of the season.

Without resorting to a match by match analysis, a look at Blackpool's results shows a gradual decline over the season; ultimately unsuccessful but with some great results along the way. They completed the league double over Liverpool – go back 25 years and it would have been impossible to conceive of circumstances in which this could have happened. They beat Tottenham too, but gradually tailed off little by little; had they completed the double over Spurs too they might have stayed up, but Defoe's late equaliser was a terrible blow. In the end they were still so close to survival, having put themselves in a strong position by beating Bolton Wanderers in a repeat of the 1953 cup final. 4-3, same score as well, although Matthews was only on the bench this time. Blackpool's final match was away to Manchester United and they even led early in the second half. Fans of other teams may have been wondering why Man Utd only seem to lose when you want them to win, but in the end another typically exciting game saw United win 4-2. Elsewhere results were not going Blackpool's way, including Wolves winning at Sunderland. Blackpool's 'dream' ended at the so-called theatre of them.

Blackpool fans were applauded away from Old Trafford that day by the home fans (United having already won the league). Perhaps with some investment it could have been them leaving in triumph but Blackpool Football Club (Stanley Matthews, Jimmy Armfield, jumpers for goalposts isn't it, hmmm?) now vie with Coventry City, Leyton Orient, Blackburn Rovers (etc!) as the supporters who most deserve to get their club back.

Focus on: Wolverhampton Wanderers

In the 1950s, *The Daily Mail*, with its usual eye for accuracy and under-statement declared Wolves to be 'Champions of the World'. Even though they had won the first division title three times under Stan Cullis it was an exaggeration which led to the formation of the European Cup to prove it wrong. Nonetheless,

Wanderers used to be big. Really big. More recently though? Poor old Wolves. Such a struggle for them. Four seasons in the Premier League including two relegations. In 2010/11 they stayed up on the final day, winning away, and even then most popular sympathy was still not with them, but with a seaside town and their slightly potty manager. In 2011/12 a point a game from their last 14 matches would probably have kept them up, but after the first of those 14 (a 1-5 home defeat to West Brom) they sacked Mick McCarthy. He may not have been 'pulling up any trees' as I've heard said in that part of the world, but there is no reason to suspect he was underperforming in historical terms either. Thereafter, Wolves' last 13 Premier League games to date finished Drew, Lost, Lost, Lost, Lost, Lost, Lost, Lost, Drew, Lost, Drew, Drew and Lost.

A spokesperson for this sorry state of affairs was eventually found in the person of Les Hurst who said:

We have a loyal following and a magnificent stadium, where we've played for more than 125 years, after being one of the founder members of the football league. Me and the Fosun Dynasty (current owners) still think Wolves best days are ahead of them. Mind you 'Champions of the World' will be difficult to beat unless the ghosts of Cullis, Swinbourne, Wright and Wilshaw can be called upon and Steve Bull be persuaded to come out of retirement.

Season's Awards

Pointless: So called 'fair play' awards. In 2007/08 Manchester City qualified for Europe via 'fair play' – evidently not in their DNA though as they had the worst disciplinary record of this campaign.

Crazy But True Facts and Statistics:

- Marc Albrighton scored the 20,000 Premier League goal. Few suspected he would go on to win the Premier League with Leicester City. Few is a huge under-estimate.

Up Next

QPR and Norwich City comfortably took the automatic spots, leaving Cardiff City and Swansea City to go into the play-offs hoping to be the first non-English side in the Premier League. However, whilst Swansea became the latest team to make the play-offs a nightmare for Nottingham Forest, Cardiff didn't manage a goal against Reading...and it was Swansea, who had finished third on goal difference, who took the third promotion spot.

Karma Police (2011-12)

Champions:	Manchester City
Relegated:	Bolton Wandererers, Blackburn Rovers, Wolverhampton Wandererers (a pair of Wanderererses infact)
Unbelievable Relegation Escape:	Queens Park Rangers (partly unbelievable for their performance in the last game when they almost broke most of a nation's hearts)

Sandbag your hearts Man U fans...what's that coming over the hill? It's the footballing Gods. The final day of this season produced the finest commentating moments of Martin Tyler's life and those familiar with this day will know about his sexual climax live on air: Aguerooooooooooooo! However, had Martin not had that opportunity I think Peter Drury's commentary five minutes from time might well have been much more famous:

'What a day to be a supporter of Manchester City! Where will they hide tonight? Where will they go? Where will they find the moral fibre to get up and go into work tomorrow morning?' P. Drury (1 minute into injury time of the last game of the season when Manchester City seemed to have thrown it all away).

Most football fans know this feeling of something happening which is so improbable and negative and happening to their team that they just don't know how to carry on existing. But I think five minutes from the end of that season must have just about been the perfect storm for Manchester City fans; everything was wrong – how long they'd waited, how wrong things had been in the interim, how big the prize, how easy the task should have been and, most of all, who was going to win instead. It was bad enough, frankly, for those of us who didn't support City.

When Arsenal won the league on Merseyside in 1989, their fans travelled without much expectation, as underdogs. They needed to win by two clear goals to take the title and any other result would see Liverpool (by then laying the final boring bricks of their own era of dominance) take the league. Of course, it was incredible, tense and exciting, and Arsenal may have missed their big chance; but if they'd lost it wasn't Spurs who were going to win the title instead and Gooners were prepared well in advance for the possibility of failure. They said nothing would top those events of 1989, but in terms of both cruelty and ecstasy, this did.

The season had ebbed and flowed but City had led United for most of it and had a superior goal difference mainly due to thrashing United 1-6 at Old Trafford early in the season. Perhaps the key game came three from the end when City beat United once more (at home, 1-0, 30 April) to go top again; but it is surprising how few 'key moments' there were prior to the last game. Balotelli scored a penalty winner deep into injury time to beat Spurs in January and added his second of the game as City came back to draw with Sunderland, having trailed 1-3 with just a few minutes left. But apart from that, City did the double against more than half the teams they played and only Sunderland (who won at the Stadium of Light) seemed to cause problems. Although the six points taken from QPR were certainly eventful.

When the final game arrived, both City and United had eminently winnable games:

- City were at home to a not very good Queen's Park Rangers
- United were away to a not very good Sunderland
- United had won the league about 2 in every 3 or 4 seasons for*ever*
- City had not won the league since 1968

So whatever Arsenal/Liverpool fans felt in the *Fever Pitch* year, I really think it is nothing to the total despair of Manchester City fans heading into added time at the end of that season. United were winning. They won. City were...err, losing 1-2 to 10 man QPR.[1] And then, like the Spanish inquisition, the footballing Gods intervened. Manchester United would have to pay for the European Cup win against Bayern Munich and all those titles and the smug certainty of their support...and City fans – though they didn't know it then – were still in credit with the *Bank of Football* (owed quite a lot in fact), even after the incredible League One play-off win against Gillingham.[2]

First Edin Dzeko (what else did he do? does anyone care?) scored a header from a corner. Then Mario Balotelli (what else sensible did he do? does anyone care?) got his only assist of the season and Aguerooooooooo scored. I don't support City, I don't even care about City, but that moment is extraordinary. It defies belief. I missed it because I had turned off the TV in disgust and tears. Many debts were settled and, even if it did make the Gallagher brothers happy, it still has to be a good thing. Goose bumps every time I watch it. Even today.

- This clip is entitled 'Martin Tyler Orgasm' and you might want to look out for the grinning Man U fan at the very start of it, as United win at Sunderland: https://www.youtube.com/watch?v=DYMDkx1qHkk

- This one is called 'Paul Merson Going Mental' and you might want to look out for the well known soothsayer's comments at the beginning about City having run out of ideas and then at the end: 'they're cuddling each other, they've got love bites and everything.' I kid ye not! https://www.youtube.com/watch?v=yO7B9ERbqdY (both clips accessed often ever since)

Anyway, Man Utd wasted effectively the final moments at the Stadium of Light but they couldn't waste those back in Manchester. Worth trawling YouTube for fan reactions too. The pain and the pleasure seemed oh so City.

---

[1] Barton sent off obviously with usual petulance at a time when his team were threatened with relegation. But as one contributor to YouTube notes, he created the drama of five minutes injury time by beating up City players, so credit where credit's due.

[2] See it here (accessed 13/1/17): **https://www.youtube.com/watch?v=JQV_PFyBLoU** but essentially Gillingham were winning 2-0 with 3 minutes left; they lost on penalties. The footballing Gods owe them big time.

Focus on: Manchester City

'Thought I'd died and gone to heaven' might have been the reaction of many a City fan at the end of the 2011/12 season, but as James Silvester explained to me it's not always been this way:

> *Don't get me wrong, being a Man City fan in this day and age is spectacular (I'm 'over the Blue Moon' etc), but for my formative years, it was a very different story. City were pants[3] in the early Premier League era, and I mean breathtakingly poor at times. Peter Reid bellowed at Keith Curle to punt a long ball downfield in the vague direction of Niall Quinn. Alan Ball sent his team out to play with no other instruction than 'Give it to Kinkladze'.[4] But then occasionally we'd produce a belter. A real diamond of a performance, in the midst of our usual crap, that would have the fans on their feet and remembering why we would always be 'City Till I Die'. We were the 'Great Unpredictables', wonderful one minute, woeful the next; the team who could unfailingly snatch defeat from the cavernous maw of victory. They brought us pain indescribable season after season, but as with the best sadomasochistic relationships, we still turned up time after time, begging for more.[5]*

> *We had our heroes of course. Some damn good players blessed our side in that time, who'd fight for the cause and the fans, and at times we played some great stuff. 1994/5 saw some of the best attacking football I've ever seen from a City side, with Rosler, Walsh and Beagrie wowing the terraces and the splendidly named Maurizio Gaudino pulling the strings in midfield. But that was hampered by a defence leakier than a Tory Cabinet in Brexit mode, and that enormous sense of 'What If?' hung around Maine Road like an asphyxiating cloud of frustration.*

> *We were just so bizarrely managed, you see? At every level. We had bugger all cash,*

---

[3] Main author's note: This is a technical term meaning 'probably not even good enough to have won the Scottish Premier League.'

[4] Curiously 'Give it to Le Tissier' had made Ball an instant hit at Southampton.

[5] Any information on where to get one of these 'best sadomasochistic relationships', please tweet @ UrbanePL25Book

but what we did have was spent in increasingly strange ways. We had dynamite players who we'd invariably sell for peanuts before shelling out huge sums (for then, and for us) on average journeymen with extortionate contracts, who'd then spend the next four of five seasons going through their increasingly ineffective and absurdly highly paid motions.

Colin Hendry, Clive Allen, Ian Bishop, Andy Hinchcliffe, Michael Hughes… just some of the names to be cast aside for small change as we pursued our apparent policy of paying 'top dollar' for 'bottom quality', or because Peter Reid had fallen out with one or other of them, or perhaps the club had just lost them in a drunken bet? It certainly felt like the important decisions were being made after, or maybe during, a heavy night down the pub. Again, 'What If we'd kept them all together?' 'What If we'd signed Trevor Sinclair when we had the chance?' 'What If Lakey hadn't got injured?'

Ah, Paul Lake. What a player… Every Club has its cult heroes and memories of players whose careers were tragically cut short, and I'd hazard a few of them are looked at through the old rose tinted glasses, but Lakey really was that good. He should have been the England Captain and everyone knew it, but it sadly wasn't to be. The last time we saw him run out for a competitive Home Game was the very first Premier League Monday Night Football Match from Sky Sports. In amongst all the showbiz glamour and ludicrously inappropriate Sky Diving exploits that heralded the game, there he was, the Number 8 shirt hanging majestically on his back, before his knee would tragically give way again in the next game and we were back in the realm of 'What If'…

For a time, we didn't realize, or didn't want to see the truth, of how far we'd fallen. As we'd labour to 1-0 wins over Bolton and Wimbledon, there were those of us who genuinely thought we were competing with that lot over the road with their trophies and their legions of southern fans.[6] All that ended when we finally slipped out of the top tier with a wheeze and a whimper in 1996; laughably playing for time thinking a draw would see us good when another goal was desperately needed. Man, how that red lot laughed as we slid down the divisions. We didn't care. We were still there, cheering on the boys. We were City, the only club from Manchester and the Best Team in the World. Forget what the league table said, it was upside down.

Nowadays it's a different story of course. Trophies are a regular treat, multi million pound deals are commonplace and the best players in the word are mentioned in the

---

[6] This is an unfair slur given strong United support in Edinburgh, Stockholm and Reykjavik.

same breath as us without the words, 'no, but seriously', immediately following, or the player himself saying, 'who?' Some of the football I've seen in the last few years would take your breath away and I don't care if the Premier League lasts for a thousand years, there will NEVER be another title deciding goal like Aguero's. It was the most wonderful way to win a title you could imagine and made fifty times sweeter by the faces of the Trafford based team who missed out at our expense.

It is real fairy tale stuff what's happened to City and I keep telling my boy he doesn't know he's born (not least because buying him a hot dog and a bottle of Coke these days involves me securing a second mortgage). But you know? I don't think any of this would have happened without the spirit of the Club being what it is, or if the fans weren't the best in the world. We were a family, we'd cry ourselves stupid at the thought of going down then hold hands and all sing together as we hung on for the ride. It was our spirit that kept us alive where other clubs might have died, and that spirit, that history, was rewarded with the takeover and the team we see today. And whether you feel it today, waltzing into Wembley for another Cup Final, or you felt it back then, drunkenly running through the back streets of Moss Side on the way to watch us lose at home to Everton, it was and is that spirit that will forever be Manchester City.

Focus on: Queens Park Rangers

Christian Wolmar is an unashamed masochist,[7] and backs that up with his repeated assertions that he's been 'QPR since 1958'. Like many fans, getting to the Premier League seems to have been the fun part, while the staying there has been painful and trickier; or at least as tricky as shooting yourself in the foot can be. He regards the Championship seemingly as a period of recuperation, after which he and his team will be ready for more pain.[8] This is what he told me:

---

[7] Actually, he may have said 'Socialist' you know?

[8] This and other points were also echoed to me by David Baker, for which thanks.

2011/12 was a fantastic year; promoted to the Premier League. As champions and with ease. Neil Warnock worked miracles, creating a wonderfully well-balanced side with mostly journeymen such as Sean Derry and Clint Hill.[9] These he moulded around the mercurial talents of Adel Taarabt (19 goals/numerous assists) and solidity of Heiðar Helgusson (eventually a fans' favourite, noted for his imperturbability and ability to read the flight of the hoofed-ball long before any defender). Even so, we had to survive a potential points' deduction scare before we could finally celebrate. We never lived up to the wonders of that season however; three Premier League seasons later (in two spells) and the bill could have run the entire education and health systems in some countries. The experience was an object lesson in how not to approach creating a sustainable base for long term top flight survival.

Sure there were fabulous moments. Coming back from 2-0 down against Liverpool with Jamie Mackie, another tireless journeyman brought in by Warnock, nutmegging Pepe Reina in injury time to give us a 3-2 victory. That was part of a sequence of five consecutive home matches that effectively kept us up. We also beat Chelsea, the rivals we hate but who hardly know who we are, twice. Sean Wright-Phillips only goal of the game at Stamford Bridge was a particular delight. His only goal for us in 67 appearances, not celebrated out of respect would you believe?

Sean is a good way into our story of serial failure and misspent millions. He was one of several players bought late in the post-promotion summer transfer window by Warnock . The lateness was the problem. The club had changed hands in August, with Bernie Ecclestone, the Formula 1 owner whose knowledge of football could be written on the petrol cap of one of his racing cars, selling his interest to Tony Fernandes, another footballing neophyte who had made his money running an Asian airline. Warnock was left scrabbling about for scraps and, although Wright-Phillips had 36 England caps, two years later a radio commentator laughed out loud at his literally pedestrian attempts to skin a lower-league full-back. Then there was Arsenal reject Armand Traoré; capable of world class crosses at times (twice in fact) and defending like a drunk donkey at most others. Luke Young did seem promising but soon disappeared to injury, once spending two years collecting his wages, suddenly turning out for one game against Blackburn and then being released. Anton Ferdinand was famously victim in the episode which ended John Terry's international career; he's unlikely to be famous for football though. It all added up to a squad barely good enough for the Premier League, even if Barton and Cissé were signings who contributed more.

By the last game of the season we had to win to guarantee survival and for a while it

---

[9] When no longer good enough for the hoops, he moved to the lesser Rangers north of the border.

looked as if we actually might. Conceding in the first half, astonishingly we equalised thanks to Cissé who took advantage of a mistake by Lescott.[10] *However, it seemed that the good work would come to nothing as Barton lost his cool and got sent off*[11] *for punching the immensely irritating Carlos Tevez and claiming himself somehow to be the victim.*[12] *But no! Here came 50% of Traoré's world class crosses, nodded in by fans' favourite Jamie Mackie.* [The story of Man City's amazing comeback, Martin Tyler's public orgasm, and both sets of fans celebrating the result is told elsewhere in this book, so I've deleted Christian's misery strewn account].

We survived! It had been the old stagers like Hill, Derry and Mackie who had kept us up, but the lesson was not learnt. Even so, nothing could ever match the stupidity of signing two international goalkeepers in the same transfer window. Rob Green had been secured early but in our first match he might just as well stayed at home as he let in five, and there was a panicked search for a second goalkeeper. Unaccountably, little QPR signed Brazil's No 1 custodian, Cesar, who was certainly no better than Green. It got us very excited but we were being foolish and never got going. Hughes went and Redknapp arrived. 'Arry's 'brilliant' strategy was to call away matches 'bonus games'; this negativity had the expected effect. Apart from pleasurable luck at Chelsea, we won only one other away match after he took over and finished bottom, 14 points from safety and won no away games while he was manager in our next stay in the Premier League either. In the winter transfer window, astonishingly we splashed out £12.5m on Christopher Samba. Redknapp said: 'Chris is just what we need. He's a monster. Great in the air, quick, a leader, strong, fantastic in both boxes, hard as nails. He's a proper centre-half. He was willing to take a massive pay cut.' Actually he made earning £100K a week look effortless. As in, he put in no effort. Amazingly he went back to Russia after our relegation for £12m. I wouldn't like an investigative journalist to look too closely at that one.[13]

Somehow, we bounced straight back. A mixture of luck and dull football; not least in the play-off final when our 10-men won with a last minute strike from Bobby Zamora, for once not hitting row Z. The footballing Gods, though, would punish us for this calumny by letting 'Arry have the cheque book again. In: fading star, Rio Ferdinand who made all of 11 appearances for us. In: Sandro injury-prone, unfit, difficult and

---

[10] Now there's a rarity.

[11] Now there's a rarity.

[12] Now there's a rarity.

[13] Author's note: Despite Christian's suspicions, as this book has taken great pains to point out elsewhere, the chances of Redknapp being involved in anything dodgy are remote. Which reminds me, I must set up a trust fund for my pet vole Colin who co-wrote this book with me and will be receiving 90% of the royalty payments.

sat in the stands for a time because he did not have a work permit. A few others with more promise – they could hardly have had less – but who didn't work out. The result was four wins all season and endless heavy away defeats – the exception being a lovely 1-4 triumph at West Brom with Bobby Zamora again missing row Z with an astonishing volley.

Back in the Championship [not really the topic of the book Christian, but we'll allow it] *we have learnt several lessons. Most importantly, not to sign surplus players from big clubs, whether Man U, Chelsea or, for chrissake, Real Madrid. You are not going to get a bargain, and you will get a pissed off failure, by definition. Who would swap the Bernabeu for Loftus Road if they had any real ambition or ability?[14]*

Three frustrating seasons, which cost Fernandes £180m in written off debts, was such an unenjoyable experience most of the time that some supporters even dread the idea of going up there again. This is not a view, incidentally, with which I concur for a single moment. If you don't want to be Champions League winners six seasons running, then you are not a true fan. We are now on the mend, having got rid all but one of the expensive signings and now focussing on picking up talent from the Championship or below, from less well established European teams and bringing on youth players. It is what we have been good at and is the formula which has worked for clubs promoted to the Premier League who have stayed there, such as Bournemouth, Swansea and Southampton. But gosh, we have learnt all this the hard way. It is fairly amazing we have survived and to that we do owe it to the fact that the owners, despite all the setbacks, have stayed firm and not flogged us off to the type of owner endured by Blackpool, Blackburn, Leyton Orient and many others. Urrrrrrs.

Season's Awards

Worthless consolation prize: United beat City in both the Community Shield and FA Cup 3rd round.

---

[14] See Ronnie Wallwork's Old Trafford to Hawthorns switch elsewhere in this book for a good example elsewhere of this phenomenon.

Crazy But True Facts and Statistics:

- Blue finished above red in both Manchester and Merseyside. First time since, I'm guessing now, 1305?

Up Next

The best three Championship sides by a distance: Reading, Southampton and West Ham...the latter's play-off victory against Blackpool probably being the final nail in the coffin for the tangerine dream team.

I ALWAYS KNEW
(2012-13)

Champions:	Manchester United
Relegated:	Wigan Athletic, Reading, Queens Park Rangers
Unbelievable Relegation Escape:	Sunderland as usual it seems and a few other teams helped by an in-form Wigan unexpectedly losing at home to Swansea near the season's end.

It's been a difficult balancing act. Manchester United have many fans, but many more despise them. On the other hand, whose fans are likely to be most interested in a book on the Premier League? Rather than approach this issue with tact and delicacy, I've decided to write whatever pops into my head, which is usually a teensy bit ABU. However, the time has come to redress the balance of all the previous bitterness and acknowledge that loathe[1] him or hate him Alex Ferguson did quite an extraordinary job. 13 of the first 21 Premier League titles, including this, the last one he competed for. Quite amazing.

We always knew that Man United would bounce back and so they did, although from seven of nine titles they were now at 13 of 21 so perhaps the 'end of era' signs were creeping in just a little, especially with Chelsea and Manchester City at least having

---

[1] Wanted to write 'love'. Couldn't.

the money to match them. This season provided a fitting tribute to Sir Alex as Robin Van Persie put in a number of outstanding performances before he stopped using the Grecian 2000 and became an old man overnight. Well they didn't win it in a long time before Ferguson so *seriously, genuinely* it was extraordinary. Perhaps the like of which will never be seen again. Fingers crossed eh?

And of course to further cement the legacy, since Fergie moved on, United managers with previously solid reputations (Moyes, Van Gaal, Mourihno) have been struggling even to qualify for Europe, let alone the Champions League or winning the Premier League. For those genuinely reading this chronologically as a history book a) sorry for the spoiler b) seriously, Wikipedia will allow you to get the facts with much less effort and irrelevant 'opinion'.[2]

Wigan (focussed on below) managed to get relegated *and* win the FA Cup. Quite a feat. Perhaps both were fated? Wigan won well at West Brom in the Premier League at the start of May, bouncing back from an own-goal 90th minute equaliser for Spurs in their previous match. But then they lost at home to Swansea despite leading 1-0 and 2-1. It feels entirely possible that victory in that match could have led to an entirely different momentum around the season, perhaps even relegation for the Saints under Pochettino. Margins are fine in football management.

Focus on: Swansea City AFC[3]

Imagine being brought up in the valleys with a name like Cedric! Well that's exactly what happened to my friend, err...Cedric Rawlings. I met him in a pub, and to be honest this book might have been a lot better if I hadn't kept meeting people in pubs. In any case, Cedric is the oldest contributor to this book. He'll be at least 79 by the time you read this, having attended his first match at the Vetch Field in 1957. Still he doesn't look a day over 99 as I start to bombard him

---

[2] These words will, I suspect, will come back to haunt me in an Amazon 1-star review from that bloke who never gets it.

[3] For proof see League of Gentlemen: **https://www.youtube.com/watch?v=mN3A0qbq6yM** There is a Swansea! (Accessed 7/4/17)

with questions. Unfortunately Cedric can really drink and I didn't take notes, so all I really got was that the Liberty Stadium is a step up in class, not least its preference for grass over mud. And that the barbed wire at the old Vetch Field was to keep people in. I made note not of the great players who wore the Swansea strip of old. So let's say Davies, A, Davies, D, Davies L and Williams (all letters). A scour of Wikipedia reminds me that one is Ivor Allchurch; scored lots of goals, got a statue.

With a name like Cedric, it's not surprising that he chose to move to England and a career in academia as soon as he could. There both his name and outrageous bow-ties were more welcome, although he never lost the familiar accent. In his local pub he was once subjected to a vitriolic tirade against the useless Welsh presence in English football. Unable to contain himself, Cedric pointed out that Cardiff City had, in fact, won the FA Cup in 1927. 'I suppose you were there were you,' was the only riposte. In fact, he was busy that day, although he is old enough to remember the days when his team were called Swansea Town.

Anyway, I kept plugging away with questions. Despite an obvious pride in Swansea's achievements, including the fairly recent League Cup win, Cedric is clearly a) downcast at the (then) possibility of relegation in 2016/17 b) more interested in whether I want another beer. So I get little in the way of strong material, although he points out that the Premier League was already ten years old when Swansea managed to stay in the whole football league only by the skin of their teeth. I finally gave up my enquiries when as an aside to a mutual acquaintance he said: *He keeps on at me with questions about football as if it were even an important game in South Wales.*

Focus on: Wigan Athletic

For some teams, the 'focus on' season has to be their one and only in the Premier League (Swindon Town, Barnsley). For others, it is the miraculous 'stay up' season before relegation the next, never to be seen again (Oldham Athletic, Bradford City). But for Wigan, the season they stopped defying the odds by staying in the Premier League was also the season they defied them even more – winning a major trophy (the FA Cup) by beating the previous and next season's champions Manchester City. David Coleman didn't, of course, commentate on Ben Watson's injury time winner, but his style would have been perfect: 'Watson! 1-0! Err...quite remarkable.'

When I were a lad, when *God Save the Queen* was a punk anthem not a national one, Wigan weren't even in the football league, let alone the Premier League. The local tastes for this town are for men with odd shaped balls grinding their flesh against each other, or so I'm told. So proper football – as opposed to so-called 'Rugby League football' – long struggled to establish itself in the charming rural idyll that isn't Wigan. Nonetheless, after a history in which they were called Wigan County, Wigan Borough, Wigan Wednesday, Wigan Falseteeth[4] etc they finally found some stability as 'Athletic' and entered the football league in 1978.

This book is not about their extraordinary rise to moderateness, but they did – in fact – play in the Premier League from 2005 to 2013. It's not inconceivable that they'll do so again, but they've already been to League One once since then and headed back after 2016/17. But from 1995 to 2013, led by the enthusiastic Chairman Dave Whelan, they scaled the heights, moving out of Springfield Park to the DW Stadium and becoming everyone's 8th or 9th favourite team.

Amazingly, Wigan were 2nd in the Premier League in November 2005, reaching the League Cup final that season and achieving their only top half finish (10th). The next season they won at Bramall Lane on the last day to stay up at the expense of their hosts. Apparently in a bunker in Berlin, Hitler was furious.[5] More close shaves and mid table miracles were accompanied by undreamt of wins against[6] the league's top teams. In May 2012 the Latics won at Ewood Park to both stay up and relegate their opponents; this was unimaginable when Rovers had won the Premier League just 17 years previously.

And then came 2012/13. It is argued that supporters would rather stay in the Premier League than win the FA Cup. True you can have the worst of all worlds (relegation and no trophy a la Newcastle), but I think it is only for the really big clubs that Premier League status is genuinely, truly, more important than the

---

[4] Thereby answering the question of whether there are any depths I won't stoop to in search of a cheap laugh?

[5] If you don't believe me: **https://www.youtube.com/watch?v=cNDRt-Ze-yU** (accessed 15/1/17)

[6] Just stopped myself writing 'the likes of' here. Phew!

FA Cup. I have supported my team for less than 30 years and not seen them win a major trophy, although they came very close in the Zenith Data Systems cup final of 1992 and EFL Cup in 2016/17 . My bestest moment in football though is still seeing my local non-league team defy the odds to win the FA Trophy at Wembley.[7]

Wigan played at home to Bournemouth in the FA Cup 3rd round, equalising in the second half to take the game to a replay which they won 0-1. The crowd was larger at Bournemouth than at the DW. The cup run didn't take them home again as visits to Macclesfield, Huddersfield and Everton all yielded victory; 3 goals in 4 first half minutes at Goodison for a 0-3 win, surely the highlight. In the semi at Wembley, everyone's 8th, now possibly 7th, favourite team beat their 88th favourite (Millwall 0-1 Wigan Athletic) before that very special injury time winner in the final.

So hats off to Wigan. Defiers of odds. Givers of hope to everyone. Wigan, whose fans still turn out even though 95% of the town would rather watch three men erotically wrestle a fourth to the ground. I doubt many Wigan fans would trade their injury time giant killing for mere Premier League football.

This impression is confirmed by Liam Sephton of Wigan fanzine *All Gone Latics* who told me that boredom with the Premier League was rife in the 2012/13 season in which Wigan were relegated. In fact around 2,500 Wigan fans travelled to Macclesfield Town in the FA Cup 4th round, but fewer than half chose to go to nearby Old Trafford or Anfield in the league.

It's clear, perhaps because of having to battle rugby league in its own town, that fans of Wigan are proudest when at their most stubborn. Liam notes that in November 2009, the club recorded its biggest ever defeat in any competition since election to the Football League in 1978. This 9-1 defeat to Tottenham threatened to crash the popular *Cockney Latic* forum with torrents of embarrassment and indignation. Like Brave Sir Robin in *Monty Python's Holy Grail*, Roberto Martinez sensibly backed out of attending the opening of the new club shop. And then? 20,447 attended the next home match v Sunderland which turned out to be a season high. *This gives you an insight into the strange mind of a Latics supporter* says Liam. Indeed.

---

[7] For the record: Bishop's Stortford 1-0 Sutton United – has a team ever played all rounds of a competition (preliminary round included) to win a trophy? The book I'd like to have written, if you need more on this story, is by Gareth Stephens (2001), *The Story of the Blues*.

As well as annoying Hitler by beating Sheffield United to stay up in 2006/07,[8] the final two games of 2010/11[9] provide another high point for Latics fans. Losing the penultimate game to West Ham, if other results had been the same, would have seen Wigan relegated that season. It's doubtful that the FA Cup would have followed in those circumstances. And losing they were (0-2) with 4,500 West Ham fans there to rub it in. However Charles N'Zogbia's winner deep into injury time completed a fine comeback, transformed the balance of gloating and saw West Ham relegated instead. Wigan meanwhile went on to confirm their safety with a win at Stoke. It was also the season in which Liverpool, Chelsea and Arsenal were all beaten at home. Indeed Wigan have had many fine odds-defying results, including a 2-3 win against Arsenal on Sky having trailed 2-0 early on.

In 2011/12 Wigan won seven of their last nine games to stay up.[10] After the final day 3-2 win over Wolves a banner was held up in the Family Stand: "Don't leave for a bigger club, stay and WE can be the bigger club." But notwithstanding the soundness of the sentiment, time was running out on the Wigan miracle. Resistance was indeed futile, despite that 'seven of nine', and relegation came in 2012/13. The final word to Liam:

> *It's a tradition to go out in Wigan on Boxing Day night in fancy dress and for as long as I can remember, Wigan Athletic supporters have opted to wear their costumes to our Boxing Day match too. In 2010 (Wolves away), 2011 (Man Utd away) and 2012 (Everton away) around 80-150 Latics fans all opted to wear banana costumes – leading to us being dubbed the 'Banana Army'.* Rumours that more recently only three fans did this leading to them being dubbed 'Bananarama' are unsubstantiated nonsense. Err...yes!

---

[8]   See elsewhere; it's a Bunker/YouTube voiceover thing.

[9]   At least I think it was 2010/11...I only just checked it on Wikipedia and I've forgotten already!

[10]   Hmmm...Seven of Nine!

Focus on: Manchester United

Notwithstanding the bitter and twisted teasing which I have regrettably sunk to, whether they be from Basel, or Edinburgh or even from Manchester itself, Man Utd fans are just regular people. Those such as Dean Hardman, who attended his first match in 1992/93, have only known Premier League and success. Dean stands here as proxy for them all and this section appears here since it was the last season at the time of publication that they won the thing.

1992/93…as an 11 year old walking up the steps from the concourse and emerging into the stadium, floodlights shining brightly onto a bowling green surface, it didn't matter that it was only the league cup against Brighton and that the Stretford End was a building site. Mark Hughes, already my hero, was the scorer that day and I was hooked.

Of course, that season was the inaugural Premier League campaign and attendance at a handful of Premier League games across each of the next few years followed, before me and my dad managed to get season tickets for 1995-96. 2009-10 was our last season as match-going Reds, after a combination of my impending fatherhood, rising ticket prices and dissatisfaction with the ownership of Glazers meant that we stopped going. That meant 18 years of watching, for the most part, incredible football and magical performances. It was literally years before I even saw United lose.

Hughes departed in 1995, as did Andrei Kanchelskis and Paul Ince. Lee Sharpe and Steve Bruce left in 1996 while Cantona lasted until 1997, yet it's those players, who I only saw play for three of four seasons, that I can still see running around the Old Trafford turf in my mind's eye. I must have only seen Hughes in the red of United in the flesh, at a guess, 10-15 times, yet my memory insists that I saw him play much more.

Old Trafford gets an undeserved reputation for being quiet, as though the fans are only vocal when the team is winning. It's a bit undeserved now and it certainly was back in the early days of the Premier League. I remember going to watch Crystal Palace v United in 1993, broadcast on a big screen to a packed Old Trafford, as we all dared to believe that the title might be coming back for the first time in 26 years.

What felt like tens of thousands sang as though the game was being played out before us and not on the back of an articulated lorry.

The best games, however, have always been against either our traditional rivals or our challengers for the title. Back in January 1995, Blackburn were the visitors and were met with the grammatically unclear "Where were you when you were shit?"[11] while, as Colin Hendry trotted over to retrieve a ball for a throw in, one chap yelled, "Here comes Shirley bleedin' temple". Those were the days and it's strange what stays with you.

Perhaps the two most electric atmospheres were against Arsenal in 2003 and then again in 2004. I've never felt injustice at a football match like I felt in the first of the games, when Ruud van Nistelrooy, one of the greats, was jostled and mocked by Martin Keown following a penalty miss in a 0-0 draw. Conversely, I don't think a win has ever felt as good as the 2-0 victory the following year, when every time Thierry touched the ball you felt he would score, although Michael Owen's winner against Manchester City in the 6th minute of injury time in 2009 comes close.

Like many people, the common denominator across my enjoyment of United's 25 years in the Premier League is the person I watched the games with. From childhood to adulthood and from getting to Old Trafford 3 hours before kick off in anticipation of Cantona's return in 1995 to being chased out of Anfield after being rumbled in the home stands because we didn't celebrate Liverpool's last minute equalizer, it's been watching with my Dad that has probably meant the most.

Season's Awards

Just keeps on scoring: Err...Giggs-wiggsy isn't it? (Allegedly)

The Britney Spears 'Oops I did it again' Award: No not Ryan obviously; that would

---

[11] Dean is a trained linguist. That's a fact rather than insult or euphemism.

be a scandalous thing to say. No, Arsenal for finishing above Spurs and pinching their Champions' League place.

Penny drops: Bale realises Saints to Spurs was to a richer club, not a bigger one. Real Madrid beckons.

Harry Houdini disappearing act: Adel Taarabt – no really, where'd he go? A Lisbon nightclub snacking heavily according to the latest reports...and they say Le Tissier wasted his talent!

Crazy But True Facts and Statistics:

- Not content with having every single Premier League record already sown-up, Manchester United used their last game of the season to claim the record for the highest scoring draw. Mind you they had to come from 2-5 up with 10 minutes left against West Brom to do it.

Up Next

After previous disappointments, Cardiff City went up as champions, followed by former clubs of Premier League status: Hull City automatically and Crystal Palace via the play-offs.

THIS CHARMING MAN
(2013-14)

Champions:	Manchester City
Relegated:	Norwich City, Fulham, Cardiff City (though they did at least get relegated having beaten the champions)
Unbelievable Relegation Escape:	No, it was too easy for the rest

In 2011/12 Manchester City were the desperate team who nearly threw away their big chance after the better part of half a century. In 2012/13 Sir Alex managed a big finale and it is not that surprising that City couldn't maintain the intensity. But by this season, City were an established force and much better equipped for the close run in, especially as this time the challenging team was not United but a more desperate team who threw away their best chance ever of winning the Premier League.[1]

There were some spooky parallels with their previous triumph. Like then a 1-0 defeat at Sunderland for City and a home draw against the same team thanks to a late equaliser. Like then, there was a league double over Manchester United by an aggregate score of 7-1. But unlike then, when nerve was needed, City won their

---

[1] Elsewhere, I noted the standard of goal-keepers winning the Premier League; this season in goal for Liverpool: Simon Mignolet

last 5 games of the season; meanwhile Liverpool who had won 11 straight to go top throughout April, slipped to defeat against Chelsea putting the ball firmly in Manchester City's court.[2] Liverpool then surrendered a 0-3 lead at Palace thanks to a late brace from Bishop's Stortford FC's leading season-long goal-scorer of all time, Dwight Gayle. But, whilst a victory in that game could have put much more pressure on Manchester City, such was the goal-difference situation that it made little difference to the outcome of the title. That damage was done, somewhat cruelly, by a slip from fans' favourite Steven Gerrard before he whiled away the remainder of his career in the United States' Major Soccer League, having fun fun fun in the warm California sun.

Incidentally, as part of my world-wide search for material for this book, I asked a fan of Toronto FC for his thoughts on the Premier League and the former players now bedazzling North American audiences in the MLS, the latest of whom is Bastian Schweinsteiger, whose name must never be translated for reasons of decency. This is what he (TFC fan) said:

> *Stevie G is a half polished $9M turd that the LA Galaxy have on their books right now. Sean Wright-Phillips is the Red Bulls' own version. Frank Lampard, Didier Drogba....ditto. If Wayne Rooney ends up here in the next 2-3 years, I will never watch another MLS game. The five polished turds mentioned above that have been [deposited] into MLS are just that. They are not diamonds that have lost a little bit of their lustre. They are pieces of [excrement] that have hardened and been polished by their personal reps and sold to a gullible American public. Having these c**** come to play in MLS is like people going to see The Stones or Paul McCartney or Elton John. People just want to say, 'I saw them play...' People don't seem to give a f*** that McCartney & Co can't f***ing sing a note anymore! Just like Stevie G and co are f***ing mailing it in to MLS fans. Sadder still is that Don Garber and his f***ing cronies at MLS are sponsoring these 'farewell tours'. They all need to F*** OFF and let others have their day. Let the game continue to grow and develop in this country, from the inside.*

Well I did ask! You can probably tell that this, err, gentleman originally hails from Glasgow. Peter, another TFC fan said 'Really hoping the rumours about Danny Rose coming to MLS/TFC are true.' They weren't. Yet.

---

[2] To be fair to Liverpool it is probably Chelsea who wasted a chance this season, since they were able to win at Anfield and do the double over City but still trail in 3rd.

Focus on: Crystal Palace[3]

Dear Liverpool fan, before ringing 606 to complain yet again about something or anything, read this from a man who supports a team who really have won f-all. Mark Newman, like many, begins his team's Premier League tale by looking back to before it started, noting (to my surprise I'll admit) that *Palace finished third in the old First Division in 1990/91, but were denied the club's first experience of European football because of the English clubs' ban after the Heysel disaster. Two years later and we were one of the first three teams to be relegated from the new Premier League. The club never recovered from the sale of their talisman, Ian Wright, to the Arsenal and went down on the last day of the season with 49 points – the highest points tally ever to relegate a team from the top flight.*[4]

And so started the yoyo years with Palace winning promotion three times in 1993/94, 1997/98 and 2003/2004 only to be relegated in the following year. Fast forward to 2017 however, and Palace were enjoying their fourth consecutive year in the Premier League. In the close season the club smashed its transfer record with the £27 million capture of Christian Benteke. In January 2017, Palace spent big; £40 million being just enough to avoid relegation.

But Palace supporters do not take their Premier-league status for granted. Many clubs have gone into administration once but it happened twice to Palace in 1999 and in 2010. The 2010 administration nearly proved terminal with the four Palace fans and local businessmen only striking a deal with Lloyd's Bank hours before the doors would have shut for the last time on Selhurst Park. That near-death experience was a

---

[3] Having been let down by someone initially very enthusiastic, Mark came along in the nick of time to save you from what I know of Palace. Namely: *Not named after a huge South London meth lab. They do seem to get relegated and promoted a lot and have annoying managers. Their female cheer leaders are actually called The Crystals but I was initially outraged as I thought they were announced as The Bristols. I once had a car-sticker that said 'I've seen the donkeys at the Selhurst Park Donkey Sanctuary' which I thought was hilarious. They have an Eagle, who may be called Eddie, who swoops from cross-bar to cross-bar before matches. Rivalry with Brighton has nothing to do with Eagles stealing Seagull eggs off Orkney.*

[4] Although there were 42 games in those days, Palace's 1.16 points per game average is still more than the 1.10 points per game that relegated West Ham in the 38 games of 2002/03. I checked cos I'm a pedant.

turning point . Selhurst Park has since won a reputation as a proper football ground with buoyant support and a knack for upsetting the big boys in the Premier League. The self-styled Holmesdale Fanatics Ultras don't quite match Juventus in the 1980s but they make a hell of a noise and their impact is recognised by the club which does what it can to accommodate them with ticket allocations. We are incredibly lucky to have them (and their excellent drummer!).

But it's rarely comfortable being a Palace fan. For most of their current spell in the Premier League they've been in – or about – the relegation zone. Just when it's looked as if we've turned a corner, another one (corner, that is) comes along. Tony Pulis's miraculous recovery looked to be heralding a new period of stability until he walked out on the club during the week before the start of the 2014/15 season. Alan Pardew's impact was miraculous during his first calendar year at the club and both the fans and management started to talk about Europe. But 2016 was an annus horibilis which left the club at the foot of the table until Pardew turned fortunes around.

We relish being an unfashionable London club. Defying the odds, we don't do mid-table anonymity. Neither are we ones for footballing purists. Pardew tried to make Palace into a top half-of-the-table club with football to match but it was not for us. Our footballing identity really hasn't changed much during the Premier League years. Wilfired Zaha will never match Ian Wright's goals but there is something about that searing pace, his directness and sublime skill which recalls Wright at his destructive best.

Best Premier League moments? It would have to be from our current four-year unbroken run in the division and that first year when Tony Pulis rescued the club from relegation. The football was pretty attritional at times[5] but it really felt that the team and the fans were as one. Players like Damian Delaney, recruited as a free agent when the wrong side of 30, and Mile Jedinak, plucked from the relative obscurity of the Turkish league, were the backbone of that team. That team is all but gone in 2017 with Joel Ward the only member who commands a regular first team place (Zaha was trying to prove himself at Man U during that first year). In their place are a squad of players assembled at a cost of more than £100 million most of whom will likely depart should Palace go back to their yo-yo days.

Should Palace retain their Premier League status most fans would put the redevelopment of Selhurst Park, and investment in a youth system which has brought through the likes of Kenny Sansom, Victor Moses and Wilf Zaha, at the top of their wish list. On the footballing front the club still awaits its first domestic trophy (I'm

---

[5]   No really?! Under Tony? Hardly believable.

not counting the now-defunct New Members Cup) and has twice fallen at the final hurdle – and in the final 10 minutes to Manchester United.

European football? Supporting the club in Europe would be special but I don't think it's something many fans spend much time worrying about. History has taught us to stay grounded and to enjoy – rather than expect – our moments in the sun. Even after four years in the top flight it still feels like a novelty to have some of the best players in the world walk out onto the Selhurst Park turf.

Focus on: Cardiff City

Just in case there are any doubts, the title of this chapter is intended as a reference to Manuel Pellegrini rather than Vincent Tan. Whatever the rights and wrongs of Tan's association with Cardiff, it does 'seem' that they 'may' have chosen the wrong multi-billionaire. Certainly changing the club's colours to red from blue seems to have been the most disastrous PR move ever and, as a football supporter with an understanding of tradition, his grinning at the camera and saying 'we'll always be red' in response to the fans' 'always be blue' campaign is difficult to watch without wanting to vomit. The use of the words 'may' and 'seem' invites you to make your own mind up. I couldn't possibly comment.[6]

2013/14 is Cardiff's sole Premier League season to date and a look at Facebook chat suggests little optimism that this will change. Alongside the clips of euphoric promotion celebrations and the party of beating Manchester City in their first Premier League home game the comment 'bloody awesome, and then Tan f***ed it up' regrettably seems to sum up the atmosphere at the club. In fact, though I will willingly put Cardiff fans into future editions of this book, I couldn't get one for this time. I mean, of course I could have driven to Cardiff, but it just didn't seem right after Tan and relegation and Swansea being in the Premier League, so I decided to experiment by getting fan feeling from fans' twitter accounts and #alwaysbeblue. This is what I learned.

---

[6] According to the publisher.

People are really, really angry about blue to red and VT, who ought to be rich enough to do his research in advance and/or employ some market research if he's just gonna trample on a century of tradition. Well done to the Cardiff City fans of the week on Soccer AM that year all in blue, but there is no comedy value here. I asked myself why he didn't just buy a team who played in red already? And then realised he'd have probably tried to buy the Welsh rugby union team...and get them to play rugby league in pink.[7]

Season's Awards (Manager Special)

Least Annoying Manager of Premier League Champions, possibly ever now I come to think about it: Manuel Pellegrini

Mr Grumpy: Ole Gunnar Solskaer (manager of Cardiff City by then) asked if Liverpool were title material said: 'I couldn't care less' before marching - nay flouncing - off.

Silliest Appointment (apart from Mr Grumpy): Pepe Mel at West Brom. As John Marks put it to me: *One of the oddest and most ill-fated of the entire Premier League era...by all accounts a likeable man, he could well be cast as a middle-aged everyman detective whose main flaw is his inherent decency, in a cult Spanish TV series. Mel was appointed half way through a season when Albion needed to survive. It was not the right moment to rethink the club's footballing philosophy. I don't actually regard him as a bona fide Albion manager, but more as a guy who sat on the bench looking bemused and homesick. I still don't know how Albion survived that season winning just 3 of his 17 matches.*

---

[7] If it's all getting too much Cardiff fans, might I suggest the Cardiff Devils ice hockey team, British Elite League champions for 2016/17.

Crazy But True Facts and Statistics:

- The lead changed hands 25 times during the season and Champions Manchester City only led the table for 14 days in total.
- Liverpool who threw away surely their best chance of a Premier League title in the latter stages scored more than 100 goals, as did the champions; this was a Premier League first.
- Average attendance (36,657) had been sneaking up over the years.

Up Next

Old faces heading back. Leicester City topped the 100 point mark as champions and some fans quaintly took the opportunity to buy 'League Champions' scarves. Surely they'd be back in the Championship very soon. Burnley also bounced and QPR hardly deserved to, but did, win the play-offs with 10 men and an uncharacteristically accurate finish from Bobby Zamora.

SPIRITS
(2014-15)

Champions:	Chelsea
Relegated:	Hull City, Burnley, Queens Park Rangers

Jose Mourinho probably felt especially pleased with himself after this season. Although since that is probably true of his entire existence, *especially, especially, especially*, pleased this season. However, the footballing Gods were to prove that not even the special one is immune from their mighty vengeance. But that's next season...

For this season though...Wow! What a roller coaster ride it was with the Premier League lead changing place no less (although also no more) than once. Chelsea finished October with seven of nine wins. They finally lost a couple of games in December (Newcastle) and January (Spurs) but then didn't lose again until the title was already theirs. The other Champions League qualifiers were Manchester City, Arsenal and Manchester United. Arsenal won the FA Cup. Chelsea won the League Cup. Wow, it wasn't half exciting though. According to Sky.

So exciting was the season that this was the stage of the book when I started watching the 'funniest moments' clips on YouTube just to make it that little bit more exciting. What I can reveal in terms of comedy value is:

- Occasionally someone gets hit in the genitals, or has them pinched or plays with their own.

- People fall over sometimes including players trying to kick the ball and officials trying to watch the ball not their feet.

- Players also fall into the crowd.

- All kinds of folk pick their nose.

- Players get arsey and children get grumpy.

- Sprinkler systems come on by mistake and people get wet.

- An animal (a bird, mouse or dog most commonly) somehow enters the field of play with hilarious consequences.

- A vole, however, has never been sighted in the EPL, even if my co-author Colin has a plan.

It's a wild and crazy league I tell you. In fact the only genuinely funny thing I could find was that Stuart Pearce was once a Premier League manager.

Focus on: Stoke City

It can be a glamorous business doing a book like this, and just 4 days after watching Barnsley take on Norwich in a Championship clogg-a-thon, I found myself travelling to sunny Stoke on a Wednesday night. Why, why, why? Delilah! Well at least this time I was going to watch my own team (not Stoke) and there was an opportunity to reacquaint myself with a Wright's meat and potato pie – the mainstay of my early 20s. So, in the mid-December gloom I headed for *The Locomotive* to meet David Wild and Paul Lewis. Normally, I would have browsed Wikipedia beforehand to get a rough idea of Stoke's history, but David is an old friend and I'd been busy, so on this occasion I thought I knew enough: Stoke used to be good, then they weren't for a long time and now they're back in the Premier League. The Chairman invests, they give free away travel to fans and the hooligan days are largely over. Oh and the made for TV film 'Marvellous' was, err, marvellous.[1]

---

[1] https://en.wikipedia.org/wiki/Marvellous (accessed 15/12/16)

In the pub, the Wright's pies were not yet hot enough. The clock ticked. David assures me Paul will have interesting anecdotes when he arrives. David doesn't seem to. We sip beer and Paul arrives. He doesn't have anecdotes either as it turns out. The next morning, I did look at Wikipedia and found my explanation for the staggering lack of enthusiasm for the Premier League. Stoke have finished 12th, 11th, 13th, 14th, 13th, 9th, 9th, 9th and 13th in their Premier League seasons.

Conversation does not flow. I found out that their old Victoria Ground was great (I liked it too) and that getting to the Cup Final (and thereby Europe) in 2010/11 was also great. But generally speaking, the slow and somewhat painful journey through second and third and second tiers was the interesting bit, not the Premier League. As with fans of other teams, there is a certain nostalgia for Saturday afternoon football. There are also complaints about train-tickets bought only for Sky to change the schedule.

When the conversation loosened up a little with beer, it became apparent that perhaps my interviewees also didn't have any special memories because they don't have any memories at all. Alcohol seemed especially prominent in their experience and some 'interesting' anecdotes were followed by a quiet aside: 'But perhaps you'd better not put that in the book eh?' So I haven't. In search of *something* we moved onto players who have played for both clubs and a couple of unforgettable moments finally emerged. Peter Crouch scoring an incredible goal against Manchester City; a brilliant control and volley from the angle of the penalty area.[2] And Ricardo Fuller giving his own club captain (Andy Griffin) a comical slap round the face and getting sent off for it.[3] But actually the conversation never really got going and we said goodbye and went to the match.

It is worth mentioning the match itself. For all the lack of passion for the Premier League, individual matches at Stoke's ground (currently Bet365 stadium) usually have a passionate atmosphere. Here though it was very quiet in the early stages, with the inevitable 'library' taunt, but came to life following the sending off of City's Arnautovic in the 24th minute. Home fans were outraged, mainly it seemed by the intervention of the linesman, and made an angry racket from that point on. Mark Hughes (Stoke manager) was equally outraged later, claiming it was because of an outmoded understanding of how

---

[2] See it here: **https://www.youtube.com/watch?v=bS9Xrme-9yA** (accessed 15/12/16)

[3] See it here: **http://www.metacafe.com/watch/2213733/ricardo_fuller_slaps_his_captain_andy_griffin_stoke_vs_west_ham_new/** (accessed 15/12/16)

Stoke play. On the one hand it was a knee high, stupid, studs-up tackle so I can't really see his point. On the other, if those challenges were penalised by sendings-off in his day, he'd hardly have been unsuspended to play, so perhaps he genuinely doesn't understand.

And if it's really a new Stoke under Mark Hughes, then the time-wasting which followed was classic Tony Pulis. It started the second Arnautovic was dismissed. His walk of shame was from one corner of the pitch to the tunnel at the other; it took so long that he put up a tent and made base camp at one point. Stoke players were constantly urging ball boys and fans not to return the ball, and finding any excuse to have a lie down on the turf. At one point Grant in the Stoke goal signalled to the crowd to delay giving the ball back. Then, when it reached him, a man paid thousands to catch footballs 'inexplicably' found that it had hit his shoulder and bounced back over the hoardings. He made himself a cup of tea and like a glacier in gloves prepared to restart. From the ball going out of play to taking the goal kick took a minute.

But not withstanding my own frustrations at the 0-0 draw, it nonetheless typified SCFC in the Premier League. Harrying to the last, with the atmosphere, which remained throughout, playing its part (although given the tension, we never got a full throttle version of 'Delilah'). You couldn't help feeling though that what Stoke fans need is a good relegation scrap to liven things up a bit. We can dream.

Focus on Burnley

More women (and indeed men) were offered the chance to contribute to this book than did so. Nonetheless, in conceding that this book regrettably mimics the gender imbalance in the game as a whole, I'm pleased that Gemma Avery has agreed to talk about her team.

Seeing your father sob into a split scarf is not a memory you forget easily, however neither is seeing your team winning the Championship Play-Off final at Wembley.

Back in 2009, a day after my 18th birthday, Wade Elliot decided to gift me with the greatest present, a peach of a goal on a gloriously sunny day under the Wembley Arch. We beat Sheffield United 1-0.⁴ We'd gone solidly 'merch-tastic' that day – even the split scarves. We've been in the Premier League a lot of my adult life, but not dad's – very special.

The Premier League era though has been a tough one for Burnley fans in general. Blackburn Rovers had been the strongest out of the East Lancs derby teams and won the Premier League of course – so last century though. Only the light relief of claret cameos from Gazza and Ian Wright gave me hope of a bright future in my early years as a fan. Stan Ternant stood at the helm (in his Reebok classics and shorts, regardless of the weather) for most of those years, making way for Steve Cotterill in 2004 and then Owen Coyle in 2007. In his first full season, Owen lead us to finish 5th in the Championship and after defeating Reading, to that fiery unforgettable final against Sheffield United.

In our first season in the Premier League, we became the first newly-promoted team to win all of their first 4 home games, including Man United and Everton. However, temporary elation soon ebbed as we sunk downwards, facing the grim realities of being the smallest club in a very rich and flashy league. Safe to say a 6-1 drubbing from Man City and 4-0 by Liverpool will never sit too well with the ego, especially of some hardy northerners who are comfortable with the wooden seats that still exist at Turf Moor. With a population of around 70,000 – equating to 1 in 4 people attending our home games – you could feel the gloominess reach every corner of the town. Brian Laws came in to band aid the problem, only for us to slip further down to our inevitable doom.

The drop became a comfortable place as we stayed in the Championship for the following seasons under new manager Eddie Howe who we assume was doing his 11+ at the time. Then came the gravelly-toned, towering man-mountain, Sean Dyche, taking the helm in 2012. Our 53rd season in top flight football commenced in 2014, Sean's first full season, only to come to an end just 9 months later with a return to the football league. Adding salt to the wound, wonder-kids Kieran Trippier and Danny Ings left Turf Moor for the lofty heights of Tottenham and Liverpool.

Despite losing key men, we returned to the 'big time' the following season, following the unusually enlightened measure of not sacking the manager who had previously

⁴ Very good. See it here: **https://video.search.yahoo.com/search/video;_ylt=A0LEVze07cdYoZYAB21XNyoA;_ ylu=X3oDMTByMjB0aG5zBGNvbG8DYmYxBHBvcwMxBHZ0aWQDBHNlYwNzYw-- ?p=2009+Championship+Play-off+final&fr=mcafee#id=1&vid=e3cb5b4950dd570459d70b3339b5 2cd5&action=view** (accessed 13/3/17)

got us there. We ended our re-promotion season on a fantastic 23-match undefeated run. Catchy chants led by Joey Barton, the born-again saint that had joined Turf Moor that season,[5] will forever ring in the ears of 'Dingles' across the town.[6] A solid season-long performance: Andre Gray netting 25 goals and winning the league's Player of the Season; a bitter rivalry with Karanka's Middlesbrough (admittedly a much larger scale club than Burnley); and the birth of the new-age Burnley that's held its own more solidly in the 2016/17 season.

What's next? We don't delude ourselves that we'll ever be favourites to win the league, qualify for the UCL or win the FA Cup, but the team that not too long ago risked dropping out the football league altogether, now puts up a serious fight with the heavyweights. Reality checks still happen (Lincoln City/FA Cup/ouch) but we've genuinely created a fortress at Turf Moor (beating Liverpool, Everton and Middlesbrough – which was nice - to name but a few).

Season's Awards

The Exciting Bit: Bradford City won 2-4 at the Bridge in the FA Cup 4th round.

---

[5] As a Saints fan, I'm not sure if this is accurate or acceptable, but I try not to censor these things!

[6] Dingles: A term of 'endearment' used by people of Blackburn and Preston for their Burnley neighbours.

Crazy But True Facts and Statistics:

- Southampton beat Sunderland 8-0 the day after I increased my daughter's pocket money by 'however many goals Saints score when they win.'[7]

- Southampton (yes really) became the first (only) team to score 5 goals in each half of a game in the same Premier League season (they were leading 3-0 at half time in the Sunderland game above, and led 5-0 at half-time versus Aston Villa near the season's end).

- Really sorry about this, but that 5-0 half time lead included a hat-trick in under 3 minutes by Sadio Mane (13, 14 and 16 minutes)

- 'I've started so I'll finish.' If you take out the time for celebrations, there are about 65 seconds between the ball hitting the net for 1st and the 3rd time.

- 'And finally Cyril.' The third goal is a thing of beauty; like Carlos Alberto for Brazil in the 1970 world cup – fluid, box to box move – except it was the Saints. Flippin' 'eck Tucker (for older readers).

Up Next

Surely the spirits of every football fan in the country were raised by the promotion of Bournemouth; no one dislikes them, not even Southampton, as much as they'd like that. Watford were pipped to the Championship title but got automatic promotion and Norwich again won the play-offs from 3rd place.

---

[7] It maintained her loyalty at a time when shirts and souvenirs were no longer enough, and became more expensive than I'd ever imagined!

BELIEVE
(2015-16)

Champions	Leicester City
Relegated	Newcastle United, Norwich City and Aston Villa (in a season which can only be described as pathetic, and was by almost all their fans)
Unbelievable Relegation Escape	Sunderland (mostly for the regularity they are able to do it and often seemingly at the expense of Newcastle!)

I don't even know if I believe!? I honestly think the Spanish Inquisition were boringly predictable in comparison with Leicester City this season.[1] Just wow! I don't even like Leicester but the whole business probably made me want to write this book. Otherwise it is a tale which could be summed up as follows: 'Manchester United won it more than half the time, were occasionally challenged by particular teams in particular phases and now more so by the teams with multi-billionaire backers.' But then Leicester effing City won it! I mean just look at the histories of 'yo-yo' clubs...if Leicester City could do this and play in the Champions League couldn't West Brom? Crystal Palace? Probably any one of about 30 teams?

---

[1] Imagine in a Monty Python style, someone says 'I only said that I didn't expect Leicester City to win the Premier League' and then Cardinal Fang jumps out and cries 'No one!!!...expected Leicester City to win the league. Their 2 chief weapons were...pace, surprise and an almost fanatical devotion to counter-attacking...err their three chief weapons were pace, surprise, counter-attacking and team spirit. Amongst their diverse strengths were such elements as...' etc

Maybe like me you watched/heard the BBC reports from Selhurst Park towards the end of the season when Leicester fans wouldn't go home and continued to sing 'Now you've gotta believe us, we're gonna win the league'. Stewards tried to remove them: 'Like the team that's gonna win the Premier League, we shall not be moved' they continued. But I don't think they did believe; that's why they milked the moment for every second they could. Leicester fans who stood to win a fortune for that sheepish bet they'd put on, more out of loyalty than belief, cashed-out for a fraction of what they'd have won if they'd held their nerve. The fact that they came up against bigger bottlers than it's possible to imagine in Spurs helped, but we all reached that point when we finally believed, and then knew. It was extraordinary.

Half way through the season there were some remarkable stats which showed, I think, that PSG, Bayern Munich and Barcelona (top of their respective leagues) were also ranked #1 for possession, total number of short-passes and pass accuracy percentage. Leicester meanwhile, top of the Premier League (which couldn't last!), were ranked 20th, 18th and 19th in the Premier League for these aspects of the game. It all added to the argument that there was a certain amount of luck in Leicester's position and that other teams would 'work them out' in the second half of the season. But that's not what happened...and though they may have had some luck, you can't lose only 3 games all season through mere luck.

The other most notable thing about this season was that although a number of teams were in contention at various points it was another team which hadn't won the Premier League that gave Leicester the sternest test. Although Manchester City dominated the early part of the season, and Arsenal went top for a few weeks mid-season it was actually Spurs who put most pressure on the Foxes, spending much of the latter part of the season in second place. They never managed to top the table however.

It was a frustrating season for the big boys. Manchester United still hadn't recovered from Ferguson's departure. Defending champions Chelsea made such a poor start to their defence that they were never in contention and had to sack their talismanic Mourinho. Manchester City were in pole position but finished fourth. Arsenal were responsible for 2 of Leicester's 3 league defeats all season and yet could not mount a challenge. But maximum frustration must be Tottenham's. They only took a point off Leicester and that was from a point at the Crisp Bowl (or whatever LCFC call their stadium nowadays) when they took the lead with 10 minutes remaining. But worse, possibly, than getting quite close to winning the EPL, on the last day of the season they went to already relegated Newcastle and went down 5-1 to surrender 2nd place to their north London rivals (again). The damage had been done previously as Spurs conspicuously failed to hold their nerve in the run in. Of course their players went on to form the 'backbone' (wrong word) of the England team which managed to take the lead and still lose to Iceland in the European championships.[2]

Focus on: Leicester City

As you all know, they came crawling out of the woodwork last year. The 'no, I never really supported United, I just liked their style of play...but my Auntie is from Hinckley' brigade. But I offer you a genuine Leicester fan. I had to laugh when Brendan sent me his contribution because it started with: *The last few years have typified what it is to be a Leicester City fan.* You mean that endless cycle of typically winning the League once in a 100 years...?

What he meant was that it has always been something of a rollercoaster ride. In actual fact the years leading up to this one had been more typical. I'll let Brendan pick up his own story:

Since I began following City in the early 60s (which makes him much older than he looks) we have had some real highs and lows. The 2014/2015 season was typical. We had won the Championship at a canter the year before, but with nine games to go in our first season back in the 'big time' we were adrift at the foot of the table. This lived up to all the pundits' predictions for us. I actually felt that our position was slightly false. We had played well all season and our defeats had all been narrow. Early in the season we had even had the fantastic sight of Man U (1-3 ahead with 20 minutes to go) losing 5-3 to a rampant City side, sparking the chant of 'Can we play you every week?' We just didn't seem to have luck on our side. Take our home game against West Brom for example. It wasn't a sparkling Leicester performance by any means but it was a very even contest. How was it decided? A Chris Brunt cross was met by

---

[2]   I think someone's done this scientifically and all that, but Iceland has a population of 300,000. Let's say 150,000 are women. Of the 150,000 men let's say that 40,000 are children and 80,000 are over 32. That leaves about 30,000 men of whom perhaps one-third played football at school with the other two-thirds doing more traditional national pastimes like being super-weird, drinking and being super-weird or being cruel to wildlife (and super-weird). In other words, allowing for all known factors, Iceland probably arrived at their squad of 23 by narrowing it down from a pool of 120 men of the right age and physique. Good grief!

a diving header from Wes Morgan which cannoned off his own team mate, Esteban Cambiasso, and past Schmeichel to give the Baggies a 1-0 win.

The last nine games saw the now well documented run of seven wins and a draw which enabled City to survive in the top flight, losing only to Champions elect Chelsea. Nigel Pearson, the engineer of this success, was then sacked and replaced, to everyone's surprise, by Claudio Ranieri. I honestly thought we would have a reasonable season but I could never have imagined it would turn out the way it did. I have bored people for years with my complaint that the Premier League is far too predictable and only four or five teams stand any chance of winning it. They just started well and built up some momentum which continued throughout the season. The highlight for me was the 3-1 away win against Manchester City where City (Leicester!) dominated from start to finish.

For me Kante was the man who made the difference. He was an outstanding tackler and reader of the game. I think his loss has contributed significantly to our poor follow up season. At least we've made some progress in the Champions League (who would ever have expected a Leicester fan to say that!).

Oddly, Brendan, who doesn't have an aunt in Hinckley, wasn't too fussed to comment on Leicester's other yo-yo-ing between divisions which have characterised their Premier League history.

Season's Awards

Overlooked in the craziness: The comfort with which Bournemouth maintained their top flight status and Watford too.

Mathematical Miracle Award: Tottenham Hotspur for finishing third in a two horse race and thus ensuring their wait to finish above Arsenal in the league would exceed 8000 days.

Crazy But True Facts and Statistics:

- The PFA team of the year contained 2 players in total from Arsenal (1), Manchester United (1), Liverpool (0), Chelsea (0) and Manchester City (0) – but 4 each from Leicester and Spurs!

Up Next

Brighton and Hove Albion came cruelly close and were cruelly close in how cruelly close they came. It was close. Another 'Smith must score' moment for older readers. Previously Premier League teams Burnley, Middlesbrough and Hull City were promoted instead.

BOYS THAT SING[1]
(2016-17)

Champions:	Chelsea
Relegated:	Sunderland, Middlesbrough and Hull City
Unbelievable Relegation Escape:	Swansea were bottom at New Year

All the other chapters here are works of history. History in the loosest possible sense of the word. Apologies are due here to those weirdoes called 'Historians' who use the word 'historiography' in all seriousness and stroke their beards sagely as someone reassesses the military strategy of Cromwell, or the place of etiquette in 15th century Venetian society, in the weekly staff/student seminar. Apologies also for calling you weirdoes, but well...you know who you are.

But what I mean is that I am writing this book as the 2016/17 season takes place, so as to have it ready for Christmas 2017.[2] It means I am not looking back on events, but chronicling them as they happen. And if the Leicester triumph was what motivated me to attempt the project in the first place, what it really needed was a multi-horse

---

[1] Given the closeness of the title race in October it was impossible to tell which boys it might be singing in May, but rather sadly it wouldn't be Viola Beach. So this is my small dedication to add to those of others.

[2] A timeless gift I think you'll find, ideal also for birthdays and many Christmases to come.

race and five teams still in with a chance come May for this final chapter. Some notes I took in mid-October suggested it might be possible.

- If Liverpool beat Manchester United on Monday[3] there will be three teams on 19 points after eight games
- Close behind are undefeated Spurs on 18 points
- Everton, Chelsea and Manchester United are all in the mix too
- Chelsea just walloped the current champions Leicester 3-0 meaning that Ranieri's side have lost more in eight games this season than in 38 last
- Could this Premier League be the most exciting ever, and who is that red and white striped outsider slowly gaining ground?

On the basis of those notes, I wrote:

I'm sure that Manchester United fans would agree that it is not 'imitation' which is the sincerest form of flattery, but 'bitter resentment'; I have demonstrated this throughout and hope it's seen as the grudging compliment it regrettably is! They're less likely to agree that the Premier League is becoming 'more' for the fact that they don't win it every season. The last four Premier League seasons have seen four different winners: Man United, Man City, Chelsea, Leicester...and with Arsenal, Liverpool and Tottenham currently doing so well, that run might even be extended to five seasons and even six or seven. Doubtless another period of 'Liverpool 1980s' and 'Manchester United Premier League' dominance will follow, and clearly money will preclude that from being Fleetwood Town or Accrington Stanley, but the competitive nature of things currently (and Leicester's triumph) have made the 'best league in the world' actually exciting.

By the weekend of 22/23 of October (when all the top teams played at different times, mostly with a chance to go top by winning) I was convinced that something special was possible:

First, undefeated Spurs went to Bournemouth for one of those rare exciting 0-0 draws, missing the chance to go top. Arsenal then did go top with a less exciting 0-0 draw at home to Middlesbrough, in which they had all the possession but fewer chances than their visitors. Liverpool then had the chance to go top if they beat West Brom by 2 clear goals; a late consolation meant they won by only

---

[3] Actual result: The most over-hyped match of the season (Red Monday!) finished 0-0 and the most over-hyped player (Zlatan) missed the best chance.

2-1. That happened on Saturday. On Sunday, Manchester City had the chance to go back to the top, and did so on goal difference, but achieved only a 1-1 draw against Southampton. Finally, Chelsea beat Manchester United 4-0; in doing so, Tottenham – who started the weekend with the chance to go top – were even pushed out of the Champions League places. So, Man City, Arsenal, Liverpool led the way, all on 20 points, followed by Chelsea and the only undefeated team left (Spurs) on 19. Everton, Man Utd, Southampton, Watford and Bournemouth followed on 15, 14, 13, 12 and 12 to complete the top half. And Leicester? Concentrating on the Champions' League – a nice luxury! So a quarter of the way into the season and five teams looking equally capable of mounting a serious challenge, with Man Utd/Mourinho never – alas – to be discounted and even Leicester...no, surely not...

And actually, who might win remained intriguing deep into December, even though the top teams began to separate from the rest and Chelsea looked to have found a winning formation. Many title winners are top at Christmas and this time it was Chelsea; indeed after ten consecutive victories for Conte's boys, what I hoped might be the closest of multi-horse races was already looking like a procession following home the team from Stamford Bridge.

By February, if I were a bookie I'd have probably paid out on Chelsea and the whole thing had ceased to interest me at all. The major talking point was whether last season's Champions would get relegated. After consecutive seasons in which they had snatched defeat from the jaws of victory in the play-off semi-finals, won the Championship, escaped inevitable relegation and won the Premier League, presumably only winning the Champions League and getting relegated could possibly top that. Although maybe the following season they would then retain the Champions League whilst going into administration and reforming as AFC Leicester in the East Midlands Alliance – Division One. Just to ensure fact was more bizarre than fiction, they sacked Ranieri; consecutive champions had now got rid of their manager less than a season after winning the thing. Claudio's sacking aroused more popular sympathy than the previous one (Mourinho), including from Mourinho himself, and those who like football spent a day shaking their heads.

In any case, even without my flights of lunacy, the story is remarkable. And remarkable enough to let someone else tell you some more about it.

Focus on Leicester City:

In 1975-76, in my school playground in Coalville, a dozen miles from Leicester, you saw plenty of Manchester United and Liverpool duffle bags, and a few bearing the name of Derby, then still basking in the afterglow of their Cloughie-inspired heyday. And then there were a few of us who preferred blue and white, with a fox's head badge. Even then, aged 7, we knew better than to expect glory. An occasional win against one of the big boys was all we asked.

We were a good side, though; good enough to finish 7th in the old Division One that year. Manager Jimmy Bloomfield had built a team that played attractive football, with Keith Weller elegant in the midfield, and Frank Worthington adding a bit of rock 'n' roll star quality up front. But the following year, Bloomfield was gone, relegation under Frank McLintock quickly followed, and that 7th place had looked like the mark of an impossibly high tide ever since.

We were the club that had never won the title, and had lost four FA Cup Finals. It says something that a Division One play-off win at Wembley over Derby in 1994 (The Silence of the Rams, as the Leicester Mercury proclaimed it), and a record of having never been outside the top two divisions, were the proudest boasts in most Leicester fans' repertoire.

To be fair, in the late 90s, Martin O'Neill gave us something else to shout about, with four consecutive top 10 finishes in the Premier League, and two Carling Cup wins, but after he left, we had years of yo-yoing (including a single season in League One – still the Third Division to me), bankruptcy, and constantly changing managers.

All of which provides some context. When Nigel Pearson completed the Great Escape of 2014-15, most of us were quietly confident that we could carry the momentum over and target a mid-table finish in 2015-16. When he was sacked a few weeks later, for reasons that still aren't clear but which probably weren't entirely to do with football, we expected a new period of instability and embarrassment. When Claudio Ranieri was appointed as his successor...

It's hard to say what I felt. I was relieved we hadn't gone for some of the other names being bandied about. Sam Allardyce, who would no doubt have been effective, but at what cost? Neil Lennon, a Foxes playing hero, but an uninspiring manager. Various unheard-of Americans and Croatians. I'd liked Ranieri at Chelsea, too, where he got too little credit for laying foundations for Mourinho. His failure as manager of Greece, much talked about by the media, seemed a bit beside the point as anyone could fail with Greece. But nevertheless, I couldn't shake off a nagging fear that he was another Sven Goran Ericsson, a big name previously brought in by the Thai owners without regard for what we really needed.

I told myself to be patient. I'm a hopeless optimist in most things, but especially where sport is concerned, so I tried to forget that we'd also lost Cambiasso, a beacon of quality during the previous season. I tried to give the new boys a chance. Early results were steady, not spectacular. Then, mid-September, home to Villa, we slipped 2-0 down on the stroke of 60 minutes. New signing Kante looked a bit lost in midfield. Our central defence looked its age. Vardy's endless running up front brought little actual end product. So easy that Villa manager Tim Sherwood saw fit to take off Sanchez, his best player on the day.

Then everything changed. Vardy, just about to embark on his long scoring run, was taken off and replaced by Leonardo Ulloa, a less dynamic striker, but one who brings other players into the game. City spent 30 minutes battering the Villa goal, and won 3-2 courtesy of a brave late header from loan signing Nathan Dyer.

All great, but it was only Villa. What was heartening, though, was that we never stopped trying to win the game. And that, I realised, is all Leicester fans generally want. We can deal with failure, given that we're so used to it. What we can't accept is the 'let's try to sneak a point' attitude that so many clubs adopt against the big boys. It was what had made O'Neill such a success, and so popular. Ignoring it was why Pearson's side had come so perilously close to relegation the previous year.

Ranieri's achievement, then, was not only to realise that he had a solid squad with two exceptional players (Kante and Mahrez) that was well capable of a top-half finish, but also that the crowd would become a 12th man if only the team could match their ambition. Risk losing, we willed them. We'll probably lose anyway. But at least give yourselves a chance of winning.

Weeks slipped by. A minor wobble around Christmas came and went, and by mid-February I dared to really hope. A fiver on us to win the league, the day before we destroyed Manchester City at the Etihad with a performance full of verve and passion. Now I really believed…although…dropped points in the return against Villa, and against Bournemouth, would surely come back to haunt us. It would be so typically Leicester to miss out at the last because of that. But putting them aside, and consigning my own partisan optimism to the mental dustbin too, I proved to my own satisfaction that we would win it.

The pressure that the pundits talked about? What was that, then? It ignored the fact that we'd faced real pressure the year before, when relegation loomed. The club might have gone into financial meltdown. Players might have spent the rest of their careers in the lower leagues. We'd faced it the year before that, getting promotion from the 24-club dogfight that is the Championship. No. Our rivals faced it, for sure. Arsenal, knowing they might not see another season in which Chelsea and Manchester United were so hopeless. Manchester City, under the weight of their enormous bank balance. Spurs, under a great weight of history.

But us? No, we could go on doing what had got us to the top of the league in the first place, knowing that even a late-season collapse would leave us at heights unheard-of by Leicester fans since before the Beatles released their first record, or the Berlin Wall went up. I have, over the years, formed a very mixed opinion of football fans as a (vastly over-generalised) whole. Loyal, yes, and willing to accept sky-high prices and shoddy treatment. But too quick to call for managers to be sacked, for players to be sold and for directors to stump up endless transfer fees. At Leicester, for many years, too impatient for any City side to build slowly from the back, preferring blood and thunder.

For once, though, the fans really do deserve a lot of the credit. Throughout the whole nine months of implausible hopes and dreams, of occasional lows and exhilarating highs, I didn't come across a single Leicester supporter who expected any more than that the players and manager should set out to win each game. If we lost, then we knew how to deal with it, after a lifetime of practice. If we kept winning, then who knew where it might end? Given that licence, the players responded, and Claudio Ranieri ditched his 'Tinkerman' image, sticking with a line-up and a game-plan that worked. The rest is the sort of history that we used to think only belonged to Forest fans.

Matt Merritt

Focus on: Bournemouth

So what could be more extraordinary than a Thai billionaire giving away free Singha and helping a smallish City in the East Midlands win the Premier League? This could. Rewind a decade and AFC Bournemouth almost went out of existence (financially) and almost out of the football league (on the field). When they finished 10th in the Championship under inspirational manager Eddie Howe in 2012/13 it was their highest ever placing in the football pyramid. It is widely believed that if Howe hadn't been putting quite so much effort into his GCSE Geography project the team might have finished even higher. Fortunately for Cherries fans, Howe the Younger decided not to stay on into the sixth form and, once he was concentrating purely on football, Bournemouth romped to the Championship in 2014/15 and stayed up the season after.

Bournemouth's traditional rivals are Poole Town. Well actually that's not true. But imagine if the Cherries got a couple of relegations and Poole were promoted a couple of times and Poole fans started talking about hating Bournemouth. It wouldn't feel right, and in a similar way Bournemouth fans, you really can't claim to hate the Saints. They're taken. In any case, my trip to the Vitality (is that a dog food?) Stadium made it clear you're too nice to hate people. There is only one south coast derby...about one a decade at the moment. Perhaps you could try hating Millwall? They'd like that.

Bournemouth is not a place I remember fondly. Rolf Harris played Southampton University's grad ball there – *can you see what I did yet?* It also gives you an idea of Southampton that the university held its grad ball in Bournemouth! Then there was the lovely Richard's funeral; he had a meeting in the twin towers on the wrong day. And then Aunty Jean's funeral, although she did have a fine, fun and event packed innings, being run out just two shy of a century. I mention this only because the latter was a chance to see people not seen for years, family visiting from New Zealand and so on and by the time I got to the club shop all the punters I'd hoped to talk to had disappeared.

In the ten minutes I had, I talked to the people who worked in the club shop instead. As I left I mentioned that I'd talked to many fans in the course of writing this book and that no-one wanted Bournemouth to go down, even Saints fans. 'We won't be going down' growled a woman. 'It's nice to know even Saints fans don't want us relegated' said a young lad.

There is, understandably an irrepressible optimism around the new Dean Court, even before they called it Vitality (for a shiny coat and a wet nose). *Eddie Howe will stay, a new stadium will be built, we've got a lovely foreign owner, the atmosphere is incredible.* Imagine the character in *The Fast Show* who just said everything was brilliant. That's Bournemouth, and terribly polite too; of course the woman didn't growl 'we won't be going down', she smiled it. And they were so nice that I was guilted into buying something from their amply stocked shop. Well I've always needed an AFC Bournemouth tea cosy.[4]

Focus on: Liverpool

For a team who so dominated football in the 1980s to then see the Premier League era dominated by their fiercest rivals will have been difficult. No season has really stood out for Liverpool in Premier League terms, even though many other teams would be delighted to have won the trophies that have come to Anfield and rarely to have even glimpsed the bottom half of the table. But the Premier League, given Liverpool's history, has been a story of disappointments, near misses, high hopes and false dawns. In recent times the painfully near miss of 2013/14 raised hopes, but that was followed by finishing 6th and then 8th.[5]

What then of Jurgen Klopp's first full season in charge? I met Dave to discuss this and see if a fan forum he was on had come up with anything. The frustration at Liverpool multiplies the frustration at Forest and provides the opposite of the bubbliness at Bournemouth. Apparently the general opinion on

---

[4] *Please be aware that nothing as useful as a tea cosy is available in any club shop, anywhere.*

[5] *Lower than Southampton for the only time in their history.*

the forum was 'why should we help someone write a book?' If you suffix 'eh?' to that and imagine one of the endless scouse whingers on 606 that'll give you more of an idea.

Although Dave is more laid back than your average fan there is no real sense of excitement about the present. Having been a free-scoring side in 2016, at the start of 2017 Liverpool suddenly drew 0-0 at home to Plymouth in one cup and failed to score over two legs in the semi-final of the other against a team with two reserve centre-halves. And although these weren't the league, the wheels also came off that campaign too. Even though Klopp is replicating his early mediocrity at Dortmund, in a reasonably amusing way, you can see in Dave's eyes no sense of optimism or excitement about the future, just a hint that it might be my round.

We go on to discuss a number of things that would have sat well in this book. The fact that Liverpool's record of trophies over the Premier League period is the envy of almost every other team in the league. How frustrating this period has been nonetheless. How much Man Utd are loathed. Why he hates Sky and the mythical excitement it pumps out. The fact that TV talks, for instance, of how many times Chelsea have won the Premier League as if winning the old first division (or not winning it) no longer counts as part of history. It would have been nice to have genuine quotes on all of this, but apart from Dave, I didn't find a spokesperson for one of the world's greatest clubs.

In answer to the question of why anyone should help with this book, the answer is of course, no reason at all. But many have done so to tell people about their team, like Liam Sephton at Wigan or David Lloyd at Fulham. Keith Wildman at Bradford would also be a good example; he helped because he is proud of his town, of his team and the history of both. He has no special love of the Premier League but feels a community bond through the football club and all its highs and considerable lows both on and off the pitch. As I sat and wondered why Liverpool fans, who after all have a special club and history, cannot share such a philosophical calmness towards the current decades' long blip, news filtered through that Leicester City had sacked Claudio Ranieri. I experienced a sense of pointlessness, interrupted only to remind Dave whose round it was. I understood in that moment the pain of football fans, and of Liverpool fans in particular. I was glad this book neared its end and heard the lure of non-league football calling me back.

As April dawned (yawned?), there was still the vaguest possibility that Spurs might overhaul Chelsea and make it necessary for me to rewrite some of this chapter, but I doubted it. In fact it all looks very predictable...so much so that I gave it a try.

April Fools' Day Predictions

Aspect of PL	Prediction	Actual
Winners	Chelsea	Chelsea
Spurs finally finish above Arsenal	Yes	Yes
Sunderland finally get relegated	Yes	Yes
Middlesbrough too	Yes	Yes
Who else?	Hull	Hull

It was that predictable.

Season's Awards

Ingratitude: Any number including Arsenal fans moaning about Wenger, Liverpool fans for moaning about only ever winning European trophies and the FA Cup and 18 league titles. Southampton fans who want to know why we can't be higher in the league as well as getting to the League Cup final, but most of all Leicester City (not the fans) for sacking Claudio. Seemed to work though...

Never Learns: I've had to self-censor. I was going to say Joey Barton for being disruptive at Rangers and for the betting and stuff. And then I read about his award-winning autobiography of which a review says 'he describes his personal crusade against the demons of violence in his nature'. So maybe there's a reflective side to his nature we don't see, but it's the violence and the disruption etc that we do. But I won't give him the award, in case he does.

Oliver Cromwell Reverential Silence Award: Although not technically the Premier League, Manchester United fans at the League Cup Final were almost fanatical in observing a monastical vow of silence throughout the match. However after 90 minutes of feeble support they finally found their voice just before victory so I'll have no truck with arguments about poor acoustics. Thereafter they were in fine and irritating voice in the tube station, offering homage to their players at exactly the point they didn't need it. What a bunch of complete.[6]

Supporters of the Century: Contrast the above with the other end of the ground. Flag-waving, scarves held aloft and balloons bouncing. And most amazingly of all, singing. Saints fans, robbed by a ridiculous linesman on the pitch, but magnificent off it.

Totally biased, bitter, twisted and sour grapes award: Me

Crazy But True Facts and Statistics:

- I'm sure there was some rule about one league club setting up too near another? Is that why Leyton Orient sportingly became a non-league team after West Ham took over the Olympic Stadium?

- Too late to make my best songs, but shortly after David Moyes managed to go down in our estimations (as if we thought that possible) by suggesting he might

---

[6] *Apparently the book has reached its word count.*

slap a female journalist, his Sunderland team trailed 2-0 to Leicester. City fans chorused 'Slapped in the morning, you're getting slapped in the morning.'

- Huddersfield were promoted to the Premier League with a goal difference across all 49 matches of minus two. They won over half their matches despite averaging only 1.16 goals per match, which is lower than Hartlepool (1.17) managed in getting relegated out of the football league. And they scored six fewer goals than 21st placed Nottingham Forest.

Up Next

Brighton and Hove Albion became the 48th team who will play in the Premier League, eventually conceding the Championship title to Newcastle in the final minutes of the season. In the play-offs, Huddersfield had the chance to become the 49th team to play in the Premier League. They squeaked past Sheffield Wednesday on penalties in the semi-final to set up a Wembley final against Reading which they sneaked through on penalties. Admirably heroic, but they won't survive on 1 goal from open play every 330 minutes (their play-off record) in the Premier League – unless they keep being award 10 penalties over the same time-frame of course.

Tranmere Rovers, who spent much of the early part of this book just missing out on promotion to the Premier League via the play-offs, finished second in the National League (sounds rather grand for 'Fifth Tier') and then lost in the play-off final. Sad face.

CONCLUSIONS

Like most genuine football fans, I have very little neutral knowledge about football. My opinions are silly, contradictory, biased and irrational. I accept this and so, for those to whom I have caused offence by having opinions at variance with your own (ridiculous) opinions, I offer an insincere apology. If I managed to actually annoy any players, I reckon you're well-rewarded enough to take it and/or deserve it, but I offer the same apology. I also wave this way and that way like tall grass in the breeze, and contradict myself depending on who my team's just lost to. At least you know I'm a proper fan who is as annoyed as you are when people say *it's only a game.* It's clearly not. (See also Kuper, 2003). But please do not send death threats. I don't mean to offend honest and, after all, *it is only a book.* In searching out amusement and provocation, I may have got it wrong, but it's more than likely I didn't mean it.

Anyway, I have gathered all my powers to try and say something sensible by way of summing up this quarter century of hype and cash. First of all, aside from the broader considerations, please be assured that wherever your team currently sits and however bleak the scenario, the footballing Gods may intervene at any second to right historical wrongs. York City may be taken over by Latin America's top llama farmer, for instance, and dominate English football for eternity.[1] Well maybe not that one, but many other scenarios are possible. And even without getting anywhere near the Premier League, sometimes fans just want their team back; admittedly starting from the 9th tier, Darlington fans have enjoyed more success in recent years than in their entire history, currently battling away in the upper reaches of National League North. And I bet it feels good after all they've been through.

Things change rapidly. Even since I started writing this conclusion, Everton have announced plans to move to a new stadium in the Mersey docks for instance. And Portsmouth are on the verge of takeover by a former head of Disney; this betrays the Gods' sense of humour of course. On the one hand he's probably very wealthy and

---

[1] And I wrote that before the Gods offered up the 2017 FA Trophy as short term compensation.

Pompey may return to the higher echelons. On the other, sponsorship by Mickey Mouse seems entirely appropriate for a club of such stature. Oh, silly people, you know I don't mean it. Much.[2]

Mark Bradley previously did lots of common sense work and training on helping businesses understand customer service. In more recent years he has been working with football at all levels on getting more people, especially families, to attend football. He styles his efforts *The Fan Experience Company* and agrees that this notion of 'experience' can annoy the hardened football fan when applied to the game. We discussed Rupert Lowe, erstwhile Chairman of Southampton Football Club, writing in his programme notes on the day Saints were relegated from the Premier League, arguing that whatever happened that day, he was sure fans would agree that the match day experience at St Mary's was second to none. Well, actually Roops, we were the fans who gave zero f***s about your 'match-day experience'; you could have sprayed us in iced water for 90 minutes if we'd beaten Man Utd that day. But we didn't. So get lost with your 'match day b****** experience'! Sorry, sidetrack of rage.

Notwithstanding Rupert though, if you want to build attendances, encourage families etc, then the 'experience' is going to be important and that's where Mark comes in. Oddly, Mark took his family to St Mary's a couple of seasons later and the experience (non-Premier then) was indeed excellent. But I asked Mark if the experience of the Premier League was 'worth it' – the money, the hassle etc, compared to just popping down to your local lower league or non-league team. Whether the pace and skill on offer compensated for not being able to wander around the ground or get away in under 2 hours. Whether watching the very best was actually worth the second mortgage required to buy a round of drinks, pies and chocolate etc?

Mark's answer took a while and meandered through his experience of watching lots of football, with a keen eye not just on but off the pitch too. Mark is a Sunderland fan (which I'm obliged to mention), but his son Luis is Bradford through and through, and Bantams fans singing when 5-0 down in the League Cup final springs to Mark's mind as a special moment. And then the Scottish 'el classico' as it's never been known, Arbroath v East Fife...amazingly one of my favourite ever fixtures too, although mine was in 1992 and his in 2013.[3] In both cases we can remember the score, but the amazing bit was the locals, the pies, the setting – rather than the football would you believe? We talked about Millwall being a family club of the year (yes really) and Durham City Ladies more or less creating a crowd and a cafe to go with it. Oh, and

---

[2] But what about the impressive supporters' trust?

[3] No seriously, you can read about it here:
  https://cloud.3dissue.com/6374/7271/131371/fcbusiness100digi/index.html

the Spanish second division; anything really apart from the Premier League.

Like many men of a certain age, Mark also wanders back 'pre-Prem' when asked about football. In this case, a Richard Shaw own goal for Crystal Palace at The Dell where Mark had gone with his best man Mark, a Palace fan and contributor to this book. Notwithstanding that it took place in the 1990/91 season, and Mark told me it was 1992, it is difficult to track down, which both Richard Shaw and Nigel Martyn's moustache must be pleased about. But you can find it.[4] I couldn't find video evidence of Mark's other claim that Glyn Hodges zipped himself up in a 'onesie' on the touchline that day; so this may be one of those cases where fact and fantasy have got confused with the passing of time. The point being though, not that Mark's dreams are strange, but that the Premier League does not make football. If your team is in it, by all means enjoy, but the experience of other levels brings other rewards, as various contributors to this book have made clear.

The above is, primarily, a 'geographical' answer; football is different but not necessarily better depending on where you are watching it at any particular time. Your finest memories may come from National League North on a Tuesday night (well they do if you've travelled from Bishop's Stortford to Workington and won 2-3 with a last minute thunderbolt) rather than the 0-0 Premier League bore draw for at Anfield. But what about a specifically 'historical' answer, which the Richard Shaw example hints at? The fact is there is both good and bad when looking at football in historical context; so the white working class ritual is no more but you see more families at games, more ethnic minorities attending games and so on. Things change and football does too.

So finally I went back where I started the book: to Oakham United, the City Ground and Meadow Lane in April and then Anfield on May 7th and St Mary's on May 21st for a final review and think. The last of these was Southampton v Stoke, the 999th paid team sporting fixture I have ever attended (mostly football). And my conclusion? Well QPR masochist Christian Wolmar is probably right; if you support your team you want them to win every game so you want them to be in the Premier League. But then again, it's not that good. Right? Well that game certainly wasn't.

In fact it is noticeable that those contributors that didn't experience the pre-Prem period are more positive about the Premier League than older contributors. Generally, older fans – and not just of Liverpool – are much more grumpy, reaching back to days when things were, well simply different. But wasn't it ever thus? Isn't football just much more fun when you're young? And although that might be a slightly down-beat note to conclude on, it does mean that this is probably the perfect Christmas or

---

[4] It can be found 35 minutes into this season long review: **https://www.youtube.com/watch?v=BhRBFX-3QhI** (accessed 31/3/17)

birthday present for your grandchildren, nephews, nieces and, indeed, anyone at all younger than you.

But then again...here's Peter Newell. Older than some, definitely wiser than many, and yet still referring to his newly promoted team as 'beloved':

Focus on: Brighton and Hove Albion

It feels unreal. My beloved Brighton and Hove Albion have been promoted to the Premier League! Even as I type that sentence I need to re-read it. It doesn't feel right - or seem at all possible. I was there 20 years ago at Hereford when we came within a whisker of falling out the league altogether.[5] It was an ugly atmosphere with so much at stake. I was in the Hereford end, unable to join the massed ranks of blue and white, and a 1-1 draw was enough to keep us up. The last ten minutes of the game were played behind riot shielded police and under supporting helicopters. It was a battle in every sense of the word.

I was also there at Wembley for the FA Cup final in 1983. The replay that is. The one we lost 4-0 and then got relegated, despite the return of the legendary Stevie Foster to the line-up. But it was still a special moment, especially back in the days when the FA Cup was still held in awe by most fans. I had a season ticket through the years at the Withdean stadium (read- athletics track). Without a roof, far from the pitch and without an atmosphere to boot. But still we won successive promotions with the great Micky Adams at the helm.

When we finally moved to the Amex stadium it was an incredibly emotional moment - a proper home of our own after so many years in the wilderness following the criminal sell off of the Goldstone ground - where I was even a ball boy once upon a time - and the ground share with Gillingham. We've then suffered three successive years of promotion challenges and play-offs to no avail and with significant heartache. The end of last season was just hideous; a horror show of misfortune and lack of grit.

---

5   Hereford themselves now play in the 7th tier.

*All of this makes this promotion success all the sweeter. Growing up alongside so many kids at school that opted to support Man Utd or Liverpool – the most successful teams in the 1980s, but in most cases without any connection to them, supporting Brighton never brought much glamour but plenty of ridicule. There will be more to come of course as we face the prospect of loses against some of the wealthy Premier League giants. But today, for now, we'll dwell on this moment, bask in the feelings of joy and celebrate this historic victory for the team, the club, the community and the global Seagulls family. We're on our way….*Very nice man, didn't even mention the possibility of Crystal Palace heading the other way.

Focus on: Sheffield Wednesday

Wednesday are the 4th oldest football team in the world, racking up their 150th year anniversary in 2017; but in 1887 they almost went under after just twenty. In that year they managed to field only 10 players in a game they lost 0-16 and the end looked nigh. What had caused this? Essentially, despite promising early years, a determination to remain amateur had seen their best players continue to leave. Fortunately they recovered from this 'short arms and long pockets' condition just in time to save the day; they agreed to pay the players. By that point the Wednesday club (initially a cricket club, then cricket and football, later just football) already had a proud history, having provided a player in the first ever international cricket match *and* first ever international football match (England v Scotland, 1872).

Yet fast forward to the present day and Sheffield Wednesday is still not quite the giant it ought to be. They lost in the Championship play-off final of 2015/16 to Hull City. In the following year the Owls never threatened automatic promotion, spending a majority of the season in 6th place. Fulham looked like they might pip Wednesday to final play-off spot at any moment, especially as the Sheffield team dropped to 7th in April. Although Fulham did indeed claim 6th spot and won at Hillsborough on the final day of the season, six successive wins had already taken Wednesday to a season high 4th spot and it was Leeds United who missed out. Even so, it was a frustrating season for Wednesday fans, starting with thoughts of automatic promotion but then knowing for most of it that the best they could hope for was a repetition of play-off agony. Perhaps that is why I found it so difficult to get a Wednesday fan to contribute? Last in this book, they were also the last team to be completed.

First I had a bus driver who was going to help, but he failed to show up. Stereotype successfully reinforced. A famous actor was keen to help, but was jetting out of the country (like they do). Nonetheless, he put me in touch with a pop star who was jetting in (ditto). My attempts to get him involved became ever more desperate, culminating in my final desperate plea: 'Don't you want me baby, don't you want me oh-oh-oh?' But no luck.[6] For a moment I thought I had a contributor as an email entitled 'Wednesday Fan' arrived in my inbox; initially suspicious as Adrian wished to remain anonymous, I decided it was definitely a spoof after reading *I only supported Wednesday at all because I was a total nerd and all the cool kids went to Bramall Lane.* In the end I did find a genuine fan - a student who was very helpful, despite the extraordinary workload they put them under at University; I mean 24 weeks every year and exams on top of that? Madness! But anyway, he pointed out that he couldn't actually remember Wednesday in the Premier League. So last century. I felt very old. *It's about time we were back where we belong* was his only, and in the circumstances quite reasonable, comment.

As a final attempt to get comment, I travelled to Hillsborough itself. These days it is a fine ground indeed. On a bright sunny day, I sneaked in through a side gate and gazed at the empty stadium and immaculate pitch. Of course football doesn't work like this (thank goodness) but it was difficult standing there not to feel that Wednesday deserve to be a top flight team. My plan had been to go to the offices and find someone to comment. But in the stillness and the sun, looking out to my left across the Leppings Lane End, I found I had not the enthusiasm to 'doorstep' people and instead spent some quiet moments thinking about not just of what happened there, but also in Bradford and Moscow[7] and elsewhere. And I'd had enough of football for that day.

As for Wednesday, the question was could they, like Brighton, put last year's near promotion agonies behind them? Well before that, I did finally talk to

---

[6] Much of the stuff in here is true, but there is the occasional gloss of artistic license; to be clear Phil Oakey did not offer or decline to be interviewed for this book. I'm not even sure who he supports because the internet doesn't know.

[7] The sad tale of Luzhniki is told here: **https://www.theguardian.com/football/2008/may/04/championsleague** (accessed 10/5/17)

a Wednesday fan, Martyn Ware, a little after the play-off first leg 0-0 draw away to Huddersfield. Like many fans, he's worried about the money and the overall effect on football of this but also proud of his team and town and what he terms a *religious connection* with his family's roots. Like so many fans, his best memories barely intersect with the Premier League at all, notwithstanding Wednesday's 'nearly' season of 1992/93. I'd seen rumours that the coach's position was in doubt so I asked about him too, but Martyn gives no sense of disgruntlement. A shame for Carvalhal that Martyn's not the Chairman I guess, although the rumours appear unfounded for now.

Despite taking the lead in the home leg of the semi-final, Sheffield Wednesday lost on penalties and I stopped pursuing their fans for comment.

AFTERWORD

Not everyone likes football. In my last book, on the Euro 2016 tournament, Nathaniel Sikand-Youngs was kind enough to offer up a defence of cricket for people who became bored of the championships (aka 'when England lost to another team they should beat').The piece was intended to appear clearly attributed to "Natty" and I offered a self-deprecating 'lead in' suggesting that here was some genuine erudition in amongst the surrounding tosh. Unfortunately, the need for speed around publication of such a product, led to a formatting error in which none of this was clear. Although Natty's name appeared in the acknowledgements his work was unclearly attributed. I would like to correct the error by including that piece here, slightly amended for a book on the Premier League. As well as it being very well written and commended by many as the best bit of writing in that book, I didn't write it - which I am now making very clear.

The Game of Football, the Life of Cricket

The roar of the crowd was a ceaseless song of devotion to the rhythm of play. It rose and fell, but never once paused, as the balance of the game swung to and fro. At the moment of kick-off, the match seized your imagination and captured your heart, carrying you with a relentless grip right up until the final whistle. Here it dropped you. The match ended and you and you fellow fans are left facing an unkind reality: It's not your season again. The Premier League glory will be won by a team from a different city (or worse, a different club from the same city). What a cruel world; how fruitless your love!

At its idyllic best, free from the interruptions of ludicrous dives, reckless tackles and unattractive hoofs up-field or out of play, football is a continuous, fluid sport. It does not stop to catch its breath, and neither can those watching. How appealing, how exhilarating, how BEAUTIFUL this all makes football, you probably think. Perhaps this is true. But to possess these qualities, a fleeting game of football sacrifices certain virtues which can only come from a longer passage of time. For a sport like a slow burning candle, unfolding in a sweeping landscape with a rhythm that breathes not races, take a seat at the pavilion end and relish in cricket.

Structurally, cricket is simply the cyclical repetition of the same formulaic "units" of play. The bowler pryingly delivers a ball of cork and leather; the batsman answers with a blade of willow. Repeat: Six times. Over. Repeat: twenty, fifty, maybe more, times. Innings. Teams swap. Repeat: from the top. For those only familiar with football, this structure can seem disjointed, impenetrable and, the word most commonly used, BORING. Each ball bowled is a singular occasion, distinct and autonomous from the deliveries that came before. In football, every pass and touch of the ball is wholly dependent on the outcome of the preceding events. The only continuity in cricket, nay, the only evidence that any play actually took place before the current moment, is the number of runs scored and wickets taken, the wear of the players' minds, and the tear in the ball and pitch. These amount to the sporting symbols of: human imperatives of measurement, understanding, and narrative writing; human capabilities of psychological and physical endurance; and human helplessness to the environment and the passing of time.

Cricket is no less than life itself played out over twenty-two yards. As such, the spectator who is bored of cricket is bored of life. No matter what the balance of the game, we cannot predict what the next delivery will bring. The strongest innings can crumble in a fraction of a session, while the weakest need only a sturdy partnership to erode away the time left in the day's play. Either way, one team will be left mourning the ruins of its once dominant position, just as human beings are so often left feeling powerless to determine their own destinies. Of course, fates twist and fortunes exchange in football, too, but the fluid structure of the sport means that such game changing moments always come out of somewhere even if they are predictable. The losing team in football still has to set up that pivotal surprise goal, whereas the underdog fielding side in cricket can produce a wicket from nowhere. Most of all, cricket pauses, composes itself, and walks back to its bowler's mark, affording the spectator the chance to absorb the full enormity of these junctures in the game.

So, by the time your team has kissed goodbye to its Premier League dreams (at either end of the table) and the excitement and enchantment of the football season have passed, turn over to the cricket. From one ball to the next, it will show you joy, monotony, surprise, defeat and success, all in a single day's play.

Nathaniel Sikand-Youngs,
November 2015

And when he puts it like that, it has to be...

The End. Almost.

PS

Focus On: Huddersfield Town

Not enough time to get hold of Patrick Stewart, but he looked very happy that the boys had made it so.

LEAGUE TABLES

1992/93

Pos	Team	Pld	W	D	L	GF	GA	GD	Pts
1	Manchester United (C)	42	24	12	6	67	31	+36	84
2	Aston Villa	42	21	11	10	57	40	+17	74
3	Norwich City	42	21	9	12	61	65	−4	72
4	Blackburn Rovers	42	20	11	11	68	46	+22	71
5	Queens Park Rangers	42	17	12	13	63	55	+8	63
6	Liverpool	42	16	11	15	62	55	+7	59
7	Sheffield Wednesday	42	15	14	13	55	51	+4	59
8	Tottenham Hotspur	42	16	11	15	60	66	−6	59
9	Manchester City	42	15	12	15	56	51	+5	57
10	Arsenal	42	15	11	16	40	38	+2	56
11	Chelsea	42	14	14	14	51	54	−3	56
12	Wimbledon	42	14	12	16	56	55	+1	54
13	Everton	42	15	8	19	53	55	−2	53
14	Sheffield United	42	14	10	18	54	53	+1	52
15	Coventry City	42	13	13	16	52	57	−5	52
16	Ipswich Town	42	12	16	14	50	55	−5	52
17	Leeds United	42	12	15	15	57	62	−5	51
18	Southampton	42	13	11	18	54	61	−7	50
19	Oldham Athletic	42	13	10	19	63	74	−11	49
20	Crystal Palace (R)	42	11	16	15	48	61	−13	49
21	Middlesbrough (R)	42	11	11	20	54	75	−21	44
22	Nottingham Forest (R)	42	10	10	22	41	62	−21	40

Champions League: Manchester United. UEFA Cup: Aston Villa, Norwich City. Cup Winners Cup: Arsenal.

1993/94

Pos	Team	Pld	W	D	L	GF	GA	GD	Pts
1	Manchester United	42	27	11	4	80	38	+42	92
2	Blackburn Rovers	42	25	9	8	63	36	+27	84
3	Newcastle United	42	23	8	11	82	41	+41	77
4	Arsenal	42	18	17	7	53	28	+25	71
5	Leeds United	42	18	16	8	65	39	+26	70
6	Wimbledon	42	18	11	13	56	53	+3	65
7	Sheffield Wednesday	42	16	16	10	76	54	+22	64
8	Liverpool	42	17	9	16	59	55	+4	60
9	Queens Park Rangers	42	16	12	14	62	61	+1	60
10	Aston Villa	42	15	12	15	46	50	−4	57
11	Coventry City	42	14	14	14	43	45	−2	56
12	Norwich City	42	12	17	13	65	61	+4	53
13	West Ham United	42	13	13	16	47	58	−11	52
14	Chelsea	42	13	12	17	49	53	−4	51
15	Tottenham Hotspur	42	11	12	19	54	59	−5	45
16	Manchester City	42	9	18	15	38	49	−11	45
17	Everton	42	12	8	22	42	63	−21	44
18	Southampton	42	12	7	23	49	66	−17	43
19	Ipswich Town	42	9	16	17	35	58	−23	43
20	Sheffield United (R)	42	8	18	16	42	60	−18	42
21	Oldham Athletic (R)	42	9	13	20	42	68	−26	40
22	Swindon Town (R)	42	5	15	22	47	100	−53	30

Champions League: Manchester United. **UEFA Cup**: Aston Villa, Blackburn Rovers, Newcastle United.
Cup Winners Cup: Arsenal, Chelsea.

1994/95

Pos	Team	Pld	W	D	L	GF	GA	GD	Pts
1	Blackburn Rovers (C)	42	27	8	7	80	39	+41	89
2	Manchester United	42	26	10	6	77	28	+49	88
3	Nottingham Forest	42	22	11	9	72	43	+29	77
4	Liverpool	42	21	11	10	65	37	+28	74
5	Leeds United	42	20	13	9	59	38	+21	73
6	Newcastle United	42	20	12	10	67	47	+20	72
7	Tottenham Hotspur	42	16	14	12	66	58	+8	62
8	Queens Park Rangers	42	17	9	16	61	59	+2	60
9	Wimbledon	42	15	11	16	48	65	−17	56
10	Southampton	42	12	18	12	61	63	−2	54
11	Chelsea	42	13	15	14	50	55	−5	54
12	Arsenal	42	13	12	17	52	49	+3	51
13	Sheffield Wednesday	42	13	12	17	49	57	−8	51
14	West Ham United	42	13	11	18	44	48	−4	50
15	Everton	42	11	17	14	44	51	−7	50
16	Coventry City	42	12	14	16	44	62	−18	50
17	Manchester City	42	12	13	17	53	64	−11	49
18	Aston Villa	42	11	15	16	51	56	−5	48
19	Crystal Palace (R)	42	11	12	19	34	49	−15	45
20	Norwich City (R)	42	10	13	19	37	54	−17	43
21	Leicester City (R)	42	6	11	25	45	80	−35	29
22	Ipswich Town (R)	42	7	6	29	36	93	−57	27

Champions League: Blackburn Rovers. **UEFA Cup**: Leeds United, Liverpool, Manchester United, Nottingham Forest **Cup Winners Cup:** Everton.

1995/96

Pos	Team	Pld	W	D	L	GF	GA	GD	Pts
1	Manchester United (C)	38	25	7	6	73	35	+38	82
2	Newcastle United	38	24	6	8	66	37	+29	78
3	Liverpool	38	20	11	7	70	34	+36	71
4	Aston Villa	38	18	9	11	52	35	+17	63
5	Arsenal	38	17	12	9	49	32	+17	63
6	Everton	38	17	10	11	64	44	+20	61
7	Blackburn Rovers	38	18	7	13	61	47	+14	61
8	Tottenham Hotspur	38	16	13	9	50	38	+12	61
9	Nottingham Forest	38	15	13	10	50	54	−4	58
10	West Ham United	38	14	9	15	43	52	−9	51
11	Chelsea	38	12	14	12	46	44	+2	50
12	Middlesbrough	38	11	10	17	35	50	−15	43
13	Leeds United	38	12	7	19	40	57	−17	43
14	Wimbledon	38	10	11	17	55	70	−15	41
15	Sheffield Wednesday	38	10	10	18	48	61	−13	40
16	Coventry City	38	8	14	16	42	60	−18	38
17	Southampton	38	9	11	18	34	52	−18	38
18	Manchester City (R)	38	9	11	18	33	58	−25	38
19	Queens Park Rangers (R)	38	9	6	23	38	57	−19	33
20	Bolton Wanderers (R)	38	8	5	25	39	71	−32	29

Champions League: Manchester United. **UEFA Cup**: Arsenal, Aston VIlla, Newcastle United. **Cup Winners Cup:** Liverpool.

1996/97

Pos	Team	Pld	W	D	L	GF	GA	GD	Pts
1	Manchester United (C)	38	21	12	5	76	44	+32	75
2	Newcastle United	38	19	11	8	73	40	+33	68
3	Arsenal	38	19	11	8	62	32	+30	68
4	Liverpool	38	19	11	8	62	37	+25	68
5	Aston Villa	38	17	10	11	47	34	+13	61
6	Chelsea	38	16	11	11	58	55	+3	59
7	Sheffield Wednesday	38	14	15	9	50	51	−1	57
8	Wimbledon	38	15	11	12	49	46	+3	56
9	Leicester City	38	12	11	15	46	54	−8	47
10	Tottenham Hotspur	38	13	7	18	44	51	−7	46
11	Leeds United	38	11	13	14	28	38	−10	46
12	Derby County	38	11	13	14	45	58	−13	46
13	Blackburn Rovers	38	9	15	14	42	43	−1	42
14	West Ham United	38	10	12	16	39	48	−9	42
15	Everton	38	10	12	16	44	57	−13	42
16	Southampton	38	10	11	17	50	56	−6	41
17	Coventry City	38	9	14	15	38	54	−16	41
18	Sunderland (R)	38	10	10	18	35	53	−18	40
19	Middlesbrough (R)	38	10	12	16	51	60	−9	39
20	Nottingham Forest (R)	38	6	16	16	31	59	−28	34

Middlesbrough were docked three points for failing to fulfil a fixture.

Champions League: Manchester United, Newcastle United. **UEFA Cup:** Arsenal, Aston VIlla, Liverpool, Leicester City
Cup Winners Cup: Chelsea.

1997/98

Pos	Team	Pld	W	D	L	GF	GA	GD	Pts
1	Arsenal (C)	38	23	9	6	68	33	+35	78
2	Manchester United	38	23	8	7	73	26	+47	77
3	Liverpool	38	18	11	9	68	42	+26	65
4	Chelsea	38	20	3	15	71	43	+28	63
5	Leeds United	38	17	8	13	57	46	+11	59
6	Blackburn Rovers	38	16	10	12	57	52	+5	58
7	Aston Villa	38	17	6	15	49	48	+1	57
8	West Ham United	38	16	8	14	56	57	−1	56
9	Derby County	38	16	7	15	52	49	+3	55
10	Leicester City	38	13	14	11	51	41	+10	53
11	Coventry City	38	12	16	10	46	44	+2	52
12	Southampton	38	14	6	18	50	55	−5	48
13	Newcastle United	38	11	11	16	35	44	−9	44
14	Tottenham Hotspur	38	11	11	16	44	56	−12	44
15	Wimbledon	38	10	14	14	34	46	−12	44
16	Sheffield Wednesday	38	12	8	18	52	67	−15	44
17	Everton	38	9	13	16	41	56	−15	40
18	Bolton Wanderers (R)	38	9	13	16	41	61	−20	40
19	Barnsley (R)	38	10	5	23	37	82	−45	35
20	Crystal Palace (R)	38	8	9	21	37	71	−34	33

Champions League: Arsenal, Manchester United. **UEFA Cup**: Aston VIlla, Blackburn Rovers, Leeds United, Liverpool. **Cup Winners Cup:** Chelsea, Newcastle United.

1998/99

Pos	Team	Pld	W	D	L	GF	GA	GD	Pts
1	Manchester United (C)	38	22	13	3	80	37	+43	79
2	Arsenal	38	22	12	4	59	17	+42	78
3	Chelsea	38	20	15	3	57	30	+27	75
4	Leeds United	38	18	13	7	62	34	+28	67
5	West Ham United	38	16	9	13	46	53	-7	57
6	Aston Villa	38	15	10	13	51	46	+5	55
7	Liverpool	38	15	9	14	68	49	+19	54
8	Derby County	38	13	13	12	40	45	-5	52
9	Middlesbrough	38	12	15	11	48	54	-6	51
10	Leicester City	38	12	13	13	40	46	-6	49
11	Tottenham Hotspur	38	11	14	13	47	50	-3	47
12	Sheffield Wednesday	38	13	7	18	41	42	-1	46
13	Newcastle United	38	11	13	14	48	54	-6	46
14	Everton	38	11	10	17	42	47	-5	43
15	Coventry City	38	11	9	18	39	51	-12	42
16	Wimbledon	38	10	12	16	40	63	-23	42
17	Southampton	38	11	8	19	37	64	-27	41
18	Charlton Athletic (R)	38	8	12	18	41	56	-15	36
19	Blackburn Rovers (R)	38	7	14	17	38	52	-14	35
20	Nottingham Forest (R)	38	7	9	22	35	69	-34	30

Champions League: Arsenal, Chelsea, Manchester United. **UEFA Cup:** Leeds United, Newcastle United, Tottenham Hotspur. **UEFA Intertoto Cup:** West Ham United.

1999/2000

Pos	Team	Pld	W	D	L	GF	GA	GD	Pts
1	Manchester United (C)	38	28	7	3	97	45	+52	91
2	Arsenal	38	22	7	9	73	43	+30	73
3	Leeds United	38	21	6	11	58	43	+15	69
4	Liverpool	38	19	10	9	51	30	+21	67
5	Chelsea	38	18	11	9	53	34	+19	65
6	Aston Villa	38	15	13	10	46	35	+11	58
7	Sunderland	38	16	10	12	57	56	+1	58
8	Leicester City	38	16	7	15	55	55	0	55
9	West Ham United	38	15	10	13	52	53	−1	55
10	Tottenham Hotspur	38	15	8	15	57	49	+8	53
11	Newcastle United	38	14	10	14	63	54	+9	52
12	Middlesbrough	38	14	10	14	46	52	−6	52
13	Everton	38	12	14	12	59	49	+10	50
14	Coventry City	38	12	8	18	47	54	−7	44
15	Southampton	38	12	8	18	45	62	−17	44
16	Derby County	38	9	11	18	44	57	−13	38
17	Bradford City	38	9	9	20	38	68	−30	36
18	Wimbledon (R)	38	7	12	19	46	74	−28	33
19	Sheffield Wednesday (R)	38	8	7	23	38	70	−32	31
20	Watford (R)	38	6	6	26	35	77	−42	24

Champions League: Arsenal, Leeds United, Manchester United. **UEFA Cup**: Chelsea, Liverpool, Leicester City.
UEFA Intertoto Cup: Aston Villa, Bradford City.

2000/01

Pos	Team	Pld	W	D	L	GF	GA	GD	Pts
1	Manchester United (C)	38	24	8	6	79	31	+48	80
2	Arsenal	38	20	10	8	63	38	+25	70
3	Liverpool	38	20	9	9	71	39	+32	69
4	Leeds United	38	20	8	10	64	43	+21	68
5	Ipswich Town	38	20	6	12	57	42	+15	66
6	Chelsea	38	17	10	11	68	45	+23	61
7	Sunderland	38	15	12	11	46	41	+5	57
8	Aston Villa	38	13	15	10	46	43	+3	54
9	Charlton Athletic	38	14	10	14	50	57	−7	52
10	Southampton	38	14	10	14	40	48	−8	52
11	Newcastle United	38	14	9	15	44	50	−6	51
12	Tottenham Hotspur	38	13	10	15	47	54	−7	49
13	Leicester City	38	14	6	18	39	51	−12	48
14	Middlesbrough	38	9	15	14	44	44	0	42
15	West Ham United	38	10	12	16	45	50	−5	42
16	Everton	38	11	9	18	45	59	−14	42
17	Derby County	38	10	12	16	37	59	−22	42
18	Manchester City (R)	38	8	10	20	41	65	−24	34
19	Coventry City (R)	38	8	10	20	36	63	−27	34
20	Bradford City (R)	38	5	11	22	30	70	−40	26

Champions League: Arsenal, Liverpool, Manchester United. **UEFA Cup:** Chelsea, Ipswich Town, Leeds United. **UEFA Intertoto Cup:** Aston VIlla, Newcastle United.

2001/02

Pos	Team	Pld	W	D	L	GF	GA	GD	Pts
1	Arsenal (C)	38	26	9	3	79	36	+43	87
2	Liverpool	38	24	8	6	67	30	+37	80
3	Manchester United	38	24	5	9	87	45	+42	77
4	Newcastle United	38	21	8	9	74	52	+22	71
5	Leeds United	38	18	12	8	53	37	+16	66
6	Chelsea	38	17	13	8	66	38	+28	64
7	West Ham United	38	15	8	15	48	57	−9	53
8	Aston Villa	38	12	14	12	46	47	−1	50
9	Tottenham Hotspur	38	14	8	16	49	53	−4	50
10	Blackburn Rovers	38	12	10	16	55	51	+4	46
11	Southampton	38	12	9	17	46	54	−8	45
12	Middlesbrough	38	12	9	17	35	47	−12	45
13	Fulham	38	10	14	14	36	44	−8	44
14	Charlton Athletic	38	10	14	14	38	49	−11	44
15	Everton	38	11	10	17	45	57	−12	43
16	Bolton Wanderers	38	9	13	16	44	62	−18	40
17	Sunderland	38	10	10	18	29	51	−22	40
18	Ipswich Town (R)	38	9	9	20	41	64	−23	36
19	Derby County (R)	38	8	6	24	33	63	−30	30
20	Leicester City (R)	38	5	13	20	30	64	−34	28

Champions League: Arsenal, Liverpool, Manchester United, Newcastle United. **UEFA Cup:** Blackburn Rovers, Chelsea, Ipswich Town, Leeds United. **UEFA Intertoto Cup:** Aston Villa, Fulham.

2002/03

Pos	Team	Pld	W	D	L	GF	GA	GD	Pts
1	Manchester United (C)	38	25	8	5	74	34	+40	83
2	Arsenal	38	23	9	6	85	42	+43	78
3	Newcastle United	38	21	6	11	63	48	+15	69
4	Chelsea	38	19	10	9	68	38	+30	67
5	Liverpool	38	18	10	10	61	41	+20	64
6	Blackburn Rovers	38	16	12	10	52	43	+9	60
7	Everton	38	17	8	13	48	49	−1	59
8	Southampton	38	13	13	12	43	46	−3	52
9	Manchester City	38	15	6	17	47	54	−7	51
10	Tottenham Hotspur	38	14	8	16	51	62	−11	50
11	Middlesbrough	38	13	10	15	48	44	+4	49
12	Charlton Athletic	38	14	7	17	45	56	−11	49
13	Birmingham City	38	13	9	16	41	49	−8	48
14	Fulham	38	13	9	16	41	50	−9	48
15	Leeds United	38	14	5	19	58	57	+1	47
16	Aston Villa	38	12	9	17	42	47	−5	45
17	Bolton Wanderers	38	10	14	14	41	51	−10	44
18	West Ham United (R)	38	10	12	16	42	59	−17	42
19	West Bromwich Albion (R)	38	6	8	24	29	65	−36	26
20	Sunderland (R)	38	4	7	27	21	65	−44	19

Champions League: Arsenal, Chelsea, Manchester United, Newcastle United. **UEFA Cup:** Blackburn Rovers, Liverpool, Manchester City, Southampton.

2003/04

Pos	Team	Pld	W	D	L	GF	GA	GD	Pts
1	Arsenal (C)	38	26	12	0	73	26	+47	90
2	Chelsea	38	24	7	7	67	30	+37	79
3	Manchester United	38	23	6	9	64	35	+29	75
4	Liverpool	38	16	12	10	55	37	+18	60
5	Newcastle United	38	13	17	8	52	40	+12	56
6	Aston Villa	38	15	11	12	48	44	+4	56
7	Charlton Athletic	38	14	11	13	51	51	0	53
8	Bolton Wanderers	38	14	11	13	48	56	−8	53
9	Fulham	38	14	10	14	52	46	+6	52
10	Birmingham City	38	12	14	12	43	48	−5	50
11	Middlesbrough	38	13	9	16	44	52	−8	48
12	Southampton	38	12	11	15	44	45	−1	47
13	Portsmouth	38	12	9	17	47	54	−7	45
14	Tottenham Hotspur	38	13	6	19	47	57	−10	45
15	Blackburn Rovers	38	12	8	18	51	59	−8	44
16	Manchester City	38	9	14	15	55	54	+1	41
17	Everton	38	9	12	17	45	57	−12	39
18	Leicester City (R)	38	6	15	17	48	65	−17	33
19	Leeds United (R)	38	8	9	21	40	79	−39	33
20	Wolverhampton Wanderers (R)	38	7	12	19	38	77	−39	33

Champions League: Arsenal, Chelsea, Liverpool, Manchester United. **UEFA Cup**: Middlesbrough, Newcastle United.

2004/05

Pos	Team	Pld	W	D	L	GF	GA	GD	Pts
1	Chelsea (C)	38	29	8	1	72	15	+57	95
2	Arsenal	38	25	8	5	87	36	+51	83
3	Manchester United	38	22	11	5	58	26	+32	77
4	Everton	38	18	7	13	45	46	−1	61
5	Liverpool	38	17	7	14	52	41	+11	58
6	Bolton Wanderers	38	16	10	12	49	44	+5	58
7	Middlesbrough	38	14	13	11	53	46	+7	55
8	Manchester City	38	13	13	12	47	39	+8	52
9	Tottenham Hotspur	38	14	10	14	47	41	+6	52
10	Aston Villa	38	12	11	15	45	52	−7	47
11	Charlton Athletic	38	12	10	16	42	58	−16	46
12	Birmingham City	38	11	12	15	40	46	−6	45
13	Fulham	38	12	8	18	52	60	−8	44
14	Newcastle United	38	10	14	14	47	57	−10	44
15	Blackburn Rovers	38	9	15	14	32	43	−11	42
16	Portsmouth	38	10	9	19	43	59	−16	39
17	West Bromwich Albion	38	6	16	16	36	61	−25	34
18	Crystal Palace (R)	38	7	12	19	41	62	−21	33
19	Norwich City (R)	38	7	12	19	42	77	−35	33
20	Southampton (R)	38	6	14	18	45	66	−21	32

Champions League: Arsenal, Chelsea, Everton, Liverpool, Manchester United. **UEFA Cup:** Bolton Wanderers, Middlesbrough. **UEFA Intertoto Cup:** Newcastle United.

2005/06

Pos	Team	Pld	W	D	L	GF	GA	GD	Pts
1	Chelsea (C)	38	29	4	5	72	22	+50	91
2	Manchester United	38	25	8	5	72	34	+38	83
3	Liverpool	38	25	7	6	57	25	+32	82
4	Arsenal	38	20	7	11	68	31	+37	67
5	Tottenham Hotspur	38	18	11	9	53	38	+15	65
6	Blackburn Rovers	38	19	6	13	51	42	+9	63
7	Newcastle United	38	17	7	14	47	42	+5	58
8	Bolton Wanderers	38	15	11	12	49	41	+8	56
9	West Ham United	38	16	7	15	52	55	−3	55
10	Wigan Athletic	38	15	6	17	45	52	−7	51
11	Everton	38	14	8	16	34	49	−15	50
12	Fulham	38	14	6	18	48	58	−10	48
13	Charlton Athletic	38	13	8	17	41	55	−14	47
14	Middlesbrough	38	12	9	17	48	58	−10	45
15	Manchester City	38	13	4	21	43	48	−5	43
16	Aston Villa	38	10	12	16	42	55	−13	42
17	Portsmouth	38	10	8	20	37	62	−25	38
18	Birmingham City (R)	38	8	10	20	28	50	−22	34
19	West Bromwich Albion (R)	38	7	9	22	31	58	−27	30
20	Sunderland (R)	38	3	6	29	26	69	−43	15

Champions League: Arsenal, Chelsea, Liverpool, Manchester United. **UEFA Cup:** Blackburn Rovers, Tottenham Hotspur, West Ham United. **UEFA Intertoto Cup:** Newcastle United.

2006/07

Pos	Team	Pld	W	D	L	GF	GA	GD	Pts
1	Manchester United (C)	38	28	5	5	83	27	+56	89
2	Chelsea	38	24	11	3	64	24	+40	83
3	Liverpool	38	20	8	10	57	27	+30	68
4	Arsenal	38	19	11	8	63	35	+28	68
5	Tottenham Hotspur	38	17	9	12	57	54	+3	60
6	Everton	38	15	13	10	52	36	+16	58
7	Bolton Wanderers	38	16	8	14	47	52	−5	56
8	Reading	38	16	7	15	52	47	+5	55
9	Portsmouth	38	14	12	12	45	42	+3	54
10	Blackburn Rovers	38	15	7	16	52	54	−2	52
11	Aston Villa	38	11	17	10	43	41	+2	50
12	Middlesbrough	38	12	10	16	44	49	−5	46
13	Newcastle United	38	11	10	17	38	47	−9	43
14	Manchester City	38	11	9	18	29	44	−15	42
15	West Ham United	38	12	5	21	35	59	−24	41
16	Fulham	38	8	15	15	38	60	−22	39
17	Wigan Athletic	38	10	8	20	37	59	−22	38
18	Sheffield United (R)	38	10	8	20	32	55	−23	38
19	Charlton Athletic (R)	38	8	10	20	34	60	−26	34
20	Watford (R)	38	5	13	20	29	59	−30	28

Champions League: Arsenal, Chelsea, Liverpool, Manchester United. **UEFA Cup:** Bolton Wanderers, Everton, Tottenham Hotspur. **UEFA Intertoto Cup:** Blackburn Rovers.

2007/08

Pos	Team	Pld	W	D	L	GF	GA	GD	Pts
1	Manchester United (C)	38	27	6	5	80	22	+58	87
2	Chelsea	38	25	10	3	65	26	+39	85
3	Arsenal	38	24	11	3	74	31	+43	83
4	Liverpool	38	21	13	4	67	28	+39	76
5	Everton	38	19	8	11	55	33	+22	65
6	Aston Villa	38	16	12	10	71	51	+20	60
7	Blackburn Rovers	38	15	13	10	50	48	+2	58
8	Portsmouth	38	16	9	13	48	40	+8	57
9	Manchester City	38	15	10	13	45	53	−8	55
10	West Ham United	38	13	10	15	42	50	−8	49
11	Tottenham Hotspur	38	11	13	14	66	61	+5	46
12	Newcastle United	38	11	10	17	45	65	−20	43
13	Middlesbrough	38	10	12	16	43	53	−10	42
14	Wigan Athletic	38	10	10	18	34	51	−17	40
15	Sunderland	38	11	6	21	36	59	−23	39
16	Bolton Wanderers	38	9	10	19	36	54	−18	37
17	Fulham	38	8	12	18	38	60	−22	36
18	Reading (R)	38	10	6	22	41	66	−25	36
19	Birmingham City (R)	38	8	11	19	46	62	−16	35
20	Derby County (R)	38	1	8	29	20	89	−69	11

Champions League: Arsenal, Chelsea, Liverpool, Manchester United. **UEFA Cup:** Everton, Manchester City, Portsmouth, Tottenham Hotspur. **UEFA Intertoto Cup:** Aston Villa.

2008/09

Pos	Team	Pld	W	D	L	GF	GA	GD	Pts
1	Manchester United (C)	38	28	6	4	68	24	+44	90
2	Liverpool	38	25	11	2	77	27	+50	86
3	Chelsea	38	25	8	5	68	24	+44	83
4	Arsenal	38	20	12	6	68	37	+31	72
5	Everton	38	17	12	9	55	37	+18	63
6	Aston Villa	38	17	11	10	54	48	+6	62
7	Fulham	38	14	11	13	39	34	+5	53
8	Tottenham Hotspur	38	14	9	15	45	45	0	51
9	West Ham United	38	14	9	15	42	45	−3	51
10	Manchester City	38	15	5	18	58	50	+8	50
11	Wigan Athletic	38	12	9	17	34	45	−11	45
12	Stoke City	38	12	9	17	38	55	−17	45
13	Bolton Wanderers	38	11	8	19	41	53	−12	41
14	Portsmouth	38	10	11	17	38	57	−19	41
15	Blackburn Rovers	38	10	11	17	40	60	−20	41
16	Sunderland	38	9	9	20	34	54	−20	36
17	Hull City	38	8	11	19	39	64	−25	35
18	Newcastle United (R)	38	7	13	18	40	59	−19	34
19	Middlesbrough (R)	38	7	11	20	28	57	−29	32
20	West Bromwich Albion (R)	38	8	8	22	36	67	−31	32

Champions League: Arsenal, Chelsea, Liverpool, Manchester United. **Europa League**: Aston Villa, Everton, Fulham.

2009/10

Pos	Team	Pld	W	D	L	GF	GA	GD	Pts
1	Chelsea (C)	38	27	5	6	103	32	+71	86
2	Manchester United	38	27	4	7	86	28	+58	85
3	Arsenal	38	23	6	9	83	41	+42	75
4	Tottenham Hotspur	38	21	7	10	67	41	+26	70
5	Manchester City	38	18	13	7	73	45	+28	67
6	Aston Villa	38	17	13	8	52	39	+13	64
7	Liverpool	38	18	9	11	61	35	+26	63
8	Everton	38	16	13	9	60	49	+11	61
9	Birmingham City	38	13	11	14	38	47	−9	50
10	Blackburn Rovers	38	13	11	14	41	55	−14	50
11	Stoke City	38	11	14	13	34	48	−14	47
12	Fulham	38	12	10	16	39	46	−7	46
13	Sunderland	38	11	11	16	48	56	−8	44
14	Bolton Wanderers	38	10	9	19	42	67	−25	39
15	Wolverhampton Wanderers	38	9	11	18	32	56	−24	38
16	Wigan Athletic	38	9	9	20	37	79	−42	36
17	West Ham United	38	8	11	19	47	66	−19	35
18	Burnley (R)	38	8	6	24	42	82	−40	30
19	Hull City (R)	38	6	12	20	34	75	−41	30
20	Portsmouth (R)	38	7	7	24	34	66	−32	19

Portsmouth were docked nine points for entering administration.

Champions League: Arsenal, Chelsea, Manchester United, Tottenham Hotspur. **Europa League**: Aston Villa, Liverpool, Manchester City.

2010/11

Pos	Team	Pld	W	D	L	GF	GA	GD	Pts
1	Manchester United (C)	38	23	11	4	78	37	+41	80
2	Chelsea	38	21	8	9	69	33	+36	71
3	Manchester City	38	21	8	9	60	33	+27	71
4	Arsenal	38	19	11	8	72	43	+29	68
5	Tottenham Hotspur	38	16	14	8	55	46	+9	62
6	Liverpool	38	17	7	14	59	44	+15	58
7	Everton	38	13	15	10	51	45	+6	54
8	Fulham	38	11	16	11	49	43	+6	49
9	Aston Villa	38	12	12	14	48	59	−11	48
10	Sunderland	38	12	11	15	45	56	−11	47
11	West Bromwich Albion	38	12	11	15	56	71	−15	47
12	Newcastle United	38	11	13	14	56	57	−1	46
13	Stoke City	38	13	7	18	46	48	−2	46
14	Bolton Wanderers	38	12	10	16	52	56	−4	46
15	Blackburn Rovers	38	11	10	17	46	59	−13	43
16	Wigan Athletic	38	9	15	14	40	61	−21	42
17	Wolverhampton Wanderers	38	11	7	20	46	66	−20	40
18	Birmingham City (R)	38	8	15	15	37	58	−21	39
19	Blackpool (R)	38	10	9	19	55	78	−23	39
20	West Ham United (R)	38	7	12	19	43	70	−27	33

Champions League: Arsenal, Chelsea, Manchester City, Manchester United. **Europa League**: Birgmingham City, Fulham, Stoke City, Tottenham Hotspur.

2011/12

Pos	Team	Pld	W	D	L	GF	GA	GD	Pts
1	Manchester City (C)	38	28	5	5	93	29	+64	89
2	Manchester United	38	28	5	5	89	33	+56	89
3	Arsenal	38	21	7	10	74	49	+25	70
4	Tottenham Hotspur	38	20	9	9	66	41	+25	69
5	Newcastle United	38	19	8	11	56	51	+5	65
6	Chelsea	38	18	10	10	65	46	+19	64
7	Everton	38	15	11	12	50	40	+10	56
8	Liverpool	38	14	10	14	47	40	+7	52
9	Fulham	38	14	10	14	48	51	−3	52
10	West Bromwich Albion	38	13	8	17	45	52	−7	47
11	Swansea City	38	12	11	15	44	51	−7	47
12	Norwich City	38	12	11	15	52	66	−14	47
13	Sunderland	38	11	12	15	45	46	−1	45
14	Stoke City	38	11	12	15	36	53	−17	45
15	Wigan Athletic	38	11	10	17	42	62	−20	43
16	Aston Villa	38	7	17	14	37	53	−16	38
17	Queens Park Rangers	38	10	7	21	43	66	−23	37
18	Bolton Wanderers (R)	38	10	6	22	46	77	−31	36
19	Blackburn Rovers (R)	38	8	7	23	48	78	−30	31
20	Wolverhampton Wanderers (R)	38	5	10	23	40	82	−42	25

Champions League: Arsenal, Chelsea, Manchester City, Manchester United. **Europa League**: Liverpool, Newcastle United, Tottenham Hotspur.

2012/13

Pos	Team	Pld	W	D	L	GF	GA	GD	Pts
1	Manchester United (C)	38	28	5	5	86	43	+43	89
2	Manchester City	38	23	9	6	66	34	+32	78
3	Chelsea	38	22	9	7	75	39	+36	75
4	Arsenal	38	21	10	7	72	37	+35	73
5	Tottenham Hotspur	38	21	9	8	66	46	+20	72
6	Everton	38	16	15	7	55	40	+15	63
7	Liverpool	38	16	13	9	71	43	+28	61
8	West Bromwich Albion	38	14	7	17	53	57	−4	49
9	Swansea City	38	11	13	14	47	51	−4	46
10	West Ham United	38	12	10	16	45	53	−8	46
11	Norwich City	38	10	14	14	41	58	−17	44
12	Fulham	38	11	10	17	50	60	−10	43
13	Stoke City	38	9	15	14	34	45	−11	42
14	Southampton	38	9	14	15	49	60	−11	41
15	Aston Villa	38	10	11	17	47	69	−22	41
16	Newcastle United	38	11	8	19	45	68	−23	41
17	Sunderland	38	9	12	17	41	54	−13	39
18	Wigan Athletic (R)	38	9	9	20	47	73	−26	36
19	Reading (R)	38	6	10	22	43	73	−30	28
20	Queens Park Rangers (R)	38	4	13	21	30	60	−30	25

Champions League: Arsenal, Chelsea, Manchester City, Manchester United. **Europa League**: Swansea City, Tottenham Hotspur, Wigan Athletic.

2013/14

Pos	Team	Pld	W	D	L	GF	GA	GD	Pts
1	Manchester City (C)	38	27	5	6	102	37	+65	86
2	Liverpool	38	26	6	6	101	50	+51	84
3	Chelsea	38	25	7	6	71	27	+44	82
4	Arsenal	38	24	7	7	68	41	+27	79
5	Everton	38	21	9	8	61	39	+22	72
6	Tottenham Hotspur	38	21	6	11	55	51	+4	69
7	Manchester United	38	19	7	12	64	43	+21	64
8	Southampton	38	15	11	12	54	46	+8	56
9	Stoke City	38	13	11	14	45	52	−7	50
10	Newcastle United	38	15	4	19	43	59	−16	49
11	Crystal Palace	38	13	6	19	33	48	−15	45
12	Swansea City	38	11	9	18	54	54	0	42
13	West Ham United	38	11	7	20	40	51	−11	40
14	Sunderland	38	10	8	20	41	60	−19	38
15	Aston Villa	38	10	8	20	39	61	−22	38
16	Hull City	38	10	7	21	38	53	−15	37
17	West Bromwich Albion	38	7	15	16	43	59	−16	36
18	Norwich City (R)	38	8	9	21	28	62	−34	33
19	Fulham (R)	38	9	5	24	40	85	−45	32
20	Cardiff City (R)	38	7	9	22	32	74	−42	30

Champions League: Arsenal, Chelsea, Liverpool, Manchester City. **Europa League**: Everton, Tottenham Hotspur, West Ham United.

2014/15

Pos	Team	Pld	W	D	L	GF	GA	GD	Pts
1	Chelsea (C)	38	26	9	3	73	32	+41	87
2	Manchester City	38	24	7	7	83	38	+45	79
3	Arsenal	38	22	9	7	71	36	+35	75
4	Manchester United	38	20	10	8	62	37	+25	70
5	Tottenham Hotspur	38	19	7	12	58	53	+5	64
6	Liverpool	38	18	8	12	52	48	+4	62
7	Southampton	38	18	6	14	54	33	+21	60
8	Swansea City	38	16	8	14	46	49	−3	56
9	Stoke City	38	15	9	14	48	45	+3	54
10	Crystal Palace	38	13	9	16	47	51	−4	48
11	Everton	38	12	11	15	48	50	−2	47
12	West Ham United	38	12	11	15	44	47	−3	47
13	West Bromwich Albion	38	11	11	16	38	51	−13	44
14	Leicester City	38	11	8	19	46	55	−9	41
15	Newcastle United	38	10	9	19	40	63	−23	39
16	Sunderland	38	7	17	14	31	53	−22	38
17	Aston Villa	38	10	8	20	31	57	−26	38
18	Hull City (R)	38	8	11	19	33	51	−18	35
19	Burnley (R)	38	7	12	19	28	53	−25	33
20	Queens Park Rangers (R)	38	8	6	24	42	73	−31	30

Champions League: Arsenal, Chelsea, Manchester City, Manchester United. **Europa League:** Liverpool, Southampton, Tottenham Hotspur, West Ham United.

2015/16

Pos	Team	Pld	W	D	L	GF	GA	GD	Pts
1	Leicester City (C)	38	23	12	3	68	36	+32	81
2	Arsenal	38	20	11	7	65	36	+29	71
3	Tottenham Hotspur	38	19	13	6	69	35	+34	70
4	Manchester City	38	19	9	10	71	41	+30	66
5	Manchester United	38	19	9	10	49	35	+14	66
6	Southampton	38	18	9	11	59	41	+18	63
7	West Ham United	38	16	14	8	65	51	+14	62
8	Liverpool	38	16	12	10	63	50	+13	60
9	Stoke City	38	14	9	15	41	55	−14	51
10	Chelsea	38	12	14	12	59	53	+6	50
11	Everton	38	11	14	13	59	55	+4	47
12	Swansea City	38	12	11	15	42	52	−10	47
13	Watford	38	12	9	17	40	50	−10	45
14	West Bromwich Albion	38	10	13	15	34	48	−14	43
15	Crystal Palace	38	11	9	18	39	51	−12	42
16	AFC Bournemouth	38	11	9	18	45	67	−22	42
17	Sunderland	38	9	12	17	48	62	−14	39
18	Newcastle United (R)	38	9	10	19	44	65	−21	37
19	Norwich City (R)	38	9	7	22	39	67	−28	34
20	Aston Villa (R)	38	3	8	27	27	76	−49	17

Champions League: Arsenal, Leicester City, Manchester City, Tottenham Hotspur. **Europa League**: Manchester United, Southampton, West Ham United.

2016/17

Pos	Team	Pld	W	D	L	GF	GA	GD	Pts
1	Chelsea (C)	38	30	3	5	85	33	+52	93
2	Tottenham Hotspur	38	26	8	4	86	26	+60	86
3	Manchester City	38	23	9	6	80	39	+41	78
4	Liverpool	38	22	10	6	78	42	+36	76
5	Arsenal	38	23	6	9	77	44	+33	75
6	Manchester United	38	18	15	5	54	29	+25	69
7	Everton	38	17	10	11	62	44	+18	61
8	Southampton	38	12	10	16	41	48	−7	46
9	AFC Bournemouth	38	12	10	16	55	67	−12	46
10	West Bromwich Albion	38	12	9	17	43	51	−8	45
11	West Ham United	38	12	9	17	47	64	−17	45
12	Leicester City	38	12	8	18	48	63	−15	44
13	Stoke City	38	11	11	16	41	56	−15	44
14	Crystal Palace	38	12	5	21	50	63	−13	41
15	Swansea City	38	12	5	21	45	70	−25	41
16	Burnley	38	11	7	20	39	55	−16	40
17	Watford	38	11	7	20	40	68	−28	40
18	Hull City (R)	38	9	7	22	37	80	−43	34
19	Middlesbrough (R)	38	5	13	20	27	53	−26	28
20	Sunderland (R)	38	6	6	26	29	69	−40	24

Champions League: Chelsea, Manchester City, Manchester United, Tottenham Hotspur. **Europa League:** Arsenal, Everton.

BEST PREMIER LEAGUE PLAYERS/TEAM

This was going to be a whole chapter, but it turns out to be less rich as a comedy seam than even singing. So here it is, stuck at the end with a few blank pages following, for you to scribble in, in preparation for your letter of complaint to the publisher. It's likely to be deleted by the publisher anyway; he's like that...ruthless and whimsical. If it does sneak in, my idea was going to be that you chose your best team without choosing players from the team you support. And if you think I've put them in the wrong category, just move them. There should be enough space for you just to write in the players that I've outrageously left out due to my small club bias. Many of these players played for several clubs, so I've designated them by nationality rather than club allegiance.

Goalkeepers

Peter Schmeichel (Denmark), Tim Flowers (England), David Seaman (England), Petr Cech (Czechia), Shay Given (Eire), Joe Hart (England), Edwin Van der Sar (Holland), David James (England), David de Gea (Spain), Nigel Martin (England), Steve Ogrizovic (England)

Defenders

Tony Adams (England), Ashley Cole (England), Lee Dixon (England), Sol Campbell (England), Leighton Baines (England), Gary Pallister (England), Jamie Carragher

(England), Ian Harte (Eire), Sami Hyypia (Finland), Steve Bruce (England), Martin Keown (England), Paul McGrath (Eire), Jose Fonte (Portugal), Rio Ferdinand (England), Francis Benali[1] (England), Virgil Van Dijk (Holland), Vincent Kompany (Belgium), Dave (Spain), Gary Neville (England), Des Walker (England)

Defensive Midfielders[2]

Paul Ince (England), Michael Essien (Ghana), Xabi Alonso (Spain), Claude Makelele (France), Patrick Vieira (France), Dennis Wise (England), N'Golo Kante (France), Steven Davis (Northern Ireland), Jack Cork (Great Britain), Victor Wanyama (Kenya)

Attacking Midfielders

Matthew Le Tissier (England), Juninho (Brazil), Ryan Giggs (Wales), Eric Cantona (France), Yaya Toure (Ivory Coast), Frank Lampard (England), Steven Gerrard (England), Georgi Kinkladze (Georgia), Paul Scholes (England), Gareth Bale (Wales), Theo Walcott (England), Mesut Ozil (Germany), Alexi Sanchez (Chile), Adam Lallana (England), Jason Koumas (Wales)[3]

Forwards (Strikers)

Les Ferdinand (England), Fabrizio Ravanelli (Italy), Robbie Fowler (England), Alan Shearer (England), Ian Wright (England), Michael Owen (England), Thierry Henry (France), Denis Bergkamp (Holland), Paolo Di Canio (Italy), Wayne Rooney (England), Ruud Van Nistelrooy (England), Robin Van Persie (Holland)

So your best team ever eleven, with traditional squad numbers:

---

[1]   This is clearly a joke but he's a good lad

[2]   If I have missed anyone out, I may just have not been very kean to include them

[3]   Roberto Martinez made me put him in.

13.	2.
18.	6.
3.	4.
37.	17.
8.	10.
9.	

Subs (up to 7): Matthew Le Tissier has to be in, just in case the game goes to penalties.[4,] [5]

---

[4] Now if only the odd England manager had thought of that

[5] Note to publisher. Well OK it's another 400 words or so but I reckon they deserve better, so don't forget to delete this prior to publication. We really can't leave this in, or it'll look like we don't know what we're doing.

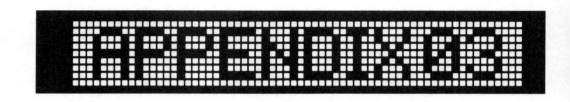

REFERENCES

Baker, C (2017), *Personal Correspondence incorporated into the text in the way it was to offer a veneer of something more solid.*

Bradley, M, (2017), 'The Service Profit Train', *FCBusiness Magazine*

The Guardian: https://www.theguardian.com/football/2009/may/18/seven-deadly-sins-roy-keane-wrath

Goldblatt, D (2015), *The Game of Our Lives: The Making and Meaning of English Football,* London: Penguin

Gros, F (2015), *A Philosophy of Walking,* London: Verso

Hamilton, A (1999), 'The unpredictability that keeps City alive. Fan's Eye View – Coventry City', *The Independent,* 13/3/1999

Kuper, S (2003), *Football Against the Enemy,* London: Orion

Pettiford, L (2005), *One Man Team: The Matt Le Tissier Story,* Cottingham: Ardra Press (now available through Urbane) – to be fair I didn't really use this, but any tenuous excuse to mention it will be taken.

Pietersen, K (2014), *KP – The Autobiography,* London: Sphere/Little-Brown – to be fair I didn't use this either, but having ploughed through a whole chapter, it developed a use for resting my laptop upon to reduce back pain.

Portnoi, G (2011), *Who Are Ya? The talkSport Book of Football's Best Ever Chants,* London: Simon and Schuster

Red Dwarf TV Series: Boxed Set (Series 4, Episode 6: Meltdown)

Shindler, C (1998), *Manchester United Ruined My Life,* London: Headline.

Stephens, G (2001), *The Story of the Blues: The Complete History of Bishop's Stortford FC since 1874,* Bishop's Stortford: BSFSC

Taylor, D and Owen, J (2016), *I Believe In Miracles: The Remarkable Story of Brian Clough's European Cup-winning Team,* London: Headline

Whiteley, P.J. (2017), *Marching on Together,* London: Urbane

Wilde, O (2015), *The Importance of Being Earnest,* London: Bloomsbury Methuen Drama

With thanks also to the Family Cat, whose songs I love. Their *Five Lives Left* double CD anthology would make a splendid Christmas present for anyone you know that doesn't like football.

APPENDIX 3

ABOUT THE AUTHOR/
FINAL MISTAKE

Sometimes the universe tells you something, but Lloyd ignored it when part of his PhD was published by the *Journal of Disasters* in 1994. From there he went on to become a Professor of International Relations, writing and publishing many books and articles on themes as diverse as teaching methods, environmental politics and terrorism. His last work as an academic was published in *World Politics* (Sage, 2017). It is strongly recommended to those doing a relevant degree - and anyone else who may be struggling to sleep.

Lloyd has occasionally been distracted by football writing since collaborating on the *World Cup: Fact and Quiz Book* (2002), publishing half a dozen books as well as articles. Urbane's back-catalogue includes the *One Man Team* (2005), an act of worship to Matt Le Tiss and Euro 2016 (2016). The latter was described by one reviewer as 'comedy non-fiction at its best' and was selling like the hottest of cakes until England were eliminated by Iceland - when sales dived off a cliff. Thanks a lot boys.

This book has been a wonderful opportunity to share the pain and excitement that is football, regardless of whether it is in the Premier League, and Lloyd is grateful both for the opportunity and all the time people have given to talk to him, as well as providing text, notes and inspiration. Updates, corrections and material for future editions will be gratefully received through Twitter @UrbanePL25Book or premierleaguefanshistory.wordpress.com - Thank you to Rachel Ward for reading draft material more than can possibly be good for one's health.

Urbane Publications is dedicated to
developing new author voices, and publishing
fiction and non-fiction that challenges, thrills and
fascinates. From page-turning novels to innovative
reference books, our goal is to publish what
YOU want to read.

Find out more at

urbanepublications.com